Lecture Notes in Computer Science 8135

Commenced Publication in 1973
Founding and Former Series Editors:
Gerhard Goos, Juris Hartmanis, and Jan van Leeuwen

Editorial Board

David Hutchison
Lancaster University, UK

Takeo Kanade
Carnegie Mellon University, Pittsburgh, PA, USA

Josef Kittler
University of Surrey, Guildford, UK

Jon M. Kleinberg
Cornell University, Ithaca, NY, USA

Alfred Kobsa
University of California, Irvine, CA, USA

Friedemann Mattern
ETH Zurich, Switzerland

John C. Mitchell
Stanford University, CA, USA

Moni Naor
Weizmann Institute of Science, Rehovot, I.

Oscar Nierstrasz
University of Bern, Switzerland

C. Pandu Rangan
Indian Institute of Technology, Madras, India

Bernhard Steffen
TU Dortmund University, Germany

Madhu Sudan
Microsoft Research, Cambridge, MA, USA

Demetri Terzopoulos
University of California, Los Angeles, CA, USA

Doug Tygar
University of California, Berkeley, CA, USA

Gerhard Weikum
Max Planck Institute for Informatics, Saarbruecken, Germany

T0226213

Kung-Kiu Lau   Winfried Lamersdorf
Ernesto Pimentel (Eds.)

Service-Oriented and Cloud Computing

Second European Conference, ESOCC 2013
Málaga, Spain, September 11-13, 2013
Proceedings

 Springer

Volume Editors

Kung-Kiu Lau
The University of Manchester, School of Computer Science
Oxford Road, Manchester M13 9PL, UK
E-mail: kung-kiu@cs.man.ac.uk

Winfried Lamersdorf
Universität Hamburg, Fachbereich Informatik/VSYS
Vogt-Kölln-Straße 30, 22527 Hamburg, Germany
E-mail: lamersd@informatik.uni-hamburg.de

Ernesto Pimentel
University of Málaga, Department of Computer Science
Boulevard Louis Pasteur 35, 29011 Málaga, Spain
E-mail: ernesto@lcc.uma.es

ISSN 0302-9743   e-ISSN 1611-3349
ISBN 978-3-642-40650-8   e-ISBN 978-3-642-40651-5
DOI 10.1007/978-3-642-40651-5
Springer Heidelberg New York Dordrecht London

Library of Congress Control Number: 2013946368

CR Subject Classification (1998): H.3.4-5, D.2.11, K.6.5, K.6.3, H.2.8, C.2.4, J.1

LNCS Sublibrary: SL 2 – Programming and Software Engineering

© Springer-Verlag Berlin Heidelberg 2013

This work is subject to copyright. All rights are reserved by the Publisher, whether the whole or part of the material is concerned, specifically the rights of translation, reprinting, reuse of illustrations, recitation, broadcasting, reproduction on microfilms or in any other physical way, and transmission or information storage and retrieval, electronic adaptation, computer software, or by similar or dissimilar methodology now known or hereafter developed. Exempted from this legal reservation are brief excerpts in connection with reviews or scholarly analysis or material supplied specifically for the purpose of being entered and executed on a computer system, for exclusive use by the purchaser of the work. Duplication of this publication or parts thereof is permitted only under the provisions of the Copyright Law of the Publisher's location, in its current version, and permission for use must always be obtained from Springer. Permissions for use may be obtained through RightsLink at the Copyright Clearance Center. Violations are liable to prosecution under the respective Copyright Law.
The use of general descriptive names, registered names, trademarks, service marks, etc. in this publication does not imply, even in the absence of a specific statement, that such names are exempt from the relevant protective laws and regulations and therefore free for general use.
While the advice and information in this book are believed to be true and accurate at the date of publication, neither the authors nor the editors nor the publisher can accept any legal responsibility for any errors or omissions that may be made. The publisher makes no warranty, express or implied, with respect to the material contained herein.

Typesetting: Camera-ready by author, data conversion by Scientific Publishing Services, Chennai, India

Printed on acid-free paper

Springer is part of Springer Science+Business Media (www.springer.com)

Preface

Service-oriented computing – together with Web services as its most important implementation platform – has become the most important paradigm for distributed software development and application for a number of years now. The former ECOWS (European Conference on Web Services) conference series addressed key issues of service-oriented computing, in particular Web services, in nine successful conferences until 2011.

In the meantime, as services are increasingly used remotely, i.e., in the "cloud," the focus of the conference series has shifted slightly. Accordingly, ECOWS was re-launched in 2012 as the "European Conference on Service-Oriented and Cloud Computing" (ESOCC) in Bertinoro, Italy, addressing the state of the art and practice of service-oriented computing and cloud computing.

The second European Conference on Service-Oriented and Cloud Computing, ESOCC 2013, was held in Málaga, Spain, during September 11–13, 2013.

This volume contains the technical papers presented at the conference. The conference consisted of two tracks: a Research Track and an Industrial Track. There were a total of 44 submissions to the Research Track, from which 11 papers were selected (yielding an acceptance rate of 25%), together with four short papers. The review and selection process was performed rigorously, with each paper being reviewed by at least three Program Committee (PC) members (sometimes with the help of additional reviewers).

The Industrial Track selected three papers for presentation, and also invited two presentations from industry.

There were three excellent invited talks at the conference, given by Gianluigi Zavattaro (University of Bologna, Italy), Kenji Takeda (Microsoft Research, Cambridge, UK), and Florian Rosenberg (IBM Thomas J. Watson Research Center, Yorktown Heights, USA).

Five workshops were co-located with the conference: Cloud for IoT (CLIoT 2013), Cloud Storage Optimization (CLOUSO 2013), Foundations of Coordination Languages and Self-Adaptive Systems (FOCLASA 2013), the First Workshop on Mobile Cloud and Social Perspectives (MoCSoP 2013), and the Third International Workshop on Adaptive Services for the Future Internet (WAS4FI 2013).

A PhD Symposium was held on the same day as the workshops.

All in all, ESOCC 2013 was a successful conference, and we owe its success to many people: all the authors who submitted papers, and those who presented papers at the conference; all the PC members who took part in the review and selection process, as well as the additional reviewers they called on for help; all the invited speakers; the members of the Organizing Committee who chaired the industrial track, the workshops and the PhD Symposium, as well as the people who helped organize these events. Last, but not least, we are grateful to the local Organizing Committee for their efficient organization and warm hospitality. To all of you: we say a heart-felt "Thank you"!

July 2013

Kung-Kiu Lau
Winfried Lamersdorf
Ernesto Pimentel

Organization

ESOCC 2013 was organized by the the Department of Computer Science of the University of Málaga, Spain.

Organizing Committee

General Chair

Ernesto Pimentel   University of Málaga, Spain

Program Chairs

Kung-Kiu Lau   University of Manchester, UK
Winfried Lamersdorf   University of Hamburg, Germany

Industrial Track Chairs

Judith Bishop   Microsoft Research USA
Aljosa Pasic   ATOS, Spain

Workshop Chairs

Massimo Villari   University of Messina, Italy
Carlos Canal   University of Málaga, Spain

PhD Symposium Chair

Wolf Zimmermann   University of Halle, Germany

Program Committee

Marco Aiello   University of Groningen, The Netherlands
Farhad Arbab   CWI and Leiden University, The Netherlands
Luciano Baresi   Politecnico di Milano, Italy
Sami Bhiri   Digital Enterprise Research Institute, Ireland
Mario Bravetti   University of Bologna, Italy
Antonio Brogi   University of Pisa, Italy
Christoph Bussler   VoxeoLabs Inc., USA
Manuel Carro   Technical University of Madrid and
                           IMDEA Software Institute, Spain
Wojciech Cellary   Poznan University of Economics, Poland
Javier Cubo   University of Málaga, Spain
Flavio de Paoli   Universita' Milano Bicocca, Italy

Juergen Dunkel	Hannover University for Applied Sciences and Arts, Germany
Schahram Dustdar	TU Wien, Austria
Rik Eshuis	Eindhoven University of Technology, The Netherlands
David Eyers	University of Otago, New Zealand
George Feuerlicht	University of Technology Sydney, Australia
Chris Giblin	IBM Research Zürich, Switzerland
Claude Godart	LORIA, France
Michael Goedicke	University of Duisburg-Essen, Germany
Thomas Gschwind	IBM Research Zürich, Switzerland
Martin Henkel	Stockholm University, Sweden
Dionisis Kehagias	Centre for Research and Technology Hellas, Greece
Ernoe Kovacs	NEC, Germany
Akhil Kumar	Penn State University, USA
Birgitta König-Ries	Friedrich Schiller University of Jena, Germany
Peep Küngas	University of Tartu, Estonia
Frederic Lang	INRIA Rhône-Alpes/VASY, France
Heiko Ludwig	IBM Almaden Research Center, USA
Welf Löwe	Linnaeus University, Sweden
Ingo Melzer	DaimlerChrysler AG, Germany
Roy Oberhauser	Aalen University, Germany
Guadalupe Ortiz	University of Cádiz, Spain
Claus Pahl	Dublin City University, Ireland
George Papadopoulos	University of Cyprus, Cyprus
Cesare Pautasso	University of Lugano, Switzerland
Wolfgang Reisig	Humboldt-Universität zu Berlin, Germany
Ulf Schreier	Furtwangen University, Germany
Rainer Unland	University of Duisburg-Essen, Germany
Massimo Villari	University of Messina, Italy
Erik Wilde	EMC Corporation, USA
Gianluigi Zavattaro	University of Bologna, Italy
Wolf Zimmermann	Universität Halle, Germany
Olaf Zimmermann	Rapperswil University of Applied Sciences, Switzerland
Christian Zirpins	University of Karlsruhe, Germany

Additional Reviewers

Vasilios Andrikopoulos	Christian Gierds	George Pallis
Juan Caballero	Eirini Kaldeli	Achille Peternier
Marco Comerio	Pedro Lopez-Garcia	Robert Prüfer
Ando Emerencia	Faris Nizamic	Jan Sürmeli

Table of Contents

Invited Talk

Aeolus: Mastering the Complexity of Cloud Application Deployment ...   1
*Michel Catan, Roberto Di Cosmo, Antoine Eiche, Tudor A. Lascu,
Michael Lienhardt, Jacopo Mauro, Ralf Treinen, Stefano Zacchiroli,
Gianluigi Zavattaro, and Jakub Zwolakowski*

Research Track

A Service Delivery Framework to Support Opportunistic
Collaborations   4
Gregory Katsaros, Erik Wittern, Birgit Gray, and Stefan Tai

Probabilistic Topic Models for Web Services Clustering and
Discovery   19
*Mustapha Aznag, Mohamed Quafafou, El Mehdi Rochd,
and Zahi Jarir*

Managing Imprecise Criteria in Cloud Service Ranking with a Fuzzy
Multi-criteria Decision Making Method   34
*Ioannis Patiniotakis, Stamatia Rizou, Yiannis Verginadis,
and Gregoris Mentzas*

Modeling Quality Attributes of Cloud-Standby-Systems: A Long-Term
Cost and Availability Model   49
Alexander Lenk and Frank Pallas

Cloud4SOA: A Semantic-Interoperability PaaS Solution for Multi-cloud
Platform Management and Portability   64
*Eleni Kamateri, Nikolaos Loutas, Dimitris Zeginis, James Ahtes,
Francesco D'Andria, Stefano Bocconi, Panagiotis Gouvas,
Giannis Ledakis, Franco Ravagli, Oleksandr Lobunets, and
Konstantinos A. Tarabanis*

Implementation and Evaluation of a Multi-tenant Open-Source ESB   79
*Steve Strauch, Vasilios Andrikopoulos, Santiago Gómez Sáez,
and Frank Leymann*

Putting the Customer Back in the Center of SOA with Service Design
and User-Centered Design   94
Arnita Saini, Benjamin Nanchen, and Florian Evequoz

RAFT-REST - A Client-Side Framework for Reliable, Adaptive
and Fault-Tolerant RESTful Service Consumption.................... 104
    Josef Spillner, Anna Utlik, Thomas Springer, and Alexander Schill

Contract Compliance Monitoring of Web Services 119
    Gregorio Díaz and Luis Llana

Service-Oriented Distributed Applications in the Future Internet:
The Case for Interaction Paradigm Interoperability.................. 134
    Nikolaos Georgantas, Georgios Bouloukakis, Sandrine Beauche,
    and Valérie Issarny

An App Approach Towards User Empowerment in Personalized Service
Environments 149
    Mario Hoffmann

Short Papers

A Life-Cycle Model for Software Service Engineering 164
    Erik Wittern and Robin Fischer

A Tale of Millis and Nanos: Time Measurements in Virtual and
Physical Machines 172
    Ulrich Lampe, Markus Kieselmann, André Miede,
    Sebastian Zöller, and Ralf Steinmetz

A UML Profile for Modeling Multicloud Applications................ 180
    Joaquín Guillén, Javier Miranda, Juan Manuel Murillo,
    and Carlos Canal

Towards Cross-Layer Monitoring of Multi-Cloud Service-Based
Applications... 188
    Chrysostomos Zeginis, Kyriakos Kritikos, Panagiotis Garefalakis,
    Konstantina Konsolaki, Kostas Magoutis, and Dimitris Plexousakis

Industrial Track

A Reliable and Scalable Service Bus Based on Amazon SQS 196
    Sergio Hernández, Javier Fabra, Pedro Álvarez, and Joaquín Ezpeleta

A Comparison of On-Premise to Cloud Migration Approaches 212
    Claus Pahl, Huanhuan Xiong, and Ray Walshe

Migration of an On-Premise Application to the Cloud:
Experience Report 227
    Pavel Rabetski and Gerardo Schneider

Author Index 243

Aeolus: Mastering the Complexity
of Cloud Application Deployment

Michel Catan[1], Roberto Di Cosmo[2], Antoine Eiche[1], Tudor A. Lascu[3],
Michael Lienhardt[2], Jacopo Mauro[3], Ralf Treinen[2], Stefano Zacchiroli[2],
Gianluigi Zavattaro[3], and Jakub Zwolakowski[2]

[1] Mandriva SA
{mcatan,aeiche}@mandriva.com
[2] Univ Paris Diderot, Sorbonne Paris Cité, PPS, UMR 7126, CNRS
roberto@dicosmo.org, michael.lienhardt@inria.fr,
{treinen,zack,zwolakowski}@pps.univ-paris-diderot.fr
[3] Lab. Focus, Department of Computer Science/INRIA, University of Bologna
{lascu,jmauro,zavattar}@cs.unibo.it

Cloud computing offers the possibility to build sophisticated software systems on virtualized infrastructures at a fraction of the cost necessary just few years ago, but deploying/maintaining/reconfiguring such software systems is a serious challenge. The main objective of the Aeolus project, an initiative funded by ANR (the French "Agence Nationale de la Recherche"), is to tackle the scientific problems that need to be solved in order to ease the problem of efficient and cost-effective deployment and administration of the complex distributed architectures which are at the heart of cloud applications.

The approach taken in Aeolus is to bridge the gap between Infrastructure as a Service and Platform as a Service. In fact, as shown in the picture, applications leveraging the power of the Cloud need to allow efficient deployment and configuration of their components at the level of IaaS and at the level of Services. For this, it is necessary to develop advanced tools that propose a deployment configuration according to the requirements of the user or of a higher level application.

Integrated solutions to this problem needs to deal at the same time with both fine grained software components, like packages to be installed on one single virtual machine, and coarse grained services possibly obtained as composition of distributed and properly connected sub-services. To this aim, in [3] we have proposed the Aeolus component model: a component is a grey-box showing relevant internal states and the actions that

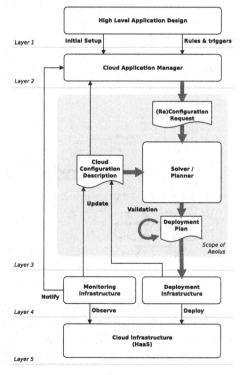

K.-K. Lau, W. Lamersdorf, and E. Pimentel (Eds.): ESOCC 2013, LNCS 8135, pp. 1–3, 2013.
© Springer-Verlag Berlin Heidelberg 2013

can be acted on the component to change state during deployment and reconfiguration, each state activates provide, require and conflict ports, active require ports must be bound to active provide ports of other components and active conflict ports prohibit the presence of components with specific active ports.

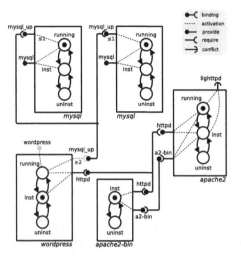

In the Aeolus component model, as depicted, one can express also numerical constraints indicating the maximal number of require ports that can be connected to a provide port, as well as a minimal number of provide ports that need to be connected to a require port. In the example, for instance, the wordpress service require two instances of the mysql database (for example, to have both a primary and a backup instance).

Based on the Aeolus formalization of software components, we have studied the *reconfigurability* problem: given an initial configuration, an universe of available components, and a target component, verify the existence of a sequence of low-level actions that bring the initial configuration to a new one in which the target component is correctly deployed. This study (see [3,2] for the details) allowed us to precisely characterize the theoretical limits of the reconfigurability problem: it is undecidable in the general case, EXP-Space hard if no numeric constraints are considered, and Polytime if also conflicts are not taken into account.

The current research in Aeolus is devoted to the identification of efficient solutions. We plan to gain effectiveness by identifying interesting sub-cases in which feasible solutions are possible. The Zephyrus tool [1] is a first achievement along this direction.

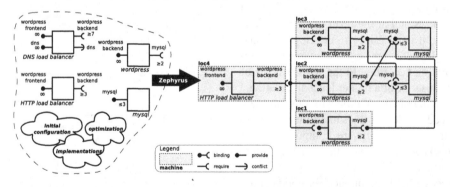

Zephyrus operates on a simplified cloud configuration model, abstracting over the dynamic aspect of Aeolus, and focusing on the problem of finding a target final configuration. When searching for such a configuration that satisfies a user reconfiguration request, Zephyrus takes into account multiple factors: the current cloud deployment status, the *software universes* (repository of available components on the different machines)

and desired optimization criteria (e.g. minimize the amount of deployed machines and, hence, the total cost of operation). Zephyrus is guaranteed to find an optimal solution if one exists, and to do so relies on an external constraint solver. Description of the software components that Zephyrus can grasp includes information about their dependencies, as well as resource consumption information (e.g. memory, bandwidth, disk space, etc.) and the distribution packages which they require to work properly. Thanks to this last piece of information, Zephyrus can assign components to virtual machines guaranteeing that they are *actually installable* there. We are currently extending Zephyrus with simple internal states like *installed*, *running*, and *stopped*. We have already implemented a prototype that computes a sequence of state transitions under the assumption that the initial configuration is empty and that the numerical constraint and the conflicts are considered only in the final configuration.

In order to practically experiment and trial our tools in an industrial environment, we are currently developing a n-tiers application deployment engine. This engine applies, on an IaaS, a final configuration proposed by the Zephyrus tool. First, this tool provisions the required virtual machines thanks to the cloud operating system Openstack. When the virtual machines are running, we go to the second step which is *installation and configuration*. In this step, the engine will connect to each virtual machine involved in the n-tiers application to install required packages and configure services. This is done using the deployment tool MSS (Mandriva Server Setup). Finally, the third step consists of launching each services in order to have an application running. These steps are performed, without any human interaction, by combining the MSS configuration informations and the Zephyrus solution. Currently, we have already deployed a varnish load balancer with several instances of Wordpress. We are now integrating more examples with complex databases configuration containing master and slave requirements.

As future work, we plan to extend the Aeolus model to deal also with different administrative domains to support a more realistic representation of complex and possibly multi-cloud applications. In fact, different administrative domains could impose to contemporaneously deal with different deployment and reconfiguration policies. At the moment, the unique form of heterogeneity that we are able to deal with in the Zephyrus model is at the level of virtual machines: those could provide different resource levels as well as different universes of basic packages depending on the installed operating system.

References

1. Di Cosmo, R., Lienhardt, M., Treinen, R., Zacchiroli, S., Zwolakowski, J.: Optimal provisioning in the cloud. Technical report, Aeolus project (Juin 2013),
   http://hal.archives-ouvertes.fr/hal-00831455
2. Di Cosmo, R., Mauro, J., Zacchiroli, S., Zavattaro, G.: Component reconfiguration in the presence of conflicts. In: Fomin, F.V., Freivalds, R., Kwiatkowska, M., Peleg, D. (eds.) ICALP 2013, Part II. LNCS, vol. 7966, pp. 187–198. Springer, Heidelberg (2013)
3. Di Cosmo, R., Zacchiroli, S., Zavattaro, G.: Towards a formal component model for the cloud. In: Eleftherakis, G., Hinchey, M., Holcombe, M. (eds.) SEFM 2012. LNCS, vol. 7504, pp. 156–171. Springer, Heidelberg (2012)

A Service Delivery Framework
to Support Opportunistic Collaborations

Gregory Katsaros[1], Erik Wittern[1], Birgit Gray[2], and Stefan Tai[1]

[1] FZI - Research Center for Information Technology, Berlin, Germany
{katsaros,wittern,tai}@fzi.de
[2] DW - Deutsche Welle, Germany
birgit.gray@dw.de

Abstract. The wide spread use of computing devices, such as smart phones, cameras, and sensors results in abundance of available information. When such information flows occur in a specific place, at a certain time, and with the participating entities working together or sharing information to achieve common goals, we refer to the outcome of an opportunistic collaboration. In this paper we define and analyse this new collaboration domain and present a framework through which opportunistic collaboration services can be provisioned. We describe in detail the processes that the framework supports, including the modeling of opportunistic collaborations, the collaboration service creation, and the participation management. We evaluate the framework through a use case scenario in the context of participatory journalism in high-profile news events.

Keywords: opportunistic collaborations, services, collaboration, model-driven engineering, Cloud platform.

1   Introduction

Collaboration is the social paradigm of people working together towards achieving a common goal. From an IT perspective, collaboration is "[...] the process in which entities share information, resources and responsibilities to jointly plan, implement and evaluate a program of activities to achieve a common goal" [1]. The same principle can be applied when describing distributed systems, with their contributing entities sharing and exchanging information, services, resources and responsibilities in order to reach a desired outcome (i.e., as outlined by the corresponding application requirements).

In collaboration networks, nowadays, human participants can exchange information through different channels, including mobile phones, tablet computers, connected cameras or wearable sensors. The adoption of such smart devices transforms each of the participants into a moving gateway of information (to be consumed or being produced), resulting in a mesh of active, communicating things. Besides, an increasing number of real-world entities are equipped with sensors and actuators and are connected with the Internet, forming the so called *Internet of Things (IoT)* [2]. Through the effective utilization of available information flows in terms of collaborations, everyday challenges can be tackled

K.-K. Lau, W. Lamersdorf, and E. Pimentel (Eds.): ESOCC 2013, LNCS 8135, pp. 4–18, 2013.
© Springer-Verlag Berlin Heidelberg 2013

and new opportunities can be realized. For example, the visitors of a high profile sports event, by sharing their position, they could create a real-time map of people participation around the stadium premises. Therefore, the digital information that is produced by all entities of a community could be exploited either for the creation of ICT services (e.g. best route), which could be offered directly back to the people, or for knowledge creation on behalf of the organizers, in a crowd-sourcing manner. [3]

These new circumstances create novel types of collaborations which are *opportunistic*. We define opportunistic collaborations in the following way:

Definition 1. *Opportunistic collaborations take place at a certain **time** and a certain **location**. In them, participants aim to achieve common and/or compatible **goals**.*

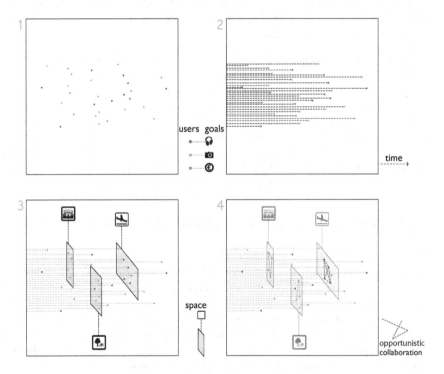

Fig. 1. The Opportunistic Collaboration realization through the intersection of goals, time and space

As depicted in Figure 1, the collaborations considered in this paper are opportunistic, in that they support participants in achieving a common or compatible goal (Figure 1, graph 1). They exist in conjunction with a timely limited occasion such as short-lived events (Figure 1, graph 2) and occur on relatively short notice, therefore, related services must be provisioned and placed quickly with little effort. On the other hand, opportunistic collaborations are linked with a certain location (Figure 1, graph 3), for example, a specific venue or geographic location. Participants may only take part in a collaboration if they are situated within the area. The high level of *volatility* of the participants even challenges the establishment of collaboration in this dynamic and constantly evolving environment. To what is more, the different technical requirements and capabilities of each participant in a collaboration hardens the interoperability, hence the increased participation. Finally, the usage patterns of an opportunistic collaboration is based on open and massive participation, thus, the mechanism serving the collaboration should be flexible in terms of capacity. Therefore, a centralized service-based solution is more appealing than an ad-hoc collaboration implementation.

In this context, our motivation for this work lies on the the need of tools and mechanisms to design and deploy *collaboration services* that support such opportunistic collaborations. These services must have short development cycles and short time-to-market, should take into consideration the diversity of data and resources, and use Cloud-enabled technologies to allow the scalability and reconfiguration during runtime.

Definition 2. *A collaboration service is an on-line offering that allows for the participants of an opportunistic situation to engage themselves in the collaboration and to share or consume information and resources in a dynamic manner.*

In this publication we present a framework which allows the modeling and provisioning of opportunistic collaboration services. In section 2 we present the framework in detail, in section 3 we validate our approach by conceptualizing a use case from the domain of participatory journalism. We discuss related work from diverse areas in section 4, before we conclude in section 5.

2   Collaboration Service Creation Framework

The proposed framework envisions the rapid development and provision of services to serve collaboration scenarios as illustrated in Figure 2. The stakeholders in the designed system are on the one hand the *participants* in the opportunistic collaboration scenario (consumers of the service) and on the other hand the *collaboration service developers*(CSDs) that are designing and offering the service.

The participants are represented by entities that offer their resources (storage, computation, video streams etc.), which make themselves available to the framework by registering through provided interfaces.

Consequently, the modeling of collaboration services and the definition of the goals are performed by the CSD. Given that the CSD identifies the opportunity, he specifies a collaboration model and rules that will guide the participants towards achieving the corresponding goals in the scenario. Therefore, the resulting *collaboration service* is owned and managed by him. One CSD can own multiple collaboration services for the same or different location, time, scenario etc.

Finally, the collaboration service will allow participants to join the collaboration network and interact with each other, following the rules and conditions that the CSD has defined in the model. Considering these entities' capabilities

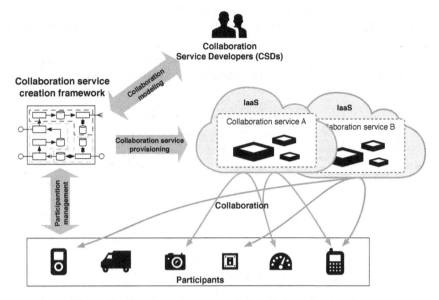

Fig. 2. Realization of opportunistic collaboration services

of producing data (for example, location data, photos and videos) and also consuming data, and based on the selected role, they can act as both *consumer* and *producer* of information.

The motivation of the CSDs in order to engage themselves and use such framework is that they could fast and simple provision custom services for specific events or situations. Those services would allow information exchange between participating entities either for enhancing the user-experience of the visitors / participants to the event or in order to assist the organizers by providing them additional information and therefore better perspective.

The incentives for participation to such collaboration would be given by the creator of the opportunistic collaboration service. To this end, for example, an opportunistic collaboration scenario during a sports event taking place in a certain location for a few days (e.g. European Basketball finals) could be based on a credit system: participants when sharing information (e.g. photos, audio stream etc.), and therefore becoming producers, they collect credits which can then spend by becoming consumers in the opportunistic collaboration, or cash into other services or presents provided by the organizers. The investigation and implementation of such incentives mechanisms is out of the scope of our work while it belongs to a business plan analysis. The focus of this work is the definition of opportunistic collaboration principles and the presentation of the framework that allows the provisioning of such services. The additional tools that could make the proposed concept a complete ready-to-use solution (e.g. mobile client application, graphical interface for modeling etc.) are not being described in this publication.

The collaboration service provisioning that is offered by the framework is divided into three major scientific and technical processes: 1) participation management, 2) collaboration modeling and 3) collaboration service provisioning. Each process is being accomplished be a set of components of the framework as is being presented in the architecture diagram illustrated in Figure 3.

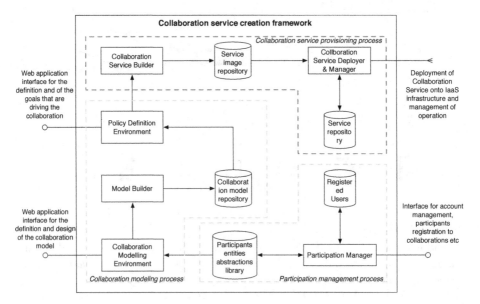

Fig. 3. Architecture of our framework for provisioning opportunistic collaboration services

In the following sections we present the framework's architecture and describe each process in detail.

2.1   Participation Management Process

The first element of the collaboration service provisioning framework is the management of participation of the framework itself as well as of the collaboration service during runtime (smart devices, IoTs etc.). All involved entities must be registered using a respective profile of participation. The *Participation Manager* component is responsible for exposing the interfaces towards the users of the framework (i.e., CSDs) as well as the possible users of a collaboration service (i.e., participants). In the case of the collaboration service participants, this profile includes an abstraction of the registered entity, which must be created for every type of entity. The objective of this registration process is twofold: (a) define and enable interfaces of several heterogeneous information and service entities, (b) create an active pool of mobile devices, sensors and actors with which future collaborations can be formed. Through this process the protocol and technology for the collaboration operation are also specified. With regard to the framework, the participation of the CSDs must be managed in order for them to have access to the tools and services of the framework. The registered users and the abstracted interfaces are being stored in the *Registered users* and *Participants entities abstractions library* repositories, as illustrated in Figure 3.

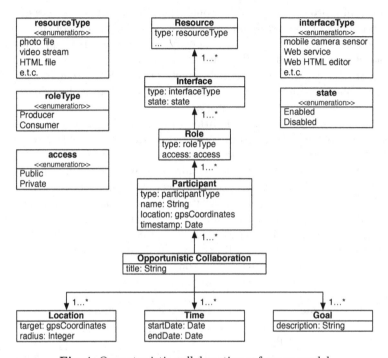

Fig. 4. Opportunistic collaboration reference model

2.2 Collaboration Modeling Process

The main offering of the framework results from its support mechanisms for CSDs to accelerate the creation of new collaboration services. The first task in that context is to identify and analyze the requirements of an opportunistic collaboration. Hence, the CSD creates a collaboration model that describes the potential participants, the information flows between them, and their roles. The time and the location factors of an opportunistic collaboration are being explicitly expressed within the model while the goal of it is being captured by the model through the constraints definition as well as by the overall model structure.

Figure 4 illustrates the reference model for modeling opportunistic collaborations. Every participant has a certain role and an interface that supports information exchange. The *resource Type* and the *interface Type* are enumeration types that are being defined during the registration process by the *Participation Manager*. Furthermore, the state of an interface can either be *enabled* (in the sense that is an active participant of the collaboration) or *disabled*. The role of a participant can formally be specified as *producer* or *consumer* of information.

To model a prosumer, the participant is modeled twice with different roles each time. Every role can be accessed publicly or privately. In a *public* role participants are allowed to join it during runtime while in a *private* one the CSD must define the participant's information during design-time. Additional roles can be defined by the CSD by extending the model.

The modeling process is realized through the *Collaboration Modeling Environment* component of the proposed framework. Using this component, the CSD can design the collaboration scenario, specify the requirements and constraints, and generate the specification file that will be used for the service development. An instance of a collaboration model depicts effectively the collaboration scenario and application that the CSD wants to realize and after the design process is being built and stored in a repository.

The application logic and coordination of any possible information processing functions is being introduced in the collaboration modeling process through the *Policy Definition Environment* component. In corresponding tasks, the CSD can add on top of the designed model certain rules and constraints that help him achieve the goals of the opportunistic collaboration. Those policies will be incorporated into the collaboration service that will be instantiated later and triggered automatically based on the information flow between the participants. The realization of this mechanism is done through a syntax inspired by the *Object Constraint Language (OCL)* [4] and adjusted to our needs. Through this descriptive syntax the CSD can define rules, operations or execute functions on top of the model. The syntax of our rule definition language is presented in Table 1.

Table 1. Rules and constraints definition notation

Predefined types	Operation
Context	Defines an operation which is being applied upon a model entity
Pre	Pre-condition with regard to an operation. Must return TRUE or FALSE. Represents what must be true before the operation is executed.
Post	Post-condition with regard to an operation. Must return TRUE or FALSE and must be evaluated after a pre-condition. Represents what will be true after the operation is executed.
Exec	Executable condition. It executes a pre-defined function and can be evaluated in relation with or without a pre- or a post-condition.
and, or, xor, not, implies, if-then-else, while	Logical operators that return a boolean value.
==,<, >, !=	Comparison operators used with logical operators.
function_name(arg1, ... , argN)	Execution of a function with the name function_name and the arguments listed in the parenthesis. The function should be found in the library, either provided by the platform or added by the CSD.

An example syntax for constraining the location of the opportunistic collaboration is the following:

```
Context: Opportunistic Collaboration
Pre: withinRange(opportunistic_collaboration->Participant.location,
  opportunistic_collaboration->Location.target,
  opportunistic\_collaboration->Location.radius)
```

In this example, the participant must be within the range of the defined location. The context specifies the entity of the model that the policy is being applied to and the *Pre* stands for a *pre-condition* constraint. There can be *post-conditions* as well as *executables* (exec). The developer, depending on the type of the resources in the modeled collaboration, can introduce, for example, a rule on a video streaming resource to not transmit the video if the brightness of the image is too low. This feature will also enable the introduction of security restrictions on the data transmitted from each information node. At this point we should note that the definition of the constraints might seem complicated and time consuming but in the final developed system such complexity would be hidden behind graphical rule definition interfaces (e.g. rule definition within email clients). Hence, here we are explaining the logic and the concept behind that functionality.

2.3   Collaboration Service Provisioning Process

In order to allow open participation, improve the interoperability and also remove the participation overhead from the end user, the realization of the collaboration is necessary to be realized through a centralized service and not in a P2P fashion. To this end, the provisioning of the opportunistic collaboration process is an important part of the framework and is being achieved through a set of components described bellow. The *Collaboration Service Builder* and the *Collaboration Service Deployer & Manager* are responsible for the respective tasks. In the beginning, the model of a scenario along with the policies defined are being transformed to a virtual machine image (VMI) through *Model Transformation Tools* integrated into the framework. This image can then be deployed to Cloud infrastructures. It includes all the necessary interfaces that are defined in the model and exist in the framework's registry and represents the collaboration service that will serve the opportunistic collaboration. Following the image creation is the deployment and management of the service. The respective component deploys the image in an Cloud provider. The details of deployment process depend on the hosting environment of the framework and therefore we will not go into details at this point. This instantiation process results in the delivery of a collaboration service, provided as a Cloud service offering, which allows for the rapid realization of the described collaborative situation. The realization of the collaboration service as a Cloud-based offering allows the CSD to modify the collaboration model and re-deploy the service during runtime. In this sense, the proposed system acts as an accelerator for the creation of services in order to harness dynamically appearing collaboration potentials.

3 Use Case: Supporting Data-Driven Reporting from Predictable, High Profile News Events

To illustrate how our framework functions with actual collaboration opportunities and to show its applicability, we here present a realistic use case from the domain of data-driven reporting [5].

3.1 The Application Domain

News events and other happenings of public interest often draw large media audiences. They include, for example, major sports championships, cultural performances, speeches by politicians, election debates, event-driven press conferences, organized demonstrations, or the aftermaths of sudden news events.

News *journalists* report from such events. They have to deal with an ever increasing volume of data in order to conduct their work in the digital age, stemming from digital devices, social networks, open sensor networks, smart city objects, or even publicly operated drones. These data sources must be managed in addition to traditional data streams from correspondents, news agencies, or outside broadcast vans. A news *editor* is regularly tasked with planning for predictable, high profile news events.

Journalists and editors should consider any available information for inclusion in their reports. They would ideally require tools, which allows them to select, combine and receive real-time data feeds from digital devices, sensor networks, or sensor-enabled objects. For the date or period in question, news editors need to know which data feeds are available, i.e. which are physically present in the location and which are reliable as well as legally compliant.

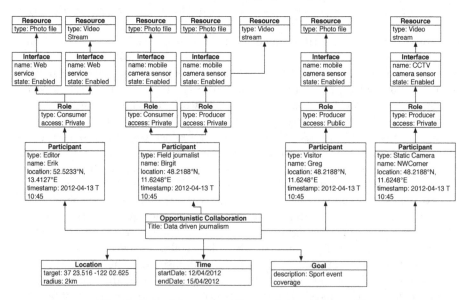

Fig. 5. Data driven journalism collaboration model

Specifying the Use Case's Collaboration

The scenario that we are going to present is referring to timely limited high profile athletics event that is taking place in a sport facility (e.g. stadium). The specified participants of this scenario are:

- **Visitors** of the sports event act as participants in the collaboration service. They dynamically enter and leave the collaboration and share resources with other participants through their mobile camera sensors, thus acting as producers of information.
- **Field journalists** located at the premises of the sport's facility report to the editor using their smart, mobile devices. They produce information using their smart phones (e.g., they stream video) and also consume information provided by visitors. Thus, field journalists obtain a real-time overview of the on-going activities and can therefore better organize the on-site coverage in total.
- **News editor** responsible for this event acts as a consumer alone. He receives the information produced by the field journalists as well as the dynamic visitor participation. By utilizing this information flow, he can orchestrate the movement of the journalist and produce in real-time the reportage for the sport event. He is also fulfilling the role of the CSD for the offline design of the collaboration model.
- **Static Camera** provided by the organizers of the sports event located in the NW corner of the stadium. It is acting as a producer participants and is able to send live video stream through its interface.

The collaboration model of the described opportunistic collaboration scenario is presented in Figure 5. We should note that for the actual implementation of this conceptual use case there might be extra tools need that are built on top of our framework. To this end we are assuming that participants (consumers or producers) of this opportunistic collaboration are using a client application to visualize the collaboration itself. Through such application the editor and the field journalist can request resources from the producer entities. The following set of constraints is defined on top of the presented scenario:

```
Context: Opportunistic Collaboration
Pre: ((opportunistic_collaboration->Participant.type == "Field Journalist")
AND (opportunistic_collaboration->Participant.type == "Visitor")
AND (opportunistic_collaboration->Participant.type == "Static Camera"))
AND (inRange(opportunistic_collaboration->Participant.location,
opportunistic_collaboration->Location.target,
    opportunistic_collaboration->Location.radius))
Post: opportunistic_collaboration->Participant->Role->Interface.state = Enabled

Context: Role
Pre: self.type=="Producer"
Exec: applyImageFilter(self->Interface)
```

The first constraint, which applies to the whole model, includes a pre-condition for the existence of the collaboration stating that the participants with the type

"Field Journalist", "Visitor" and "Static Camera" must be within the range of the defined collaboration location (Interface.state=Enabled). As a result the "Editor" of the scenario could be in a different location but still receive the feeds from the information producers which are restricted to a certain location. The second constraint applies to the Role entity of the model and has the precondition that the role type should be "Producer". In that case the exec condition must be applied as well, which in this case is the execution of the function "applyImageFilter" on the interface of the "Producer" role. In other words, the content transmitted from the producers will subject to an image correction filter that will be applied by this function. The function is being provided by the CSD during the constraint definition step and is being incorporated within the collaboration service image.

Through this conceptual validation of the opportunistic collaboration modeling we can verify the applicability of the proposed approach in scenarios with certain usage patterns. The *location and time specific requirements* of the news event are captured by the model and the presented constraint. The participants, the field journalists and the static camera must be within the specified range, while the editor could be anywhere. The concrete realization of information transmission, on the other hand, depends on the implementation of the *information interfaces*. Thus, our model is principally capable of handling diverse information transmission technologies by defining specific interfaces in the respective entities. To what is more, successful adaptation of collaboration services in the data-driven journalism context requires processing of *real-time information flows*. Our model specifies the creation and transfer of information in terms of involved roles being producer or consumer. In addition, handling potentially *tremendous amounts of information* requires effective processing means like filtering of legally or quality-wise inappropriate information. Using our framework's proposed constraint definition, we are able to specify the (automatic) pre-processing of information, which can be used for the outlined purposes.

4   Related Work

We focus related work on two areas: first, we consider existing approaches in the area of *collaboration modeling*, which is at the heart of our approach. Second, we consider related work regarding *Cloud service deployment*.

4.1   Collaboration Modeling

A fundamental question addressed in related work regarding **generic collaboration models** is whether modeling approaches can support the development of collaboration technologies [6], corresponding to the premise of our collaboration reference model. The authors present eight collaboration modeling approaches, and conclude that with them can contribute to the requirements analysis, choosing or developing new collaboration capabilities, adoption, and maximizing benefit from technologies. In this sense, the authors support our idea of utilizing modeling approaches to improve the realization of collaboration scenarios. "A

Reference Model for Collaborative Networks" (ARCON) is a modeling framework for capturing collaborative networks [7]. Its goal is to provide a generic abstract representation of collaborative networks a) to better understand their involved entities and relations among them and b) to provide basis for more specific models for manifestations of collaborative networks. While ARCON provides a very complete reference model, it does not specifically focus on opportunistic collaborations. In the field of ad-hoc networks there have been modeling structures presented for workflows[8] as well as opportunistic service compositions[9]. Such solutions usually propose decentralized strategies, which in our case could not fulfill our requirements as we explained in previous section. Other approaches focus more specifically on modeling the collaboration in the context of **collaboration models for the Internet of Things**. It has been proposed to use agent models to capture how sensors in a network can collaborate [10]. The model includes various types of software agents that realize sensor collaboration. Other approaches model collaboration between Internet of Things (IoTs) entities [11]. For collaborations, devices are abstracted as device-oriented Web services which are composed in process models. Further, this approach does not include aspects like temporal or local validity, which we address. The "pervasive computing supported collaborative work" model (PCSCW) aims to seamlessly integrate smart devices to enable the collaboration of users [12]. A *task model* defines collaboration processes that make use of resources defined in a *resource model*, under consideration of device collaboration rules [13]. These rules define behavior of resources within a collaboration, for example, to switch the means of data communication given a certain threshold is reached. Despite not targeting opportunistic collaborations specifically, PCSCW's approach is very similar to our perception of collaboration modeling and did and will continue to influence our work.

Some ideas exist with regard to **utilizing smart phones (and their various sensors) in collaboration scenarios**. It is proposed to use smart phone cameras for collaborative road advisories [14], or in combination with online social networks for collaboration in the context of opportunistic scenarios [15].

4.2   Cloud Service Delivery

Cloud service delivery requires the creation of a service in the sense of a virtual machine image, which can be run on Cloud infrastructure or platforms. Our framework utilizes *model-driven engineering (MDE)* approaches for this purpose. In MDE, models describing software are created instead of manually implementing software. The main goal of MDE is to better cope with increasing development complexities, avoiding for example errors or memory leaks introduced through manual software implementation [16]. The created models are automatically transferred to executable software. Arguments for MDE include the increased abstraction from the software's underlying computing environment, allowing engineers to focus on the software solution instead of the details of the implementation [17].

Cloud computing can be beneficially combined with MDE in two ways [18]: First, MDE can be utilized to automate the development of Cloud services. On the infrastructure level, it has been proposed to use MDE for the configuration, deployment, and management of virtual machines [19]. The approach uses feature models from the software engineering domain to capture the configuration options of virtual machines and uses these models to drive the deployment process. On the application level, for example, the "model-driven approach for the design and execution of applications on multiple Clouds" (MODAClouds) has been presented [20]. By using MDE, the approach aims to enable the creation of services specific for different (and potentially multiple) Clouds. Second, MDE can be performed using Cloud services. Multiple service providers offer integrated development environments that can be accessed as Software-as-a-Service [1]. Also, modeling capabilities can be offered as Software-as-a-Service [2]. Related research addresses questions like collaboration, revision control, and continuous integration [21]. In the context of IoT, it has been proposed to simplify the development and deployment of radio-frequency identification (RFID) related applications [22]. The approach uses blueprints, which act as architectural patterns, to abstract from and ease the utilization of Cloud services. Software modules, representing for example the RFID sensors, can then be combined using a Cloud-based mash-up editor.

As far as the services lifecycle concerns specifications from OSLC (Open Services for Lifecyle Collaboration) have being proposed for the development of model-based methodologies for service discovery[23]. The proposed technique for code generation and service orchestration would be considered for the implementation of the Collaboration Service Manager component of our framework. Our framework foresees both approaches to combine MDE and Cloud computing for Cloud service delivery: a platform that provides means for the model-driven development of opportunistic collaboration services, using MDE to automatically create, deploy, and operate the resulting services in the Cloud.

5   Conclusion

The high dynamics in which nowadays devices are created and their increased interconnectedness, enabled by their interfaces, result in an active information mesh. The effective collaboration between the members of that mesh could be highly productive and raise new opportunities.

To this end, we presented an architectural framework through which one can develop services to support opportunistic collaborations. The suggested methodology incorporates three processes: (a) the participation management, (b) the opportunistic collaboration modeling, and (c) the service provisioning. In this context, we designed and proposed a reference model for opportunistic collaborations. On top of that model, we defined a constraint language and syntax

---

[1] For example the "Cloud9 IDE", see: https://c9.io/

[2] For example Signavio's BPMN process modeling offers, see: http://www.signavio.com/products/process-editor/process-modeling/

that can be used in order to express the logic and operation of an opportunistic collaboration.

Furthermore, we performed a conceptual validation of the proposed methodology by applying the modeling process of the suggested system on a use case from the data-driven reporting sector. In the specific scenario an opportunistic collaboration between the field journalists, the visitors and the editor of a media/news agency is formed in order to facilitate and enhance the coverage of a high-profile sports event. Using our modeling approach we were able to capture all the necessary interactions that characterize the scenario. The time and location constraints could be effectively expressed through the policy definition language that we introduced.

Our future steps include the implementation of a user friendly interface [3] for the modeling of opportunistic collaborations through which even non-experts could design a collaboration scenario. In addition, we aim at implementing the management components (participation and service manager) as RESTful services that would keep resources for every entity. The evaluation of the proposed implementation will be done in terms of: (a)time to publish a collaboration service, (b) ease of collaboration modeling methodology, (c) capacity of participation, and (d) communication interfaces supported.

Overall, we strongly believe that our framework could be the baseline of a platform to accelerate the development of opportunistic collaborations.

References

[1] Camarinha-Matos, L., Afsarmanesh, H.: Taxonomy of Collaborative Networks. Technical report, Future Internet Enterprise Systems (FInES) Task Force on Collaborative Networks (March 2012)

[2] Kortuem, G., Kawsar, F., Sundramoorthy, V., Fitton, D.: Smart objects as building blocks for the internet of things. IEEE Internet Computing 14(1), 44–51 (2010)

[3] Leimeister, J.M., Huber, M., Bretschneider, U., Krcmar, H.: Leveraging crowdsourcing: Activation-supporting components for it-based ideas competition. J. Manage. Inf. Syst. 26(1), 197–224 (2009)

[4] OMG: Object Constraint Language v2.0. Technical report, Object Management Group (2006)

[5] Mirko, L.: Status and Outlook for data-driven journalism. European Journalism Center: Data-Driven Journalism: What is there to learn? A Paper on the Data-Driven Journalism Roundtable Held in Amsterdam on 24 August (2010)

[6] Poltrock, S., Handel, M.: Modeling Collaborative Behavior: Foundations for Collaboration Technologies. In: Proceedings of the 42nd Hawaii International Conference on System Sciences (HICSS), pp. 1–10 (2009)

[7] Camarinha-Matos, L., Afsarmanesh, H.: The ARCON modeling framework. In: Collaborative Networks: Reference Modeling. Springer, New York (2008)

[8] Huth, C., Smolnik, S., Nastansky, L.: Applying topic maps to ad hoc workflows for semantic associative navigation in process networks. In: Proceedings of the Seventh International Workshop on Groupware, pp. 44–49 (2001)

---

[3] Such as Oryx Editor, https://code.google.com/p/oryx-editor/

[9] Groba, C.: Towards opportunistic service composition in dynamic ad hoc environments. In: Pallis, G., et al. (eds.) ICSOC 2011 Workshops. LNCS, vol. 7221, pp. 189–194. Springer, Heidelberg (2012)

[10] Biswas, P.K., Qi, H., Xu, Y.: A Mobile-Agent-Based Collaborative Framework for Sensor Network Applications. In: 2006 IEEE International Conference on Mobile Adhoc and Sensor Systems (MASS), pp. 650–655 (October 2006)

[11] Chen, F., Ren, C., Dong, J., Wang, Q., Li, J., Shao, B.: A Comprehensive Device Collaboration Model for Integrating Devices with Web Services under Internet of Things. In: Proceedings of the 19th IEEE International Conference on Web Services (ICWS). IEEE Computer Society, Los Alamitos (2011)

[12] Hamadache, K., Lancieri, L.: Role-Based Collaboration Extended to Pervasive Computing. In: International Conference on Intelligent Networking and Collaborative Systems (INCOS 2009), pp. 9–15. IEEE Computer Society (November 2009)

[13] Hamadache, K., Lancieri, L.: Dealing with device collaboration rules for the PC-SCW model. In: Kolfschoten, G., Herrmann, T., Lukosch, S. (eds.) CRIWG 2010. LNCS, vol. 6257, pp. 233–248. Springer, Heidelberg (2010)

[14] Koukoumidis, E., Martonosi, M., Peh, L.S.: Leveraging Smartphone Cameras for Collaborative Road Advisories. IEEE Transactions on Mobile Computing 11(5), 707–723 (2012)

[15] Liu, C.H., Hui, P.: Mobile Sensing for Social Collaborations. Technical report, Deutsche Telekom Laboratories (2011)

[16] Schmidt, D.C.: Model-Driven Engineering. IEEE Internet Computing 39(2), 25–31 (2006)

[17] Sommerville, I.: Software Engineering, 9th edn. Addison-Wesley (2011)

[18] Bruneliere, H., Cabot, J., Jouault, F., et al.: Combining Model-Driven Engineering and Cloud Computing. In: Modeling, Design, and Analysis for the Service Cloud-MDA4ServiceCloud 2010: Workshop's 4th edn. (Co-Located with the 6th European Conference on Modelling Foundations and Applications-ECMFA 2010) (2010)

[19] Le Nhan, T., Sunyé, G., Jézéquel, J.-M.: A Model-Driven Approach for Virtual Machine Image Provisioning in Cloud Computing. In: De Paoli, F., Pimentel, E., Zavattaro, G. (eds.) ESOCC 2012. LNCS, vol. 7592, pp. 107–121. Springer, Heidelberg (2012)

[20] Ardagna, D., Di Nitto, E., Mohagheghi, P., Mosser, S., Ballagny, C., D'Andria, F., Casale, G., Matthews, P., Nechifor, C.S., Petcu, D., et al.: MODAClouds: A model-driven approach for the design and execution of applications on multiple Clouds. In: 2012 ICSE Workshop on Modeling in Software Engineering (MISE). IEEE Computer Society (2012)

[21] Mikkonen, T., Nieminen, A.: Elements for a cloud-based development environment: online collaboration, revision control, and continuous integration. In: Proceedings of the WICSA/ECSA 2012 Companion Volume, WICSA/ECSA 2012. ACM, New York (2012)

[22] Guinard, D., Floerkemeier, C., Sarma, S.: Cloud Computing, REST and Mashups to Simplify RFID Application Development and Deployment. In: Proceedings of the 2nd International Workshop on the Web of Things (WoT 2011). ACM, San Francisco (2011)

[23] Biehl, M., Gu, W., Loiret, F.: Model-based service discovery and orchestration for OSLC services in tool chains. In: Brambilla, M., Tokuda, T., Tolksdorf, R. (eds.) ICWE 2012. LNCS, vol. 7387, pp. 283–290. Springer, Heidelberg (2012)

Probabilistic Topic Models
for Web Services Clustering and Discovery

Mustapha Aznag[1], Mohamed Quafafou[1], El Mehdi Rochd[1], and Zahi Jarir[2]

[1] Aix-Marseille University, LSIS UMR 7296, France
{mustapha.aznag,mohamed.quafafou,el-mehdi.rochd}@univ-amu.fr
[2] University of Cadi Ayyad, LISI Laboratory, FSSM, Morocco
jarir@uca.ma

Abstract. In Information Retrieval the Probabilistic Topic Models were originally developed and utilized for topic extraction and document modeling. In this paper, we explore several probabilistic topic models: Probabilistic Latent Semantic Analysis (PLSA), Latent Dirichlet Allocation (LDA) and Correlated Topic Model (CTM) to extract latent factors from web service descriptions. These extracted latent factors are then used to group the services into clusters. In our approach, topic models are used as efficient dimension reduction techniques, which are able to capture semantic relationships between word-topic and topic-service interpreted in terms of probability distributions. To address the limitation of keywords-based queries, we represent web service description as a vector space and we introduce a new approach for discovering web services using latent factors. In our experiment, we compared the accuracy of the three probabilistic clustering algorithms (PLSA, LDA and CTM) with that of a classical clustering algorithm. We evaluated also our service discovery approach by calculating the precision (P@n) and normalized discounted cumulative gain (NDCGn). The results show that both approaches based on CTM and LDA perform better than other search methods.

Keywords: Web service, Data Representation, Clustering, Discovery, Machine Learning, Topic Models.

1 Introduction

The Service Oriented Architecture (SOA) is a model currently used to provide services on the internet. The SOA follows the find-bind-execute paradigm in which service providers register their services in public or private registries, which clients use to locate web services. SOA services have self-describing interfaces in platform-independent XML documents. Web Services Description Language (WSDL) is the standard language used to describe services. Web services communicate with messages formally defined via XML Schema. Different tasks like matching, ranking, discovery and composition have been intensively studied to improve the general web services management process. Thus, the web services community has proposed different approaches and methods to deal with these

K.-K. Lau, W. Lamersdorf, and E. Pimentel (Eds.): ESOCC 2013, LNCS 8135, pp. 19–33, 2013.
© Springer-Verlag Berlin Heidelberg 2013

tasks. Empirical evaluations are generally proposed considering different simulation scenarios. Nowadays, we are moving from web of data to web of services as the number of UDDI Business Registries (URBs) is increasing. Moreover, the number of hosts that offer available web services is also increasing significantly. Consequently, discovering services which can match with the user query is becoming a challenging and an important task. The keyword-based discovery mechanism supported by the most existing services search engines suffers from some key problems: (1) User finds difficulties to select a desired service which satisfies his requirements as the number of retrieved services is huge. (2) Keywords are insufficient in expressing semantic concepts. This is due to the fact that the functional requirements (keywords) are often described by natural language. To enrich web service description, several Semantic Web methods and tools are developed, for instance, the authors of [9,19,1] use ontology to annotate the elements in web services. Nevertheless, the creation and maintenance of ontologies may be difficult and involve a huge amount of human effort [2,12].

To address the limitation of keywords-based queries, we represent web service description as a vector and introduce a new approach for discovering web services using a semantic clustering approach. Service Clustering aims to group together services which are similar to each other. Our clustering approach is based on probabilistic topic models. By organizing the web service data into clusters, services become easier and therefore faster to be discovered and recommended [17].

Probabilistic topic models are a way to deal with large volumes of data by discovering their hidden thematic structure. Their added value is that they can treat the textual data that have not been manually categorized by humans. The concept of "topic" consists on discovering clusters of textual data on similar subjects. These clusters are obtained by calculating the occurrences of words emerging together frequently in different independent texts. Formally, probabilistic topic models use their hidden variables to discover the latent semantic structure in large textual data.

In this paper we investigate using probabilistic machine-learning methods to extract latent factors $z_f \in Z = \{z_1, z_2, ..., z_k\}$ from service descriptions. We will explore several probabilistic topic models : PLSA (Probabilistic latent semantic analysis), LDA (Latent Dirichlet Allocation) and CTM (Correlated Topic Model) and use them to analyze search in repository of web services and define which achieves the best results. By describing the services in terms of latent factors, the dimensionality of the system is reduced considerably. The latent factors can then also be used to efficiently cluster services in a repository. In our experiments, we consider that web services are mixtures of hidden topics, where a topic defines a probability distribution over words.

The rest of this paper is organized as follows. Section 2 provides an overview of related work. In Section 3 we describe in detail our service clustering and discovery approach. Section 4 describes the experimental evaluation. Finally, the conclusion and future work can be found in Section 5.

2   Related Work

In this section, we briefly discuss some of research works related to discovering Web services. Although various approaches can be used to locate and discover Web services on the web, we have focused our research on the service discovery problem using a clustering method. The clustering methodology is a technique that transforms a complex problem into a series of simpler ones, which can be handled more easily. Specifically, this technique re-organizes a set of data into different groups based on some standards of similarity. Clustering analysis has been often used in computer science, as in data mining, in information retrieval, and in pattern classification.

In [1], the authors proposed an architecture for Web services filtering and clustering. The service filtering mechanism is based on user and application profiles that are described using OWL-S (Web Ontology Language for Services). The objectives of this matchmaking process are to save execution time and to improve the refinement of the stored data. Another similar approach [15] concentrates on Web service discovery with OWL-S and clustering technology. Nevertheless, the creation and maintenance of ontologies may be difficult and involve a huge amount of human effort [2,12].

Generally, every web service associates with a WSDL document that contains the description of the service. A lot of research efforts have been devoted in utilizing WSDL documents [8,2,12,13,7,14,17]. Dong et al. [8] proposed the Web services search engine Woogle that is capable of providing Web services similarity search. However, their engine does not adequately consider data types, which usually reveal important information about the functionalities of Web services [11]. Liu and Wong [13] apply text mining techniques to extract features such as service content, context, host name, and service name, from Web service description files in order to cluster Web services. They proposed an integrated feature mining and clustering approach for Web services as a predecessor to discovery, hoping to help in building a search engine to crawl and cluster non-semantic Web services. Elgazzar et al. [7] proposed a similar approach which clusters WSDL documents to improve the non-semantic web service discovery. They take the elements in WSDL documents as their feature, and cluster web services into functionality based clusters. The clustering results can be used to improve the quality of web service search results.

Some researchers use the proximity measures to cluster web services. Measuring the proximity between a service and other services in a dataset is the basic step of most clustering techniques [15,17]. If two vectors are closed to each other in vector space, then they have similar service descriptions or functional attributes depending on characteristics used for constructing the model. Various techniques exist to measure the proximity of two vectors. Nayak et al. [15] proposed a method to improve the Web service discovery process using the Jaccard coefficient to calculate the similarity between Web services. Multidimensional Angle is an efficient measure of the proximity of two vectors. It is used in various clustering approaches [17]. This proximity measure applies cosine of the angle between two vectors. It reaches from the origin rather than the distance between the absolute position of the two points in vector space.

Ma et al. [14] proposed an approach similar to the previously discussed approaches [8,1,15] where the keywords are used first to retrieve Web services, and then to extract semantic concepts from the natural language descriptions in Web services. Ma et al. presented a service discovery mechanism called CPLSA which uses Probabilistic Latent Semantic Analysis (PLSA) to extract latent factors from WSDL service descriptions after the search is narrowed down to a small cluster using a K-Means algorithm. The PLSA model represents a significant step towards probabilistic modelling of text, it is incomplete in that it provides no probabilistic model at the level of documents [3]. The Latent Dirichlet Allocation (LDA) [3] is an attempt to improve the PLSA by introducing a Dirichlet prior on document-topic distribution.

Cassar et al. [5,6] investigated the use of probabilistic machine-learning techniques (PLSA and LDA) to extract latent factors from semantically enriched service descriptions. These latent factors provide a model which represents any type of service's descriptions in a vector form. In their approach, the authors assumed all service descriptions were written in the OWL-S. In [5], Cassar et al. showed how latent factors extracted from service descriptions can be used directly to cluster services in a repository; obtaining a more efficient clustering strategy than the one obtained by a K-Means algorithm. The results obtained from comparing the two methods (PLSA and LDA) showed that the LDA model provides a scalable and interoperable solution for automated service discovery in large service repositories. The LDA model assumes that the words of each document arise from a mixture of topics, each of which is a distribution over the vocabulary. A limitation of LDA is the inability to model topic correlation [4]. This limitation stems from the use of the Dirichlet distribution to model the variability among the topic proportions.

The Correlated Topic Model (CTM) has been developed to address the limitation of LDA [4]. In CTM, topic proportions exhibit correlation via the logistic normal distribution. One key difference between LDA and CTM is the independence assumption between topics in LDA, due to the Dirichlet prior on the distribution of topics (under a Dirichlet prior, the components of the distribution are independent whereas the logistic normal models correlation between the components through the covariance matrix of the normal distribution). However, in the CTM model, a topic may be consistent with the presence of other topics. In this paper, we exploit the advantages of CTM to propose an approach for web service discovery and use a novel semantic clustering algorithm to cluster web services. In our approach, we utilized CTM to capture the semantics hidden behind the words in a query, and the descriptions of the services. Then, we extracted latent factors from web service descriptions. The latent factors can then be used to efficiently cluster services in a repository.

3   Web Service Clustering and Discovery Approach

In this section, we will first describe the necessary pre-processing of WSDL document to construct a web service representation. We then discuss the probabilistic machine-learning techniques used to generate the latent factors. Finally we explain how these latent factors are used to provide an efficient clustering and discovery mechanism.

3.1   Web Service Representation

Generally, every web service has a WSDL (Web Service Description Language) document that contains the description of the service. The WSDL document is an XML-based language, designed according to standards specified by the W3C, that provides a model for describing web services. It describes one or more services as collections of network endpoints, or ports. It provides the specifications necessary to use the web service by describing the communication protocol, the message format required to communicate with the service, the operations that the client can invoke and the service location. Two versions of WSDL recommendation exist: the 1.1[1] version, which is used in almost all existing systems, and the 2.0[2] version which is intended to replace 1.1. These two versions are functionally quite similar but have substantial differences in XML structure.

To manage efficiently web service descriptions, we extract all features that describe a web service from the WSDL document. We recognize both WSDL versions (1.1 and 2.0). During this process, we proceed in two steps. The first step consists of checking availability of web service and validating the content of WSDL document. The second step is to get the WSDL document and read it directly from the WSDL URI to extract all information of the document.

Before representing web services as TF-IDF (Text Frequency and Inverse Frequency) [18] vectors, we need some preprocessing. There are commonly several steps:

- *Features extraction* extracts all features that describe a web service from the WSDL document, such as service name and documentation, messages, types and operations.
- *Tokenization:* Some terms are composed by several words, which is a combination of simple terms (*e.g.*, *get_ComedyFilm_MaxPrice_Quality*). We use therefore regular expression to extract these simple terms (*e.g.*, *get, Comedy, Film, Max, Price, Quality*).
- *Tag and stop words removal:* This step removes all HTML tags, CSS components, symbols (punctuation, etc.) and stop words, such as 'a', 'what', etc. The Standford POS Tagger[3] is then used to eliminate all the tags and stop words and only words tagged as nouns, verbs and adjectives are retained. We also remove the WSDL specific stopwords, such as *host, url, http, ftp, soap, type, binding, endpoint, get, set, request, response*, etc.

---

[1] http://www.w3.org/TR/wsdl
[2] http://www.w3.org/TR/wsdl20/
[3] http://nlp.stanford.edu/software/tagger.shtml

– *Word stemming*: We need to stem the words to their origins, which means that we only consider the root form of words. In this step we use the Porter Stemmer [16] to remove words which have the same stem. Words with the same stem will usually have the same meaning. For example, 'computer', 'computing' and 'compute' have the stem 'comput'. The Stemming process is more effective to identify the correlation between web services by representing them using these common stems (root forms).

– *Service Matrix construction*: After identifying all the functional terms, we calculate the frequency of these terms for all web services. We use the Vector Space Model (VSM) technique to represent each web service as a vector of these terms. In fact, it converts service description to vector form in order to facilitate the computational analysis of data. In information retrieval, VSM is identified as the most widely used representation for documents and is a very useful method for analyzing service descriptions. The TF-IDF algorithm [18] is used to represent a dataset of WSDL documents and convert it to VSM form. We use this technique, to represent a service description in the form of *Service Matrix*. In the service matrix, each row represents a WSDL service description, each column represents a word from the whole text corpus (vocabulary) and each entry represents the TF-IDF weight of a word appearing in a WSDL document. TF-IDF gives a weight w_{ij} to every term j in a service description i using the equation: $w_{ij} = tf_{ij} \cdot \log(\frac{n}{n_j})$. Where tf_{ij} is the frequency of term j in WSDL document i, n is the total number of WSDL documents in the dataset, and n_j is the number of services that contain term j.

3.2 A Probabilistic Topic Model Approach

In our approach, we apply probabilistic machine-learning techniques; Probabilistic Latent Semantic Analysis (PLSA), Latent Dirichlet Allocation (LDA) and Correlated Topic Model (CTM); to extract latent factors $z_f \in Z = \{z_1, z_2, ..., z_k\}$ from web service descriptions (i.e., *Service Matrix*). We use then the extracted latent-factors to group the services into clusters. In our work, topic models are used as efficient dimension reduction techniques, which are able to capture semantic relationships between *word-topic* and *topic-service* interpreted in terms of probability distributions. In our context, an observed event corresponds to occurrence of a word w in a service description s.

The Probabilistic Latent Semantic Analysis (PLSA) is a generative statistical model for analyzing co-occurrence of data. PLSA is based on the aspect model [10]. Considering observations in the form of co-occurrences (s_i, w_j) of words and services, PLSA models the joint probability of an observed pair $P(s_i, w_j)$ obtained from the probabilistic model is shown as follows [10]:

$$P(s_i, w_j) = \sum_{f=1}^{k} P(z_f)P(s_i|z_f)P(w_j|z_f) \tag{1}$$

We assume that service descriptions and words are conditionally independent given the latent factor. We have implemented the PLSA model using the

PennAspect[4] model which uses maximum likelihood to compute the parameters. The dataset was divided into two equal segments which are then transformed into the specific format required by the PennAspect. We use words extracted from service descriptions and create a PLSA model. Once the latent variables $z_f \in Z = \{z_1, z_2, ..., z_k\}$ are identified, services can be described as a multinomial probability distribution $P(z_f|s_i)$ where s_i is the description of the service i. The representation of a service with these latent variables reflects the likelihood that the service belongs to certain concept groups [14]. To construct a PLSA model, we first consider the joint probability of an observed pair $P(s_i, w_j)$ (Equation 1). The parameters $P(z)$, $P(s|z)$ and $P(w|z)$ can be found using a model fitting technique such as the Expectation Maximization (EM) algorithm [10]. The learned latent variables can be used to cluster web services. If a probability distribution over a specific z_f when given a web service s is high, then the service s can be affected to the cluster z_f.

The Latent Dirichlet Allocation (LDA) is a probabilistic topic model, which uses a generative probabilistic model for collections of discrete data [3]. LDA is an attempt to improve the PLSA by introducing a Dirichlet prior on service-topic distribution. As a conjugate prior for multinomial distributions, Dirichlet prior simplifies the problem of statistical inference. The principle of LDA is the same as that of PLSA: mapping high-dimensional count vectors to a lower dimensional representation in latent semantic space. Each word w in a service description s is generated by sampling a topic z from topic distribution, and then sampling a word from topic-word distribution. The probability of the ith word occurring in a given service is given by Equation 2:

$$P(w_i) = \sum_{f=1}^{k} P(w_i|z_i = f)P(z_i = f) \tag{2}$$

Where z_i is a latent factor (or topic) from which the ith word was drawn, $P(z_i = f)$ is the probability of topic f being the topic from which w_i was drawn, and $P(w_i|z_i = f)$ is the probability of having word w_i given the fth topic.

Let $\theta^{(s)} = P(z)$ refer to the multinomial distribution over topics in the service description s and $\phi^{(j)} = P(w|z = j)$ refer to the multinomial distribution over words for the topic j. There are various algorithms available for estimating parameters in the LDA: Variational EM [3] and Gibbs sampling [20]. In this paper, we adopt an approach using Variational EM. See [3] for further details on the calculations. For the LDA training, we used Blei's implementation[5], which is a C implementation of LDA using Variational EM for Parameter Estimation and Inference. The key objective is to find the best set of latent variables that can explain the observed data. This can be made by estimating $\phi^{(j)}$ which provides information about the important words in topics and $\theta^{(s)}$ which provides the weights of those topics in each web service. After training the LDA model, we use the learned latent factors to cluster web services. If a probability distribution $\theta^{(s)}$ over a specific z_f when given a web service s is high, then the service s can be affected to the cluster z_f.

---

[4] http://cis.upenn.edu/~ungar/Datamining/software_dist/PennAspect/
[5] http://www.cs.princeton.edu/~blei/lda-c/

The Correlated Topic Model (CTM) is another probabilistic topic model that enhances the basic LDA [3], by modeling of correlations between topics. One key difference between LDA and CTM is that in LDA, there is an independence assumption between topics due to the Dirichlet prior on the distribution of topics. In fact, under a Dirichlet prior, the components of the distribution are independent whereas the logistic normal used in CTM, models correlation between the components through the covariance matrix of the normal distribution. However, in CTM, a topic may be consistent with the presence of other topics. Assume we have S web services as a text collection, each web service s contains N_s word tokens, T topics and a vocabulary of size W. The Logistic normal is obtained by :

- For each service, draw a K-dimensional vector η_s from a multivariate Gaussian distribution with mean μ and covariance matrix Σ : $\eta_s \sim \mathcal{N}(\mu, \Sigma)$
- We consider the mapping between the mean parameterization and the natural parameterization: $\theta = f(\eta_i) = \frac{\exp \eta}{\sum_i \exp \eta_i}$
- Map η into a simplex so that it sums to 1.

The main problem is to compute the posterior distribution of the latent variables given a web service : $P(\eta, z_{1:N}, w_{1:N})$. Since this quantity is intractable, we use approximate techniques. In this case, we choose variational methods rather than gibbs sampling because of the non-conjugacy between logistic normal and multinomial. The problem is then to bound the log probability of a web service :

$$\log P(w_{1:N}|\mu, \Sigma, \beta) \geq E_q[\log P(\eta|\mu, \Sigma)] + \sum_{n=1}^{N} E_q[\log P(z_n|\eta)] \\ + \quad \sum_{n=1}^{N} E_q[\log P(w_n|z_n, \beta)] + H(q) \tag{3}$$

The expectation is taken with respect to a variational distribution of the latent variables :

$$q(\eta, z|\lambda, \nu^2, \phi) = \prod_{i=1}^{K} q(\eta_i|\lambda_i, \nu_i^2) \prod_{n=1}^{N} q(z_n|\phi_n) \tag{4}$$

and $H(q)$ denotes the entropy of that distribution (See [4] for more details).

Given a model parameters $\{\beta_{1:K}, \mu, \Sigma\}$ and a web service $w_{1:N}$, the variational inference algorithm optimizes the lower bound (Equation 3)) with respect to the variational parameters using the variational EM algorithm. In the E-step, we maximize the bound with respect to the variational parameters by performing variational inference for each web service. In the M-step, we maximize the bound with respect to the model parameters. The E-step and M-step are repeated until convergence. For the CTM training, we used the Blei's implementation[6], which is a C implementation of Correlated Topic Model using Variational EM for Parameter Estimation and Inference. We estimate the *topic-service* distribution by computing: $\theta = \frac{\exp(\eta)}{\sum_i \exp(\eta_i)}$. Where $\exp(\eta_i) = \exp(\lambda_i + \frac{\nu_i^2}{2})$ and the variational parameters $\{\lambda_i, \nu_i^2\}$ are respectively the mean and the variance of the normal distribution. Then, we estimate the *topic-word* distribution ϕ by calculating the

---

[6] http://www.cs.princeton.edu/~blei/ctm-c/index.html

exponential of the log probabilities of words for each topic. As already mentioned, the learned latent factors can be used to cluster web services. Thus, if a probability distribution θ over a specific z_f when given a web service s is high, then the service s can be affected to the cluster z_f.

The three topic models were trained using different number of classes (e.g 5 to 100) to compare the results (See Section 4).

The key idea of our approach is to cluster the services into a group of learned latent variables, which can be achieved by computing the probability $P(latent\_variable|service)$ for each latent variable. The rationale for this is that the dimensionality of the model is reduced as every web service can be described in terms of a small number of latent factors (topics) rather than a large number of concepts. With the maximum value of the computation used for the cluster for a service, we can categorize services into their corresponding group. Consequently, searching for a service inside a cluster can be performed by searching for matching topics rather than matching the text describing the web service to a set of keywords extracted from the user query.

Based on the clustered service groups, a set of matched services can be returned by comparing the similarity between the query and the related topic, rather than computing the similarity between query and each service in the dataset. If the retrieved services are not compatible with user's query, the second best cluster would be chosen and the computing proceeds to the next iteration.

Service discovery aims to find web services with user required functionalities. The service discovery process assumes that services with similar functionalities should be discovered. In our work, we propose to use the probabilistic topic model to discover the web services that match with the user query. Let $Q = \{w_1, w_2, \ldots, w_n\}$ be a user query that contains a set of words w_i produced by a user. In our approach, we propose to use the generated probabilities θ and ϕ as the base criteria for computing the similarity between a service description and a user query. For this, we model information retrieval as a probabilistic query to the topic model. We note this as $P(Q|s_i)$ where Q is the set of words contained in the query. Thus, using the assumptions of the topic model, $P(Q|s_i)$ can be calculated by equation 5.

$$P(Q|s_i) = \prod_{w_k \in Q} P(w_k|s_i) = \prod_{w_k \in Q} \sum_{z=1}^{T} P(w_k|z_f)P(z_f|s_i) \tag{5}$$

The most relevant services are the ones that maximize the conditional probability of the query $P(Q|s_i)$. Consequently, relevant services are ranked in order of their similarity score to the query. Thus, we obtain automatically an efficient ranking of the services retrieved.

4   Evaluation

Our experiments are performed out based on real-world web services obtained from [21]. The WSDL corpus consists of over 1051 web services from 8 different application domains. Each web service belongs to one out of eight service domains named as: Communication, Education, Economy, Food, Travel, Medical and Military. Table 1 lists the number of services from each domain.

Before applying the proposed service clustering and discovery, we deal the WSDL corpus. The objective of this pre-processing is to identify the functional terms of services, which describe the semantics of their functionalities. WSDL corpus processing consists of several steps: *Features extraction, Tokenization:, Tag and stop words removal, Word stemming* and *Service Matrix construction* (See Section 3.1).

Table 1. Domains of Web services

Domain	Services	Domain	Services
Communication	59	Geography	60
Economy	354	Medical	72
Education	264	Travel	161
Food	41	Military	40

4.1   Web Service Clustering Evaluation

In order to evaluate the effectiveness of the clustering technique, we use two different measures: *entropy* and *purity* [23,22]. Suppose q classes represent the partitioned web services (service domains), k clusters produced by our clustering approach and n the total number of services.

– *Entropy*: The entropy measures how the various semantic classes are distributed within each group (cluster). Given a particular cluster C_j of size n_j, the *entropy* of this cluster is defined to be:

$$E(C_j) = -\frac{1}{log(q)} \sum_{i=1}^{q} \frac{n_j^i}{n_j} log(\frac{n_j^i}{n_j}) \qquad (6)$$

Where q is the number of domains in the dataset, and n_j^i is the number of services of the ith domain that where assigned to the jth cluster. The averaged entropy of the clustering solution is defined to be the weighted sum of the individual cluster entropies (Equation 7). In general, smaller entropy values indicate better clustering solutions.

$$Entropy = \sum_{j=1}^{k} \frac{n_j}{n} E(C_j) \qquad (7)$$

– *Purity*: The purity measure evaluates the coherence of a cluster. It is the degree to which a cluster contains services from a single domain. The purity of C_j is formally defined as:

$$P(C_j) = \frac{1}{n_j} max_i(n_j^i) \qquad (8)$$

Where $max_i(n_j^i)$ is the number of services that are from the dominant domain in cluster C_j and n_j^i represents the number of services from cluster C_j assigned to domain i.

The purity gives the fraction of the overall cluster size that the largest domain of services assigned to that cluster. For a clustering solution, the overall purity is then again the weighted sum of the individual cluster purities (Equation 9). In general, larger purity values indicate better clustering solutions.

$$Purity = \sum_{i=1}^{k} \frac{n_i}{n} P(C_i) \qquad (9)$$

In our experiment, we compared the accuracy of three probabilistic clustering algorithms (PLSA, LDA and CTM) to that of a classical clustering algorithm (K-means). The eight service domains described previously (Table 1), are used as the base classes to evaluate *Purity* and *Entropy* of clusters. Thus, we generate k clusters using each algorithm starting with 5 clusters and increasing in steps of 5 up to 100 clusters. The results of Entropy and Purity for clustering solutions are shown respectively in Figure 1(a) and 1(b). The results show that the clustering method based on the CTM performs significantly than others algorithms. We also note that LDA performs better than PLSA and K-means. The K-means is a simple algorithm and does not an always converge in an optimal way. It depends on the random factor of where the initial cluster centroids are generated. As can be seen from Figure 1, CTM and LDA perform better than PLSA and K-means for a large number of clusters. This makes them ideal solutions for web services clustering in large dataset. The Correlated Topic Model allows each service to exhibit multiple topics with different proportions. Thus, it can capture the heterogeneity in grouped data that exhibit multiple latent factors.

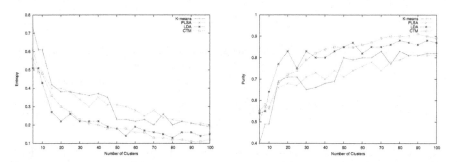

Fig. 1. (a) Entropy of clusters for the proposed clustering solutions. (b) Purity of clusters for the proposed clustering solutions.

4.2 Web Service Discovery Evaluation

We also evaluated the effectiveness of web service discovery based on the three probabilistic topic models (labeled *PLSA*, *LDA* and *CTM*). The probabilistic methods are compared with a text-matching approach (labeled *Text-Search*). For this experiment, we use the services description collected from the WSDL corpus. As described previously, the services are divided into eight domains and some queries templates are provided together with a relevant response set for each query. The relevance sets for each query consists of a set of relevant service and each service s has a graded relevance value $relevance(s) \in \{1, 2, 3\}$ where 3 denotes *high relevance* to the query and 1 denotes a *low relevance*.

In order to evaluate the accuracy of our approach, we compute two standard measures used in *Information Retrieval*: *Precision at n* (*Precision@n*) and *Normalised Discounted Cumulative Gain* (*NDCG$_n$*). These evaluation techniques are used to measure the accuracy of a search and matchmaking mechanism.

– *Precision@n*: In our context, *Precision@n* is a measure of the precision of the service discovery system taking into account the first n retrieved services. Therefore, *Precision@n* reflects the number of services which are relevant to the user query. The precision@n for a list of retrieved services is given by Equation 10:

$$Precision@n = \frac{|RelevantServices \cap RetrievedServices|}{|RetrievedServices|} \quad (10)$$

Where the list of relevant services to a given query is defined in the test collection. For this evaluation, we have considered only the services with a graded relevance value of 3 and 2.

– *Normalised Discounted Cumulative Gain*: $NDCG_n$ uses a graded relevance scale of each retrieved service from the result set to evaluate the gain, or usefulness, of a service based on its position in the result list. This measure is particularly useful in Information Retrieval for evaluating ranking results. The $NDCG_n$ for n retrieved services is given by Equation 11.

$$NDCG_n = \frac{DCG_n}{IDCG_n} \quad (11)$$

Where DCG_n is the Discounted Cumulative Gain and $IDCG_n$ is the Ideal Discounted Cumulative Gain. The $IDCG_n$ is found by calculating the DCG_n of the first n returned services. The DCG_n is given by Equation 12.

$$DCG_n = \sum_{i=1}^{n} \frac{2^{relevance(i)} - 1}{log_2(1 + i)} \quad (12)$$

Where n is the number of services retrieved and $relevance(s)$ is the graded relevance of the service in the ith position in the ranked list.

We evaluated our service discovery approach by calculating the *Precision@n* and *NDCG$_n$*. In this experiment, we have selected randomly 12 queries from the test collection. The text description is retrieved from the query templates and used as the query string. We consider that the size of the services to be returned was set to 50. The average *Precision@n* and *NDCG$_n$* are obtained over all 12 queries for CTM, LDA, PLSA and Text-Search. The results are shown in Figure 2(a) and 2(b).

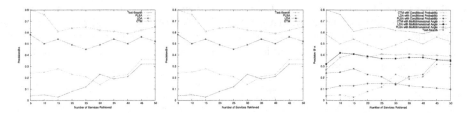

Fig. 2. (a) Comparaison of average Precision@n values over 12 queries. (b) Comparaison of average $NDCG_n$ values over 12 queries. (c) Comparaison of average Precision@n values over 12 queries for all methods using both Conditional Probability and Multi-dimensional Angle.

The comparison of *Precision@n* shows that the CTM and LDA perform better than Text-Search and PLSA. The probabilistic methods based on CTM and LDA used the information captured in the latent factors to match web services based on the conditional probability of the user query. Text-Search and PLSA were unable to find some of the relevant web services that were not directly related to the user's queries through CTM and LDA. The low precision results obtained by probabilistic method based on PLSA are due to limited number of concepts used for training the model. In this context, web service descriptions are similar to short documents. Therefore, the method based on PLSA model is not able to converge to a high precision using these limited concepts.

In Information retrieval, $NDCG_N$ gives higher scores to systems which rank a search result list with higher relevance first and penalizes systems which return services with low relevance. The $NDCG_n$ values for all queries can be averaged to obtain a measure of the average performance of a ranking algorithm. In our experiments, we consider services with graded relevance values from 3 (high relevance) to 1 (low relevance) for this evaluation. $NDCG_n$ values vary from 0 to 1. The results obtained for $NDCG_n$ show that the both CTM and LDA perform better than the other search methods. Thus, the probabilistic methods based on both CTM and LDA give a higher $NDCG_n$ than all other methods for any number of web services retrieved. This reflects the accuracy of the ranking mechanism used by our method. Text-Search and PLSA methods have a low $NDCG_n$ because, as shown in the *Precision@n* results, both methods are unable to find some of the highly relevant services.

In order to compare the accuracy of our approach with existing approaches, we have implemented the approach proposed by Cassar et al. [6], which uses the proximity measure called *Multidimensional Angle* (also known as *Cosine Similarity*); a measure, which uses the cosine of the angle between two vectors [17]. In the first time, we represent the user's query as a distribution over topics. Thus, for each topic z_f we calculate the relatedness between query Q and z_f based on *topic − word* distribution ϕ using Equation 13.

$$P(Q|z_f) = \prod_{w_i \in Q} P(w_i|z_f)$$ (13)

Then, we calculate the similarity between the user's query and a web service by computing the Cosine Similarity between a vector containing the query's distribution over topics q and a vector containing the service's distribution over topics p. The multidimensional angle between a vector p and a vector q can be calculated using Equation 14:

$$Cos(p,q) = \frac{p.q}{\| p \| \cdot \| q \|} = \frac{\sum_{i=1}^{t} p_i q_i}{\sqrt{\sum_{i=1}^{t} p_i^2 \sum_{i=1}^{t} q_i^2}} \tag{14}$$

where t is the number of topics.

The comparison of average *Precision@n* (See Figure 2(c)) shows that the probabilistic method CP (i.e. Conditional Probability) performs better than the MA (i.e. Multidimensional Angle) for all the probabilistic topic models. The results show that the CTM and LDA perform better than Text-Search and PLSA.

5 Conclusion

In this paper, we have used several probabilistic topic models (i.e. PLSA, LDA and CTM) to extract latent factors from web service descriptions. Then, the learned latent factors are used to group services into clusters. Indeed, the categorization of services is often done with human intervention. To overcome this limitation, we propose to vary the number of topics (which can be considered as clusters, with one difference, which is that we can model the observations in a more compressed way than it would be if the model was based on clusters) to automatically obtain the categories to which services belong. The accuracy of the three probabilistic clustering algorithms is compared with a classical clustering algorithm (i.e. K-means). The results show that the clustering method based on both CTM and LDA perform better than PLSA and K-means. In our work, we propose also to use the probabilistic topic models to discover the web services that match with the user query. We evaluated our service discovery approach by calculating the *Precision@n* and $NDCG_n$. The comparison of *Precision@n* and $NDCG_n$ show that the CTM and LDA perform better than the other search methods (i.e. Text-Search and PLSA). This reflects the accuracy of the ranking mechanism used by our method. The probabilistic methods based on both CTM and LDA used the information captured in the latent factors to match web services based on the conditional probability of the user query. The obtained results show that the topic models provide a scalable and interoperable solution for automated service discovery in large service repositories. Future work will focus on developing a new probabilistic model based on the latent factors to tag web services automatically.

References

1. Abramowicz, W., Haniewicz, K., Kaczmarek, M., Zyskowski, D.: Architecture for Web services filtering and clustering. In: ICIW 2007 (2007)
2. Atkinson, C., Bostan, P., Hummel, O., Stoll, D.: A Practical Approach to Web service Discovery and Retrieval. In: ICWS 2007 (2007)

3. Blei, D., Ng, A.Y., Jordan, M.I.: Latent dirichlet allocation. J. Mach. Learn. Res. 3, 993–1022 (2003)
4. Blei, D., Lafferty, J.D.: A Correlated Topic model of Science. In: AAS 2007, pp. 17–35 (2007)
5. Cassar, G., Barnaghi, P., Moessner, K.: Probabilistic methods for service clustering. In: Proceeding of the 4th International Workshop on Semantic Web Service Match-making and Resource Retrieval, Organised in conjonction the ISWC 2010 (2010)
6. Cassar, G., Barnaghi, P., Moessner, K.: A Probabilistic Latent Factor approach to service ranking. In: ICCP 2011, pp. 103–109 (2011)
7. Elgazzar, K., Hassan, A., Martin, P.: Clustering WSDL Documents to Bootstrap the Discovery of Web Services. In: ICWS 2010, pp. 147–154 (2010)
8. Dong, X., Halevy, A., Madhavan, J., Nemes, E., Zhang, J.: Similarity Search for Web Services. In: VLDB Conference, Toronto, Canada, pp. 372–383 (2004)
9. Heß, A., Kushmerick, N.: Learning to Attach Semantic Metadata to Web Services. In: Fensel, D., Sycara, K., Mylopoulos, J. (eds.) ISWC 2003. LNCS, vol. 2870, pp. 258–273. Springer, Heidelberg (2003)
10. Hofmann, T.: Probabilistic Latent Semantic Analysis. In: UAI, pp. 289–296 (1999)
11. Kokash, N.: A Comparison of Web Service Interface Similarity Measures. Frontiers in Artificial Intelligence and Applications, vol. 142, pp. 220–231 (2006)
12. Lausen, H., Haselwanter, T.: Finding Web services. In: European Semantic Technology Conference, Vienna, Austria (2007)
13. Liu, W., Wong, W.: Web service clustering using text mining techniques. IJAOSE 2009 3(1), 6–26 (2009)
14. Ma, J., Zhang, Y., He, J.: Efficiently finding web services using a clustering semantic approach. In: CSSSIA 2008, pp. 1–8. ACM, New York (2008)
15. Nayak, R., Lee, B.: Web service Discovery with Additional Semantics and Clustering. In: IEEE/WIC/ACM 2007 (2007)
16. Porter, M.F.: An Algorithm for Suffix Stripping. Program 1980 14(3), 130–137 (1980)
17. Platzer, C., Rosenberg, F., Dustdar, S.: Web service clustering using multidimensional angles as proximity measures. ACM Trans. Internet Technol. 9(3), 1–26 (2009)
18. Salton, G.: Automatic Text Processing: The Transformation, Analysis, and Retrieval of Information by Computer. Addison-Wesley Longman Publishing Co., Inc., Boston (1989)
19. Sivashanmugam, K., Verma, A.P., Miller, J.A.: Adding Semantics to Web services Standards. In: ICWS 2003, pp. 395–401 (2003)
20. Steyvers, M., Griffiths, T.: Probabilistic topic models. In: Landauer, T., Mcnamara, D., Dennis, S., Kintsch, W. (eds.) Latent Semantic Analysis: A Road to Meaning. Lawrence Erlbaum (2007)
21. Yu, Q.: Place Semantics into Context: Service Community Discovery from the WSDL Corpus. In: Kappel, G., Maamar, Z., Motahari-Nezhad, H.R. (eds.) ICSOC 2011. LNCS, vol. 7084, pp. 188–203. Springer, Heidelberg (2011)
22. Zhao, Y., Karypis, G.: Empirical and theoretical comparisons of selected criterion functions for document clustering. In: Machine Learning 2004, vol. 55, pp. 311–331 (2004)
23. Zhao, Y., Karypis, G.: Evaluation of hierarchical clustering algorithms for document datasets. In: CIKM 2002 (2002)

Managing Imprecise Criteria in Cloud Service Ranking with a Fuzzy Multi-criteria Decision Making Method

Ioannis Patiniotakis[1], Stamatia Rizou[2], Yiannis Verginadis[1], and Gregoris Mentzas[1]

[1] Institute of Communications and Computer Systems,
National Technical University of Athens
9 Iroon Polytechniou Str., Athens, Greece
{ipatini,jverg,gmentzas}@mail.ntua.gr
[2] European Projects Department, Singular Logic S.A.,
Al. Panagouli & Siniosoglou Ste., Athens, Greece
srizou@singularlogic.eu

Abstract. The increase of cloud technology solutions has made the evaluation and selection of desired cloud services, a cumbersome task for the user. In particular, the lack of standard mechanisms that allow the comparison of cloud service specifications against user requirements taking into account the implicit uncertainty and vagueness is a major hindrance during the cloud service evaluation and selection. In this paper, we discuss an alternative classification of metrics used for ranking cloud services based on their level of fuzziness and present an approach that allows cloud service evaluation based on a heterogeneous model of service characteristics. Our approach allows the multi-objective assessment of cloud services in a unified way, taking into account precise and imprecise metrics. We use fuzzy numbers to model the imprecise service characteristics and vague user preferences and we validate a fuzzy AHP approach that solves the problem of service ranking.

Keywords: Cloud Services, Ranking, Imprecise Criteria, Fuzzy, MCDM.

1 Introduction

As the complexity of cloud services increases, the role of cloud brokers in the cloud service ecosystems becomes increasingly important. More specifically, with the increase of cloud technologies adoption, the number of services offered in the cloud market also raises. Thus, the evaluation of the available cloud services could be a cumbersome task for the user due to the plethora of the offered services in the cloud market and the lack of standard mechanisms that allow their comparison against user requirements. In that respect, there is an increasing need for user guidance during the service selection process. Cloud brokers that mediate between the service user and the service provider, assist the service user in selecting the most appropriate service.

Recent work has focused on developing methods and mechanisms to allow the comparison and ranking of competitive cloud services and help the user during the cloud service selection. As a first step towards this goal, researchers identified the

K.-K. Lau, W. Lamersdorf, and E. Pimentel (Eds.): ESOCC 2013, LNCS 8135, pp. 34–48, 2013.
© Springer-Verlag Berlin Heidelberg 2013

evaluation criteria that can be used as comparison dimensions to enable the service ranking [1], [2]. According to this existing work, the service evaluation may be affected by a set of quantitative and qualitative service characteristics. Quantitative characteristics are those that can be measured, e.g. response time, while qualitative characteristics cannot be quantified in an objective manner and are based typically on user experience such as service usability. Although the existence and significance of qualitative characteristics are identified, existing approaches up to now do not provide models and methods to handle the qualitative service characteristics. Furthermore, current approaches use quantitative models to insert user requirements. However, imprecise models are closer to the human perception since they can express the vagueness of the user requirements. For instance, while price is a quantitative metric, it is obviously more intuitive for the user to express his requirements by using expressions such as cheap or expensive, rather than by specifying definite numerical thresholds.

In this paper, we aim to tackle the aforementioned limitations of the existing approaches in cloud service ranking by providing an approach that allows cloud service evaluation based on a heterogeneous model of service characteristics. We categorize service characteristics in two categories according to the most appropriate modeling (precise or imprecise) of the service specification and requirements. In more detail, we focus on imprecise metrics and on a unified method to manage them along with the precise ones (i.e. measurable without uncertainty) for providing cloud service rankings. Given the proposed model, we present a fuzzy AHP approach that solves the problem of service ranking and allows the multi-objective assessment of cloud services. In addition, this approach provides a more expressive and unified way to capture and process user opinions and preferences, both precise and imprecise, than traditional service ranking methods. Finally we apply our approach in an example extracted from the literature and we demonstrate its validity.

The rest of the paper is structured as follows: In Section 2 a discussion of the problem space is given, while in Section 3, we detail our proposed service ranking approach. In Section 4, we give an illustrative example. In Section 5, we present the related work and we conclude this paper and discuss the next steps in Section 6.

2   Problem Space

Several attempts have been made to provide taxonomies of the various attributes that can characterize a cloud service. One of most important works in that direction is the SMICloud [1], [3] which distinguishes between qualitative and quantitative metrics. For instance, cost could be classified in quantitative metrics since it can be measured in local currency, while reputation could be classified in qualitative characteristics since it is based on the user experience and word of mouth. It is also evident from the literature review that most of these efforts focus only on the quantitative (or at least on quantifiable metrics) and all of them use only measurable and precise metrics (i.e. crisp numbers) in the methods and techniques implemented for ranking cloud services [1].

However, sometimes it can be hard to classify the characteristics in one of the two categories, since even for some quantitative attributes it makes sense that the users express their preferences in a qualitative manner. There are a number of metrics that can be seen as qualitative but at the same time with some reasonable assumptions they can be precisely quantified (e.g. Interoperability, Usability etc.) or that they can be resolved in a number of lower level metrics, involving both quantitative and qualitative attributes (e.g. Serviceability etc.) or including both precise and imprecise values. For instance, usability metric has been defined as a quantifiable attribute [1] in the sense of average time experienced by users of the cloud service to install, learn, understand and operate it. But, often this average time is not enough to define how usable a cloud service is, since this information is often vague and imprecise. It might be the case that the average installation or learn time for a cloud customer about a specific service is relative short because of the customer's huge experience in the specific domain and not because the service is really usable for an average user. It would be an oversight to ignore the degree of difficultness that previous users experienced based on their degree of expertise, when they tried to install, learn, understand and operate the specific cloud service. This value is highly subjective, uncertain and often is available through linguistic terms when previous users are expressing their opinions.

Therefore, we believe that a distinction between precise and imprecise metrics is more meaningful for characterizing and ranking a cloud service. Most of the related work focused on the precise metrics that can be objectively measured with high degree of certainty using specific software and hardware monitoring tools (e.g. Service Response Time, On-going Cost, Stability, Availability etc.). In this paper, we focus on imprecise metrics and on a unified method to manage them along with the precise ones for providing cloud service rankings. Imprecise metrics cannot be measured accurately, they present a high degree of uncertainty and their value is usually subjective (e.g. Provider Brand Name, Service Reputation, Support Satisfaction, Documentation Readability etc.). For example, regarding the Service Reputation it is more realistic for cloud customers to express their opinions verbally (i.e. Bad, Ok, Good) thus inducing in a cloud service ranking system a vagueness that should not be ignored. Cloud customers need to declare their preferences in a way that retains their inherent vagueness, such as using linguistic terms, which are easier, more intuitive and more comprehensible than using numbers.

So, there is a need for a more realistic approach that takes under consideration the implicit vagueness in certain criteria along with the fuzziness when coping with user's preferences or requirements, expressed with words and terms common in human language. In the next section, we present our approach for addressing the cloud service ranking based on both precise and imprecise criteria in unified way. We use a fuzzy MCDM approach that may also take into account cases where cloud customers would like to declare their preferences for precise criteria in a fuzzy way.

3   Proposed Service Ranking Approach

Before detailing with our proposed service ranking approach some essential concepts will be briefly presented.

3.1   Preliminaries on Fuzzy Numbers

Fuzzy numbers are based on Zadeh's pioneer work on Fuzzy Set Theory [4]. Fuzzy sets are sets of ordered pairs $A = \{(x, \mu_A(x)), x \in A, \mu \in \mathbb{R}\}$, where $\mu(x)$ is called the membership function. They extend the notion of membership of an element in a set, from binary (belongs or not belongs) to a grade of membership, expressed as a real number, usually in *[0,1]* interval (called normalized fuzzy set).

Fuzzy numbers are defined as convex, normalized fuzzy sets on the Real axis, whose membership functions $\mu: R \rightarrow [0,1]$ are at least segmentally continuous and have membership value 1 at precisely one element. A special class of fuzzy numbers is Triangular Fuzzy Numbers (TFNs) seen in figure 1. Their membership function is defined as in (1) and they are graphically rendered as triangles (see Fig.1). They are usually represented as triplets $\tilde{a} = (l, m, u)$ or (a^l, a^m, a^u), $s.t. l \leq m \leq u$. When $l=m=u$ the number becomes an ordinary number, called crisp number.

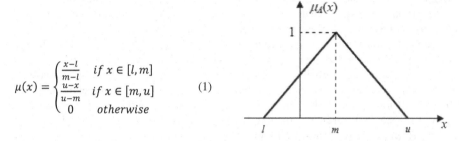

$$\mu(x) = \begin{cases} \frac{x-l}{m-l} & if\ x \in [l, m] \\ \frac{u-x}{u-m} & if\ x \in [m, u] \\ 0 & otherwise \end{cases} \qquad (1)$$

Fig. 1. Triangular Fuzzy Number

In our work we will only consider positive TFNs, where $l, m, u > 0$. For them the four arithmetic operations are defined as in equations (2) – (5).

$$\tilde{A} \oplus \tilde{B} = (a^l, a^m, a^u) \oplus (b^l, b^m, b^u) = (a^l + b^l, a^m + b^m, a^u + b^u) \qquad (2)$$

$$\tilde{A} \ominus \tilde{B} = (a^l, a^m, a^u) \ominus (b^l, b^m, b^u) = (a^l - b^u, a^m - b^m, a^u - b^l) \qquad (3)$$

$$\tilde{A} \otimes \tilde{B} = (a^l, a^m, a^u) \otimes (b^l, b^m, b^u) = (a^l \cdot b^l, a^m \cdot b^m, a^u \cdot b^u) \qquad (4)$$

$$\tilde{A} \oslash \tilde{B} = (a^l, a^m, a^u) \oslash (b^l, b^m, b^u) = (a^l/b^u, a^m/b^m, a^u/b^l) \qquad (5)$$

An important operation on fuzzy numbers is fuzzy comparison. In crisp numbers a natural order exists, but in fuzzy numbers this is not the case. An approach widely used to compare fuzzy numbers is by defuzzying them; i.e. mapping them onto real numbers. Several defuzzification techniques have been proposed in literature (see [5]). In our work we choose Chan et al. [8] technique:

$$\hat{a} = (\widehat{l, m, u}) = \frac{l + 4 \cdot m + u}{6} \qquad (6)$$

Fuzzy intervals are also defined. They are intervals on Real axis where one or both of their boundaries are fuzzy. Two important operations on fuzzy intervals are *union* and *intersection*. A way to apply them is by defuzzifying the fuzzy interval into a crisp one, by defuzzifying the fuzzy bounds into crisp bounds. In this work we specifically consider a class of fuzzy intervals, called trapezoidal fuzzy intervals.

3.2   Proposed Service Ranking Method

The proposed method aims at providing a cloud service ranking technique capable to leverage both crisp and fuzzy information. It extends the SMI approach [1], which is based on the Service Measurement Index (SMI) [3], a set of business-relevant Key Performance Indicators (KPIs).

SMICloud proposes a set of quantifiable metrics (KPIs) capable to measure several aspects of cloud services. A modified Analytical Hierarchy Process (AHP) is used for ranking cloud services, but instead of requiring experts to compare them, it uses service KPIs to achieve the same purpose, thus reducing experts' effort and alleviating subjective judgment errors. Garg et al. [1] have proposed certain techniques to derive the relative service importance values from KPIs, required in AHP. Furthermore, they have distinguished between essential, where KPI values are required, and non-essential attributes. They have also explained how to handle the lack of KPI values for non-essential attributes. This approach [1] considers only crisp values. In the following paragraphs we explain how we extend SMICloud approach in order to handle fuzzy values too.

We propose a method where service KPI and user requirement values can be fuzzy numbers and intervals, or linguistic terms. In the latter case linguistic terms are mapped onto fuzzy numbers in order to ensure unified processing, both of the imprecise and precise in nature, user provided values. Imprecise values usually pertain to qualitative attributes or attributes where uncertainty in measurements is involved. Precise values pertain to accurately measured attribute values. Using techniques similar to SMICloud's we derive fuzzy comparison matrices and subsequently using a fuzzy AHP we rank services. Buckley [6] has proposed such a fuzzy AHP method. Kwong & Bai [7] have introduced a process that transforms the problem into a crisp ranking problem. Chan et al. [8] have proposed an enhancement on the former approach using extend analysis method [9], thus avoiding some of its shortcomings.

In our work we have selected the method presented in [8], appropriately adapted for service ranking purposes. We have also chosen to use triangular fuzzy numbers and trapezoidal intervals due to their simplicity and broad use. Our approach provides a more expressive and unified way to capture user opinions and preferences, both precise and imprecise, than traditional service ranking methods. In the following paragraphs we present the four phases of the proposed service ranking method.

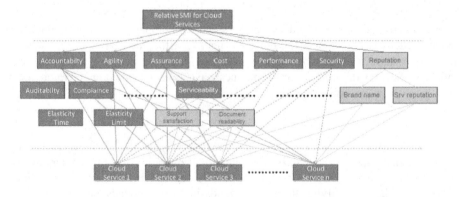

Fig. 2. Extended SMICloud Attribute Hierarchy for Cloud computing

Phase 1: Expressing ranking problem into a hierarchal structure

The goal of the cloud service ranking is captured into a hierarchical model (Fig. 2). Goal is decomposed into service attributes contributing to goal achievement. Attributes can be further decomposed into sub-attributes at any number of levels. Eventually, the cloud services are related to the lowest-level (leaf) attributes. Our model extends the hierarchical structure, presented in Fig.2, by enabling the addition of imprecise attributes in different levels (e.g. Reputation).

Phase 2: Computation of relative QoS attribute weights

Next the relative importance of each attribute in hierarchical model, compared to its siblings, must be calculated. Siblings are those attributes at the same level and with the same parent attribute/goal. The approach proposed in original AHP [10] and used in SMICloud, is through pairwise comparisons between all sibling attributes. Every comparison yields the relative importance of an attribute over another one, expressed in a scale of 1 (equal importance) to 9 (extremely more important).

However, since the input might be fuzzy, a more appropriate approach would be the use of fuzzy importance values. The work in [8] proposed a scale of fuzzy importance values, but other variations also appear in literature, for instance [7], [11].

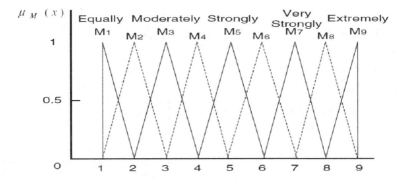

Fig. 3. The membership functions of the fuzzy relative importance values [8]

Having the relative importance values, a fuzzy AHP method is applied to calculate the relative weights of the attributes, for every level and group of siblings. A detailed presentation of the method is given in next section. Obviously, if any of the service attributes in hierarchical model is of no interest in a particular case of service ranking then it can be omitted from the process, implying a zero weight.

Phase 3: Computation of relative service performances

The original AHP method would require expert(s) to pairwise compare all services for every lowest-level attribute, using a 1 to 9 scale. Contrary, SMICloud proposes that relative service performances can be deduced from KPI values. Four types of KPIs are considered; Boolean, Numeric, Unordered Sets and Range KPIs. It also distinguishes attributes to essential, where KPI values must be provided, and non-essential. For every essential attribute a user requirement must be provided. Services failing to comply with all essential requirements are excluded from the ranking process. We extend SMICloud approach in order to handle fuzzy KPIs and user requirements. Specifically, they are defuzzified before applying SMICloud techniques.

Let services S_i and S_j and their respective KPI values v_i and v_j for an attribute q. v_r is the user requirement value that represents a fuzzy constraint above (or below) which the service KPI values (for a criterion) must reside in order to accept the corresponding service for ranking. w_q is the weight of the attribute from phase 2. For range attributes, KPI values and user requirements are ranges rather than single numbers. In this case the limits of the ranges can be fuzzy numbers, meaning the ranges have imprecise boundaries.

Table 1. Relative service performance values for the four attribute types

Boolean KPI attributes	Numeric KPI attributes
$$S_i/S_j = \begin{cases} 1 & if\ v_i \equiv v_j \\ w_q & if\ v_j = 1\ and\ v_i = 0 \\ 1/w_q & if\ v_j = 0\ and\ v_i = 1 \end{cases}$$	$$S_i/S_j = \begin{cases} v_i/v_j & if\ higher\ is\ better \\ v_j/v_i & if\ lower\ is\ better \\ w_q & if\ v_i\ is\ not\ provided \\ 1/w_q & if\ v_j\ is\ not\ provided \end{cases}$$
Unordered set KPI attributes *if an essential attribute* $$S_i/S_j = \frac{size(v_i)}{size(v_j)}$$ *if a non-essential attribute* $$S_i/S_j = \begin{cases} \frac{size(v_i \cap v_r)}{size(v_j \cap v_r)} & if\ v_j \cap v_r \neq \emptyset\ and\ v_i \cap v_r \neq \emptyset \\ 1 & if\ v_j \cap v_r \equiv \emptyset\ and\ v_i \cap v_r \equiv \emptyset \\ w_q & if\ v_j \cap v_r \neq \emptyset\ and\ v_i \cap v_r \equiv \emptyset \\ 1/w_q & if\ v_j \cap v_r \equiv \emptyset\ and\ v_i \cap v_r \neq \emptyset \end{cases}$$	**Range KPI attributes** *if an essential attribute* $$S_i/S_j = \frac{len(v_i \cap v_r)}{len(v_j \cap v_r)}$$ *if a non-essential attribute* $$S_i/S_j = \begin{cases} \frac{len(v_i \cap v_r)}{len(v_j \cap v_r)} & if\ v_j \cap v_r \neq \emptyset\ and\ v_i \cap v_r \neq \emptyset \\ 1 & if\ v_j \cap v_r \equiv \emptyset\ and\ v_i \cap v_r \equiv \emptyset \\ w_q & if\ v_j \cap v_r \neq \emptyset\ and\ v_i \cap v_r \equiv \emptyset \\ 1/w_q & if\ v_j \cap v_r \equiv \emptyset\ and\ v_i \cap v_r \neq \emptyset \end{cases}$$ We define length of a fuzzy interval as the length of the defuzzified interval, i.e. $len(\tilde{X}) = len(\hat{X})$.

The resulting relative service performances formulate a comparison matrix for each attribute. Then a fuzzy AHP method is applied to derive the relative service weights for each one. A detailed description of the method is given in the next section.

Phase 4: Aggregation of relative service weights

The relative service weights of each attribute, computed in phase 3, are aggregated using their corresponding relative weights computed in phase 2. The aggregation operation is a weighted average between sibling-attributes. This process is repeated bottom-up at all levels of the hierarchical model. The result will be the overall relative service weights, which can be used to rank the cloud services.

If more than one user contribute their opinions/preferences on service KPI attribute values and/or requirements, then it is imperative to aggregate them into single values per service, requirement and attribute in order to apply the described method. As Meixner [22] explained the use of the geometric mean yields satisfactory fuzzy value aggregations and also geometric mean is commonly used in AHP applications where group decision making is involved. Let N be the number of user values and $k=1..N$

$$\overline{\tilde{V}_{ij}} = \left(\left(\prod_{k=1}^{N} l_{ijk}\right)^{1/N}, \left(\prod_{k=1}^{N} m_{ijk}\right)^{1/N}, \left(\prod_{k=1}^{N} u_{ijk}\right)^{1/N}\right)$$

3.3   Brief Description of Fuzzy AHP with Extend Analysis

The fuzzy AHP with extend analysis method proposed in [8] is applied in phases 2 and 3. It takes a comparison matrix of attributes or services, and determines their weight vector using the extend analysis method [9]. The process starts by obtaining the fuzzy synthetic degree D_i for each matrix row, using the next equations. Let $\tilde{A}^k = [\tilde{a}_{ij}^k]$ be the fuzzy comparison matrix, and $i,j=1..N$.

$$\tilde{D}_i = \left(D_i^l, D_i^m, D_i^u\right) = \sum_{j=1}^{N} a_{ij} \otimes \left(\sum_{i=1}^{N} \sum_{j=1}^{N} a_{ij}\right)^{-1} \tag{7}$$

Next, we find the attributes or services with the higher fuzzy synthetic degree D. The degree of possibility that D_i is greater than D_j is:

$$V(D_i \geq D_j) = \begin{cases} 1 & if\ D_i^m \geq D_j^m \\ \frac{D_j^l - D_i^u}{\left(D_i^m - D_i^u\right) - \left(D_j^m - D_j^l\right)} & if\ D_i^m \leq D_j^m\ and\ D_j^l \leq D_i^u \\ 0 & otherwise \end{cases} \tag{8}$$

The degree of possibility that a fuzzy synthetic degree D_i is greater than the rest D_k where $k=1..N$ and $k \neq i$, is:

$$d_i = V(D_i \geq D_k\ \forall k = 1..N, k \neq i) = min\ V(D_i \geq D_j) \tag{9}$$

Eventually, the weights vector is the normalized vector of d_i.

$$w = [w_1 \cdots w_N]^T\ where\ w_i = d_i / \sum_{k=1}^{N} d_k \tag{10}$$

The proposed method is explained in the next section through an example.

4   Use Case Example

We extend the example of [1] in three ways. First we add *Reputation*, as a new (top-level) QoS group and adjust QoS group weights accordingly. Reputation encompasses two attributes, *Brand-name* and *Service reputation*, which can be fuzzy numbers or linguistic terms mapped onto fuzzy numbers. Second, we extend the pre-existing

Serviceability attribute by adding two new second-level, fuzzy attributes. Thus Serviceability encompasses both crisp and fuzzy attributes. The new attributes are *Support satisfaction* and *Document readability*. Third, we convert two user requirements into fuzzy, namely *Memory Capacity* and *Service response time range*.

The resulting example is shown in Table 3. The user weights are supposed to have been derived using the process described in phase 2. However in this example we have used random weights. The linguistic terms used for the four new attributes are mapped onto triangular fuzzy numbers as shown next:

Table 2. Mapping of linguistic terms onto fuzzy numbers

Brand name		Service rep.		Support satisfaction				Doc. readability	
BELOW	(0,3,5)	BAD	(0,3,5)	VERY LOW	(0,3,4)	HIGH	(5,6,7)	BAD	(0,3,5)
OK	(4,5,7)	OK	(4,5,7)	LOW	(3,4,5)	VERY HIGH	(6,7,8)	OK	(4,5,7)
ABOVE	(5,7,9)	GOOD	(5,7,9)	MEDIUM	(4,5,6)	PERFECT	(7,8,9)	GOOD	(5,7,9)

In the following we briefly explain the calculations used in phases 3 and 4 of the proposed method, on a specific fuzzy attribute. For instance we choose Brand-name in Reputation QoS group, which is an essential attribute.

Using the input of Table 3 and the mapping of Table 2 we have: S_1 is OK: *(3,5,7)*, S_2 is ABOVE: *(5,7,9)* and S_3 is OK: *(3,5,7)* and user requirement is OK: *(3,5,7)* or better. We remind that fuzzy KPI values express single but imprecise values. With equation (6) we defuzzify service brand-name KPI values in order to check whether they meet the user requirement,

$$\widehat{S_1} = \widehat{S_3} = \widehat{v_r} = (\widehat{3,5,7}) = \frac{3 + 4 \cdot 5 + 7}{6} = 5 \ and \ \widehat{S_2} = 7$$

Obviously all three services meet the user requirement since S_1 and S_3 are on par with constraint whereas S_3 is clearly above. Since Brand-name is effectively a numeric constraint, in order to compute the relative service importance, we select the equation for numeric attributes in Table 1. Fuzzy division is given by equation (5).

$$S_1/S_2 = (4,5,7) \oslash (5,7,9) = (0.44, 0.71, 1.40)$$

We also calculate relative service importance for S_1/S_3, S_2/S_3 and their inverses. The fuzzy relative service ranking matrix for Brand-name is:

$$F.RSRM_{brand} = \begin{bmatrix} (1,1,1) & (0.44, 0.71, 1.40) & (0.57, 1.00, 1.75) \\ (0.71, 1.40, 2.25) & (1,1,1) & (0.71, 1.40, 2.25) \\ (0.57, 1.00, 1.75) & (0.44, 0.71, 1.40) & (1,1,1) \end{bmatrix}$$

Continuing, the fuzzy synthetic degree for each service is computed, using Fuzzy RSRM data and equation (7). The fuzzy synthetic degrees for the three services are:

Table 3. Case Study Example (based on [1])

Top level QoS Groups	First level Attributes	Second level Attributes	Service 1 (S1)	Service 2 (S2)	Service 3 (S3)	Value Type	User Required Value
Accountability (0.05)	level: 0-10 (1)		4	8	4	Numeric	4
Agility (0.1)	Capacity (0.8)	CPU (0.4)	9.6	12,8	8,8	Numeric	4 x 1.6 GHz
		Memory (0.5)	15	14	15	Fuzzy Num	(9,10,15) GB
		Disk (0.1)	1690	2040	630	Numeric	500 GB
	Elasticity (0.2)	Time (1)	80-120	520-780	20-200	Range	60-120 msec
Assurance (0.2)	Availability (0.5)		99,95%	99,99%	100%	Numeric	99,90%
	Service Stability (0.3)	Upload Time (0.3)	13,6	15	21	Numeric	
		CPU (0.2)	17,9	16	23	Numeric	
		Memory (0.5)	7	12	5	Numeric	
	Serviceability (0.2)	Free Support (0.4)	0	1	1	Boolean	
		Type of Support (0.2)	24/7, Diagnostic tools, Phone, Urgent Response	24/7, Diagnostic tools, Phone, Urgent Response	24/7, Phone, Urgent Response	Unordered Set	24/7, Phone
		Support satisfaction (0.3)	VERY HIGH	HIGH	MEDIUM	Linguistic	MEDIUM
		Document readability (0.1)	GOOD	OK	OK	Linguistic	≥ OK
Cost (0.4)	On-Going Cost (1)	VM Cost (0.6)	0,68	0,96	0,96	Numeric	< 1 $/hour
		Data – inbound (0.1)	10	10	8	Numeric	100 GB/month
		Data – outbound (0.1)	11	15	18	Numeric	200 GB/month
		Storage (0.2)	12	15	15	Numeric	1000 GB
Performance (0.1)	Service Response Time (1)	Range (0.2)	80-120	520-780	20-200	Fuzzy Range	(50,60, 115,125) msec
		Average Value (0.8)	100	600	30	Numeric	
Security (0.05)	level: 0-10 (1)		4	8	4	Numeric	4
Reputation (0.1)	Brand Name (0.35)		OK	ABOVE	OK	Linguistic	≥ OK
	Service Reputation (0.65)		GOOD	OK	OK	Linguistic	≥ OK

$$D_{S1} = \sum_{j=1}^{3} a_{1j} \otimes \left(\sum_{i=1}^{3} \sum_{j=1}^{3} a_{ij} \right)^{-1} = (0.15, 0.29, 0.64)$$

$$D_{S2} = \sum_{j=1}^{3} a_{2j} \otimes \left(\sum_{i=1}^{3} \sum_{j=1}^{3} a_{ij} \right)^{-1} = (0.18, 0.41, 0.85)$$

$$D_{S3} = \sum_{j=1}^{3} a_{3j} \otimes \left(\sum_{i=1}^{3} \sum_{j=1}^{3} a_{ij} \right)^{-1} = (0.15, 0.29, 0.64)$$

With equations (8) and (9) we get the possibility a service is better than the rest.
$$d(S_1) = \min V(S_1 \geq S_2, S_3) = 0.80, d(S_2) = 1.00 \text{ and } d(S_3) = 0.80$$

Eventually, the normalized relative weights vector of services for brand-name is:

$$W_{brand} = [0.31 \quad 0.38 \quad 0.31]^T$$

Similarly we calculate the relative service weight vectors for all lowest-level attributes, either fuzzy or crisp. The higher-level attribute vectors can be computed as explained in phase 4. For instance, for *Service Reputation* weight vector is:

$$W_{serv.reput.} = [0.38 \quad 0.31 \quad 0.31]^T$$

Then the relative service weight vector for Reputation can be derived from the vectors of brand-name and service reputation as shown next.

$$W_{Reputation} = [W_{brand} \quad W_{serv.reput.}] \times \begin{bmatrix} 0.35 \\ 0.65 \end{bmatrix} = \begin{bmatrix} 0.31 & 0.38 \\ 0.38 & 0.31 \\ 0.31 & 0.31 \end{bmatrix} \times \begin{bmatrix} 0.35 \\ 0.65 \end{bmatrix} = \begin{bmatrix} 0.36 \\ 0.33 \\ 0.31 \end{bmatrix}$$

Repeating the process for every attribute we get the relative service weights for the overall goal. Then the ranking of the three cloud services is $S_1 > S_3 > S_2$.

$$W_{overall} = [0.45 \quad 0.20 \quad 0.35]^T$$

5   Related Work

In the area of web services, there are existing works that model the nfp (non-functional properties) and considerate them during service ranking. In particular, some existing approaches have used fuzzy models for matchmaking of user requirements to service specifications and for service discovery [16], [17], [18]. More relevant to the service ranking problem, several selection methods have been proposed in the literature based on fuzzy sets in an effort to model imprecise metrics [19], [21], [14]. However, in these approaches the optimal solution is computed based on classical summations of weighted functions that do not allow the representation of the trade-offs among the different attributes. Some recent works have tried to address this limitation. Benouaret et al. [15] proposed a fuzzification of Pareto dominance to compute the top-k service composition. Liu et al. [20] proposed a method for service selection based on personalized preference and trade-offs among QoS factors and price. However, none of these works intended to propose a model for handling heterogeneous quantitative and qualitative service attributes. Our proposed solution based on AHP, allows the expression of trade-offs using pairwise comparisons of service attributes. Moreover our method enables the modeling of both functional and non-functional metrics, proposing thus a unified model for cloud service ranking.

Closer to our goal, existing works in the area of cloud service optimization have mainly focused on the modeling and assessment of quantitative (precise) characteristics to enable automatic service optimization in infrastructure layer. For instance, CloudCmp has proposed a measurement methodology for quantifying and comparing the performance of cloud services in IaaS layer. In that respect, authors have first identified common services e.g. elastic compute cluster or persistent storage, offered by different providers that can be subject to comparison. Then, for each service, they have defined a set of low-level performance metrics such as benchmark finishing time, costs and scaling latency. Similarly, Han et al. [12] have proposed a service recommender framework using network QoS and Virtual Machine (VM) platform factors for assisting user's decisions when it comes to the selection of cloud provider. In their work, they do not consider user preferences and they limit their evaluation criteria only to IaaS specific factors. In an effort to provide automatic cloud service adaptation across different cloud platforms, Pawluk et al. [13] have presented the STRATOS cloud brokerage framework which addresses the problem of dynamically selecting resources from multiple cloud providers at runtime by calculating the induced costs and lock-in effect using a quantitative model. These approaches focus on the service optimization in IaaS layer and they do not address the problem of service evaluation in multiple quantitative and qualitative dimensions taking into account the uncertainty or vagueness.

Beyond the service optimization in IaaS layer, which uses typically low-level performance metrics, some existing approaches have attempted to provide a classification of service characteristics and attributes in order to enable the comparison of cloud services. To this end, SMICloud [1] proposes the SMI Index, which classifies the service characteristics in a hierarchy of top-level attributes that are further divided in first- and second-level attributes. For instance, cost is a top-level attribute with acquisition and ongoing costs as first-level attributes. SMICloud presents also a framework that enables the ranking of services based on a multi-dimensional model by using an Analytical Hierarchical Process (AHP) ranking mechanism. However, this ranking mechanism supports only quantifiable (precise) measures and does not allow the comparison of services based on imprecise metrics. Similarly, Godse et al. [2] applied an AHP algorithm for ranking SaaS products and presented a hierarchy of top-level and first-level service characteristics.

To the best of our knowledge, there is no existing work that attempts to address imprecise criteria and vagueness on user expressed preferences in a unified service ranking mechanism. To this end, in this paper we present a model that extends the SMICloud approach and provides a mechanism that enables the ranking of services based on precise as well as imprecise characteristics and information regarding user preferences.

6   Conclusions

In this paper, we discussed the limitations of the existing approaches in cloud service ranking domain. We introduced an alternative classification of metrics used for ranking cloud services based on their level of fuzziness. In order to address these limitations, we presented an approach that allows cloud service evaluation based on a heterogeneous model of service characteristics. Based on this approach, we allowed the fuzzy expression of user preferences even for the quantitative characteristics, while we use also fuzzy numbers to model the qualitative characteristics in a more intuitive way. In addition, we used a fuzzy AHP approach that solves the problem of service ranking and allows the multi-objective assessment of cloud services in a unified way (taking into account precise and imprecise metrics). Although tracing its roots in existing service ranking methods, our approach provides a more expressive and unified way to capture user opinions and preferences, both precise and imprecise. In addition, the use of linguistic terms in place of fuzzy numbers reduces the apparent complexity of the approach and makes its use more intuitive.

Moreover, we have illustrated the usage of our approach by applying it on an extended version of the example in [1]. Further comparison between the proposed approach and traditional approaches using solely crisp values for criteria evaluation is not considered meaningful at this stage of our research. This is because the traditional approaches make assumptions and approximations for addressing the imprecise nature of criteria while in our approach we cope with this issue by taking into account their real nature (i.e. considering their fuzziness). In addition, we provide with the means for addressing both precise and imprecise criteria in a unified way. However, in order to validate our approach we plan to conduct relevant experiments with the participation of industrial users.

In our short-term future work, we plan to examine a fuzzy extension of the Analytic Network Process (ANP) method in order to cope with cases where there are interdependent relationships among criteria. In our current approach the criteria must be independent and this is a restriction posed by AHP method. Furthermore, we plan to integrate and validate the proposed framework in a dedicated optimization mechanism that will address the need for continuous optimization in cloud service brokers. Taking into account imprecise information regarding the cloud service ranking can lead to a more realistic, user-friendly and valuable solution for enhancing cloud brokerage capabilities.

Acknowledgment. The research presented in this paper is supported by the European Union within the FP7 Marie Curie Initial Training Network "RELATE" and the FP7 ICT Broker@Cloud project.

References

1. Garg, S.K., Versteeg, S., Buyya, R.: SMICloud: A Framework for Comparing and Ranking Cloud Services. Presented at the Fourth IEEE International Conference on Utility and Cloud Computing, Victoria, NSW, pp. 210–218 (2011), doi:10.1109/UCC.2011.36

2. Godse, M., Mulik, S.: An Approach for Selecting Software-as-a-Service (SaaS) Product. In: 2009 IEEE International Conference on Cloud Computing (2009)
3. Cloud Service Measurement Index Consortium (CSMIC) (n.d.). SMI Framework. Introducing the Service Measurement Index, `http://www.cloudcommons.com/web/cc/SMIintro` (retrieved)
4. Zadeh, L.A.: Fuzzy sets. Information and Control 8(3), 338–353 (1965)
5. Ross, T.J.: Fuzzy Logic with Engineering Applications, 3rd edn. John Wiley & Sons (2010)
6. Buckley, J.J.: Ranking alternatives using fuzzy numbers. Fuzzy Sets Systems 15(1), 21–31 (1985)
7. Kwong, C.K., Bai, H.: A fuzzy AHP approach to the determination of importance weights of customer requirements in quality function deployment. Journal of Intelligent Manufacturing 13(5), 367–377 (2002), doi:10.1023/A:1019984626631
8. Chan, K.Y., Dillon, T.S., Kwong, C.K.: An Enhanced Fuzzy AHP Method with Extent Analysis for Determining Importance of Customer Requirements. In: Chan, K.Y., Kwong, C.K., Dillon, T.S. (eds.) Comput. Intell. Techniques for New Product Design. SCI, vol. 403, pp. 79–94. Springer, Heidelberg (2012)
9. Chang, D.-Y.: Applications of the extent analysis method on fuzzy AHP. European Journal of Operational Research 95(3), 649–655 (1996), doi:dx.doi.org/10.1016/0377-2217(95)00300-2
10. Saaty, T.L.: The Analytic Hierarchy Process. McGraw-Hill International (1980)
11. Durán, O., Aguilo, J.: Computer-aided machine-tool selection based on a Fuzzy-AHP approach. Expert Systems with Applications 34(3), 1787–1794 (2008), doi:dx.doi.org/10.1016/j.eswa.2007.01.046
12. Han, S.-M., Hassan, M.M., Yoon, C.-W., Huh, E.-N.: Efficient service recommendation system for cloud computing market. In: 2nd International Conference on Interaction Sciences: Information Technology, Culture and Human (2009)
13. Pawluk, P., Simmons, B., Smit, M., Litoiu, M., Mankovski, S.: Introducing STRATOS: A Cloud Broker Service. In: 5th IEEE International Conference on Cloud Computing (CLOUD), pp. 891–898 (2012)
14. Almulla, M., Almatori, K., Yahyaoui, H.: A QoS-based Fuzzy Model for Ranking Real WorldWeb Services. Presented at the IEEE International Conference on Web Services (2011)
15. Benouaret, K., Benslimane, D., Hadjali, A., Barhamgi, M.: Top-k Web Service Compositions using Fuzzy Dominance Relationship. Presented at the IEEE International Conference on Services Computing (2011)
16. Chao, K.-M., Younas, M., Lo, C.-C., Tan, T.-H.: Fuzzy Matchmaking for Web Services. Presented at the 19th International Conference on Advanced Information Networking and Applications, AINA 2005 (2005)
17. Huang, C.-L., Chao, K.-M., Lo, C.-C.: A Moderated Fuzzy Matchmaking for Web Services. Presented at the the Fifth International Conference on Computer and Information Technology, CIT 2005 (2005)
18. Lin, M., Xie, J., Guo, H., Wang, H.: Solving QoS-driven Web Service Dynamic Composition as Fuzzy Constraint Satisfaction. Presented at the IEEE International Conference on e-Technology, e-Commerce and e-Service (EEE 2005). (2005)
19. Lin, W.-L., Lo, C.-C., Chao, K.-M., Younas, M.: Fuzzy Consensus on QoS in Web Services Discovery. Presented at the 20th International Conference on Advanced Information Networking and Applications, AINA 2006 (2006)

20. Liu, X(F.), Fletcher, K.K., Tang, M.: Service Selection based on Perso-nalized Preference and Trade-Offs among QoS. Presented at the IEEE First International Conference on Service Economics (2012)
21. Nepal, S., Sherchan, W., Hunklinger, J., Bouguettaya, A.: A Fuzzy Trust Management Framework for Service Web. Presented at the IEEE International Conference on Web Services (2010)
22. Meixner, O.: Fuzzy AHP Group Decision Analysis and its Application for the Evaluation of Energy Sources. Presented at the 10th International Symposium on the Analytic Hierarchy/Network Process Multicriteria Decision Making, Pittsburgh, Penn-sylvania, USA (2009)

Modeling Quality Attributes
of Cloud-Standby-Systems
A Long-Term Cost and Availability Model

Alexander Lenk and Frank Pallas

FZI Forschungszentrum Informatik
Friedrichstr. 60
10117 Berlin, Germany
{lenk,pallas}@fzi.de

Abstract. Contingency plans for disaster preparedness and concepts for resuming regular operation as quickly as possible have been an integral part of running a company for a long time. Today, large portions of revenue generation are taking place over the Internet and it has to be ensured that the respective resources and processes are secured against disasters, too. Cloud-Standby-Systems are a way for replicating an IT infrastructure to the Cloud. In this work, a Markov-based model is presented that can be used to analyze and configure such systems on a long term basis. It is shown that by using a Cloud-Standby-System the availability can be increased, how configuration parameters like the replication interval can be optimized, and that the model can be used for supporting the decision whether the infrastructure should be replicated or not.

Keywords: Cloud-Standby, Cold-Standby, BCM, Cloud Computing, IaaS.

1 Introduction

The effort of companies to protect their production facilities, distribution channels or critical business processes against possible risks is not a new phenomenon. Instead, contingency plans for disaster preparedness and concepts for resuming regular operation as quickly as possible have been an integral part of running a company since the times of the industrial revolution. In this context, disasters are fire, earthquakes, terrorist attacks, power outages, theft, illness, or similar circumstances. The respective measures that must be taken in order to being prepared for such disasters and for keeping up critical business processes in the event of an emergency are commonly referred to as "Business Continuity Management" (BCM) [1] in economics. The effectiveness of BCM can be controlled via the key figures "Recovery Time Objective" (RTO) and "Recovery Point Objective" (RPO) [2]. RTO refers to the allowed time for which the business process may be interrupted and the RPO relates to the accepted amount of produced units or data that may be lost by an outage.

Today, with the Internet being production site as well as distribution channel, BCM faces different challenges. One of the most important tasks in IT-related emergency

K.-K. Lau, W. Lamersdorf, and E. Pimentel (Eds.): ESOCC 2013, LNCS 8135, pp. 49–63, 2013.
© Springer-Verlag Berlin Heidelberg 2013

management is the redundant replication of critical systems. Depending on the system class, different mechanisms are used to secure a system against prolonged outages. In this regard the RTO specifies the maximum allowed time within which the IT system must be up again and the RPO is the accepted period of data updates that may be lost, i.e. generally the time between two backups [2].

This work presents an approach for the calculation based on Markov chains [6]. The basic idea is to carry out a "random walk" [6] on the system's state graph according to defined transition probabilities. The costs and the availability can then be calculated by means of the Markov chain and the probability distribution for staying in each state. The presented model is illustrated by means of a simple example and it is shown that the model can be used to calculate optimal configuration options, like the replication interval, of the Cloud-Standby-Systems.

The remainder of this paper is structured as follows: First the related work and a brief description of the Cloud-Standby-System-Class is presented. Then the quality model itself is developed and it is shown how it can be used to make deliberate configuration decisions on the basis of a simple example. Finally, the conclusion sums up the paper and gives an outlook to future work in this field.

2   Related Work

The recovery of IT systems can be achieved through different replication mechanisms [10][11]. "Hot standby" is on the one side of the spectrum: A second data center with identical infrastructure is actively operated on another site with relevant data being continuously and consistently mirrored in almost real-time from the first to the second data center. The operating costs of such a hot standby system, however, amount to the operating costs of the secondary system plus the cost of the mirroring. On the other side of the spectrum is the "cold standby", the low-cost backup, e.g. on tape, without retaining a second site with backup infrastructure resources. A tape backup is not possible during productive operation and is usually done at times of low load like at night or during weekends. In this case, a RPO of days or weeks is common. Due to the fact that the IT infrastructure has to be newly procured in case of a disaster, an RTO of several days to months is possible. Between these two extremes lies the concept of "warm standby". Although a backup infrastructure is kept at another location in this case, it is not fully active and must be initially put into operation in case of a disaster. A warm standby system usually has a RPO and RTO between minutes and hours.

The calculation of quality metrics addressed in this paper can generally be subdivided into the two fields of cost and availability calculation. Regarding these calculations, related work already exists in the field of virtualized infrastructures, Cloud Computing, and warm standby systems.

The approach of Alhazmi et al. [8] describes a way of evaluating disaster recovery plans by calculating the costs. The approach is of generic nature and is not focusing on the field of Cloud Computing with its own specific pricing models. Wood et al. [2] describe a way of replicating the data from one virtual machine to a replica machine.

The respective cost calculation is focusing on this specific approach and cannot be adapted to Cloud-Standby-Systems like the ones considered in this paper.

Dantas et al. [12] present an Markov-based approach to model the availability of a warm-standby Eucalyptus cluster. Even if the approach is related to the work presented herein with regards to the used mathematical model and also shows that Markov chains can be used to model availabilities in Cloud Computing, it is not used to model the costs and the calculation of the availability is restricted to a single Eucalyptus installation with different clusters and does not consider settings with several cloud providers.

Klems et al. [4] present an approach for calculating the downtime of a Cloud-Standby-System. This approach evaluates the system in general but is a rather simplistic short term approach, comparing a Cloud-Standby-System with a manual replication approach.

3   Cloud-Standby-System

A common option for reducing the operating costs of only sporadically used IT infrastructure, such as in the case of the "warm standby" [10][11], is Cloud Computing. As defined by NIST [3], Cloud Computing provides the user with a simple, direct access to a pool of configurable, elastic computing resources (e.g. networks, servers, storage, applications, and other services, with a pay-per-use pricing model). More specifically, this means that resources can be quickly (de-)provisioned by the user with minimal provider interaction and are also billed on the basis of actual consumption. This pricing model makes Cloud Computing a well-suited platform for hosting a replication site offering high availability at a reasonable price. Such a warm standby system with infrastructure resources (virtual machines, images, etc.) being located and updated in the Cloud is herein referred to as a "Cloud-Standby-System". The relevance and potential of this cloud-based option for hosting replication systems gets even more obvious in the light of the current situation in the market. Only fifty percent of small and medium enterprises currently practice BCM with regard to their IT-services while downtime costs sum up to $12,500-23,000 per day for them [9].

The calculation of quality properties, such as the costs or the availability of a replication system, and the comparison with a "base system" without replication is an important basis for decision-making in terms of both the introduction and the configuration of Cloud-Standby-Systems. However, due to the structure and nature of replication systems, this calculation is not trivial, as in each replication state different kinds of costs (replication costs, breakdown costs, etc.) with different cost structures incur. Furthermore, determining the quality of the system is difficult due to the long periods of time and the low probability of disasters (e.g. only one total outage every 10 years). A purely experimental determination by observing a reference system over decades is therefore not feasible. Instead, a method for simulating and calculating the long-term quality characteristics of different configurations is needed.

Cloud-Standby is a Cloud based warm standby approach where the virtual machine images of a Primary System (PS) are periodically synced to a standby-site in the Cloud – the Replication System (RS). The states of a generic Cloud-Standby-System [2][7] are depicted in Fig. 1.

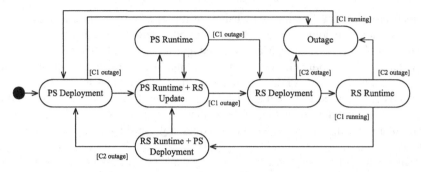

Fig. 1. State chart of a Cloud-Standby-System

It is assumed that the PS needs to be deployed on Cloud 1 (C1) at first and goes into runtime after the deployment. During runtime, the RS on Cloud 2 (C2) is periodically started, updated and then shut down again. In case of an outage on C1, the RS takes over and only if during this time an outage also takes place on C2 the whole system is unavailable. As soon as C1 rises up again, the PS can be redeployed and then takes over. A more detailed description of the Cloud-Standby-System-Class is subject to future publications.

In order to provide decision support regarding the question whether the introduction of such a Cloud Standby System is useful or not, the states need to be transferred into to a mathematical model first. In the next chapter we build such a quality model using a graph and Markov chain, based on the UML chart in Fig.1.

4   Quality Model

In order to facilitate the calculation of quality properties at all, some variables must be defined and parameterized for calculation. Some of the parameters are defined in the use case, or of experimental origin, others are taken from external sources and some can only be estimated. Together with results from previous experiments, average start times can then be calculated. Table 1 represents the time variables to be parameterized as well as the underlying source for its parameterization.

To calculate the total costs, the costs for the run-time of each server must be known. These data can be found in the offers of the Cloud providers. For some evaluations, the costs / loss of profit faced by the company in the case of system unavailability must also be known or at least estimated. All types of costs included in the following analysis are summarized in Table 1. The availability of the Cloud provider is an important basis for the calculation of the overall availability of the system and thus also of the costs. Many Cloud providers declare such availability levels in their SLA. However, this availability is less interesting in the context of this calculation because this work focuses on global, long-term outages caused by disasters that

Table 1. Parameters

Type	Variable	Unit	Source
Duration of the initial deployment	t_{depl}	min.	Experiment / calculation
Backup interval	$t_{updateInt}$	min.	Specification
Backup time	t_{backup}	min.	Experiment / calculation
Duration of the replica deployment	$t_{replica}$	min.	Experiment / calculation
Transition from emergency to normal state	t_{error}	min.	Assumption / historical
Primary Cloud provider costs	$cost_1$	Euro/h/ server	Offer
Secondary Cloud provider costs	$cost_2$	Euro/h/ server	Offer
Unavailability costs	$cost_e$	Euro/h	Assumption / historical
Primary Cloud availability	$avail_1$	years	Assumption / historical
Secondary Cloud availability	$avail_2$	years	Assumption / historical

cannot be handled by traditional backup techniques. The availability described in the third part of Table 1 indicates the average time period in which exactly one such global outage of the respective Cloud provider is likely to be expected.

Even if elasticity [3] is a key concept of Cloud Computing and although the prices for cloud resources constantly changed during the past years, we use static values for the average amount of servers and for the costs over the years. These dynamic aspects could nonetheless easily be added in future work by not having constant prices and servers but functions representing these values. For a first step towards modelling the costs of Cloud-Standby-Systems, however, the use of static values appears acceptable.

4.1 Units

The states for the state graph that should represent the basis for further calculations can be directly derived from the different states of the UML state chart (Fig. 1). In that regard, S_i corresponds to the description of the state i from the state space I. To calculate the quality properties of the system, stopping times must be assigned to each of the states (see Table 2). It is assumed that the step length of the Markov chain is one minute and the stopping time is $d_i \ \forall \ i \in I$ in a state S_i.

Table 2. Designation of the states from the process steps

Process Step	Model State
PS Deployment	S_1
PS Runtime	S_2
PS Runtime + RS Update	S_3
RS Deployment	S_4
RS Runtime	S_5
RS Runtime + PS Deployment	S_6
Outage	S_7

$$\vec{d} := \begin{bmatrix} t_{depl} \\ t_{updateInt} \\ t_{update} \\ t_{replDepl}(t_{updateInt}) \\ t_{error} - t_{replDepl}(t_{updateInt}) - t_{restore} \\ t_{restore} \\ t_{error} \end{bmatrix}$$

As shown in the definition of the stopping times $\vec{d}$, all times except those of d_2, d_4 and d_5 can be determined from the previously set parameters (Table 1). The update interval $t_{updateInt}$ is part of the configuration and has a major influence on the costs and the availability of the system. The time it takes to start the replica deployment (d_4) strongly depends on when the server has last been updated. Consequently, the start time of the replica is increased by a long update interval. Hence, an increase of the backup interval results in a reduction of the deployment time and accordingly the function $t_{replDepl}(t_{updateInt})$ is increasing monotonically. For d_5 it is assumed that the time t_{error} is constant, regardless of the use of a replication system. The run-time of the replication system is therefore made up of the outage time less replication deployment time (d_4) and the time for the return to the production system (d_6).

4.2   Markov Chain and Transition Graph

The quality properties of the replication system can be calculated by modeling the states as a Markov chain and a long-term distribution of the stopping time probabilities in the states S. Due to the lack of memory of the Markov chain (Markov property) it is not possible to directly model the stopping times. The stopping times must be transferred into recurrence probabilities. These must be designed so that, on average, in d_i of the cases the state is maintained and in one case the state is left. It follows that the total number of possible cases is $d_i + 1$. Thus, the recurrence probabilities have to be calculated with $\lambda_i \; \forall \; i \in I$:

$$\lambda_i = \frac{d_i}{d_i+1} \forall \, i \in I$$

In addition to the recurrence probabilities, the probabilities of an outage are required. These are calculated analogously to the recurrence probabilities. On the average, normalized to the iteration step of the Markov chain of one minute, one outage in the period of $avail_i, i \in \{1,2\}$ should incur:

$$\varepsilon_i = \frac{1}{avail_i*365*24*60} \, , i \in \{1,2\}$$

Replication system

Considering these probabilities, the Markov chain MC_1 for the replication system can now be established as follows:

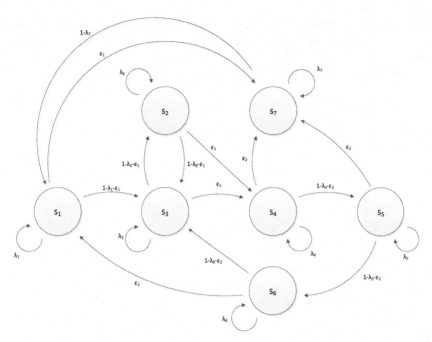

Fig. 2. States of the replication system as a Markov chain (MC_1)

The transition matrix P_1 can be read directly from the Markov chain in Fig. 2:

$$\begin{pmatrix} \lambda_1 & 0 & 1-\lambda_1-\varepsilon_1 & 0 & 0 & \varepsilon_1 & 0 \\ 0 & \lambda_2 & 1-\lambda_2-\varepsilon_1 & \varepsilon_1 & 0 & 0 & 0 \\ 0 & 1-\lambda_3-\varepsilon_1 & \lambda_3 & \varepsilon_1 & 0 & 0 & 0 \\ 0 & 0 & 0 & \lambda_4 & 1-\lambda_4-\varepsilon_2 & 0 & \varepsilon_2 \\ 0 & 0 & 0 & 0 & \lambda_5 & 1-\lambda_5-\varepsilon_2 & \varepsilon_2 \\ \varepsilon_2 & 0 & 1-\lambda_6-\varepsilon_2 & 0 & 0 & \lambda_6 & 0 \\ 1-\lambda_7 & 0 & 0 & 0 & 0 & 0 & \lambda_7 \end{pmatrix}$$

Base system

As the properties of the replication system should in the end be compared to the original system, now the Markov chain MC_2 and the transition matrix P_2 must be created as a reference for the system without replication. The two chains only differ in the fact that no update is performed, which means $t_{updateInt} \to \infty$, the stopping time in the states $S_3 - S_6$ are equal to zero and no second provider exists, the probability of outage ε_2 is therefore 1. In case these parameters are applied to MC_1, the states S_5 and S_6 are no longer obtainable. With a probability of 1 the state of S_4 merges directly with S_7 and can thus be combined with S_7.

Due to the fact that the update interval is infinite, the recurrence probability of S_2 is one[1]. This also results in a negative transition probability from S_2 to S_3. However,

---

[1] $\lim\limits_{t_{updateInt} \to \infty} \lambda\big(t_{updateInt}\big) = \lim\limits_{t_{updateInt} \to \infty} \dfrac{t_{updateInt}}{t_{updateInt}+1} = 1.$

as the recurrence probability of S_3 is zero, this negative transition probability can be resolved by combining the vertices S_2 and S_3 to S_2. Eventually, this results in a new recurrence probability for S_2 of $1 - \varepsilon_1$.

The new Markov chain is therefore MC_2:

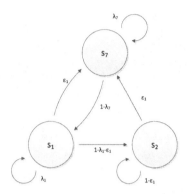

Fig. 3. States of the base system as a Markov chain (MC_2)

The transition matrix P_2 was created similarly to P_1 as a $\mathbb{R}^{7 \times 7}$ matrix, so that the same algorithms are applicable on both matrices. The transitions to and from the states $S_3 - S_6$ have a probability of zero:

$$
\begin{pmatrix}
\lambda_1 & 1 - \lambda_1 - \varepsilon_1 & 0 & 0 & 0 & 0 & \varepsilon_1 \\
0 & 1 - \varepsilon_1 & 0 & 0 & 0 & 0 & \varepsilon_1 \\
0 & 0 & 0 & 0 & 0 & 0 & 0 \\
0 & 0 & 0 & 0 & 0 & 0 & 0 \\
0 & 0 & 0 & 0 & 0 & 0 & 0 \\
0 & 0 & 0 & 0 & 0 & 0 & 0 \\
1 - \lambda_7 & 0 & 0 & 0 & 0 & 0 & \lambda_7
\end{pmatrix}
$$

4.3   Long-Term Distribution

The stationary distribution of a Markov chain MC can be calculated in order to reach a long-term distribution of the system. This distribution π_i , $i \in I$ states the probability of the system to be in the state S_i , $i \in I$ at any given time $n \in \mathbb{N}$. With the help of the probability distribution, long-term quality properties such as the cost of γ and the overall availability of α can easily be calculated. The algorithm for determining the stationary distribution is represented in shortened form as follows[2]. In this case E_r is the unit matrix and $\overrightarrow{b_r}$ is the unit vector with the rank r.

$$Q = P - E_7$$

---

[2]   A detailed description of the calculation of the stationary distribution is given in [6].

$$Q' = \begin{pmatrix} q_{1,1} & \cdots & q_{1,7} & 1 \\ \vdots & \ddots & \vdots & \vdots \\ q_{7,1} & \cdots & q_{7,7} & 1 \end{pmatrix}^T$$

The result of the equation system

$$Q' * \vec{\pi} = \vec{b_7}$$

is the stationary distribution $\vec{\pi}$. This distribution is a vector of which point $\pi_i \in I$ indicates the probability to be in the state S_i at a given step n.

5   Quality Metrics and Decision Support

After defining the stationary distribution π_i, $i \in I$, the quality properties of costs and availability can be determined.

5.1   Cost

The costs c_1 for provider 1 result from the sum of the costs in the states S_1, S_2, S_3, S_6. The costs c_2 incur for provider 2 during the update, in the emergency mode in S_3, S_4, S_5 and the recurrence via state S_6. The costs c_ε for the non-availability of the system incur in the states S_1, S_4, S_7.

$$\gamma(\vec{\pi}, \vec{c}, n_{server}) := c_1 n_{server} \overset{i \in \{1,2,3,6\}}{\sum_i} \pi_i + c_2 n_{server} \overset{i \in \{3,4,5,6\}}{\sum_i} \pi_i + c_\varepsilon \overset{i \in \{1,4,7\}}{\sum_i} \pi_i \quad (1)$$

5.2   Availability

The availability results from the sum of the probabilities of the states in which the system is available (S_2, S_3, S_4, S_6) or from the recurrence probability for the states in which the system is unavailable (S_1, S_4, S_7):

$$\alpha(\vec{\pi}) := \overset{i \in \{2,3,5,6\}}{\sum_i} \pi_i = 1 - \overset{i \in \{1,4,7\}}{\sum_i} \pi_i \quad (2)$$

5.3   Decision Support Based on the Quality Metrics

In case of a decision having to be made whether the replication system should be used in a particular configuration or not, it is useful to compare the quality properties of the different options. Especially during the introduction phase such a direct comparison between the base system and the replication system makes sense.

In many cases companies cannot accurately predict certain parameters such as the cost of an outage ($cost_e$) and can only make estimations in a specific interval. Therefore, it is appropriate to make quality properties not only dependent on the update interval, but also on other parameters.

Ratio of Outage Costs to Replication Interval

To perform a comparison of the total costs in relation to the outage costs and update interval, the total costs with variable outage costs ($cost_e$) and update interval ($t_{updateInt}$) have to be calculated first. We represent these total costs as:

$$\gamma_i\left(t_{updateInt}, cost_e\right) := \gamma\left(\vec{\pi}_i(t_{updateInt}), \vec{c}(cost_e), n_{server}\right), i \in \{1,2\} \tag{3}$$

By using these variable cost calculation functions the area in which the two systems have the same cost can be determined. This is achieved by sectioning the functions:

$$cost_e\left(t_{updateInt}\right) := \gamma_1\left(t_{updateInt}, cost_e\right) \cap \gamma_2\left(t_{updateInt}, cost_e\right) \tag{4}$$

The function will facilitate the consideration of the limit of value. In this case limits for the update interval are the value of continuous updates and an update interval tending to infinity. Due to the cost structure of the Cloud provider (billing period of an hour) the continuous replication is to be equated with a replication interval of 1 hour or 60 minutes:

$$cost_e^{min} := \lim_{t_{updateInt} \to \infty} cost_e\left(t_{updateInt}\right) \tag{5}$$

$$cost_e^{max} := \lim_{t_{updateInt} \to 60} cost_e\left(t_{updateInt}\right) \tag{6}$$

Outside of the interval [$cost_e^{min}, cost_e^{max}$] a Cloud-standby replication such as described in this work doesn't make sense. Should the costs $cost_e^{min}$ decrease, the base system is always cheaper and should the update interval be 60 minutes, two systems are operated in parallel. In this case, there would be a direct transition to a hot standby approach because it guarantees an even higher availability.

Ratio of Availability to the Replication Interval

To establish a ratio between availability and replication interval, the availability α is represented as a function that is dependent on $t_{updateInt}$:

$$\alpha_i\left(t_{updateInt}\right) := \alpha(\vec{\pi}_i), i \in \{1,2\} \tag{7}$$

This ratio allows a determination of the interval in which the replication system can ensure availability:

$$\alpha_1^{min} := \lim_{t_{updateInt} \to \infty} \alpha_1\left(t_{updateInt}\right) \tag{8}$$

$$\alpha_1^{max} := \lim_{t_{updateInt} \to 60} \alpha_1\left(t_{updateInt}\right) \tag{9}$$

The system without replication availability is independent of $t_{updateInt}$:

$$\overline{\alpha}_2 = \alpha_2\left(t_{updateInt}\right)$$

As the availability function $\alpha_1\left(t_{updateInt}\right)$ is convex, $\alpha_1^{min} < \alpha_1^{max}$ always applies. Furthermore, it also applies:

$$\overline{\alpha}_2 \leq \alpha_1^{min} \tag{10}$$

This connection which is surprising at first glance can be explained by the fact that in case of an error in the base system it will be directly changed to the state S_7, while in case of a replication the outage time can be bridged by using Cloud provider 2. Only in case of $t_{error} = 0$ applies:

$$\overline{\alpha}_2 = \alpha_1^{min}$$

i.e. for $t_{error} > 0 \ \lor \ t_{updateInt} > 60$ applies:

$$\overline{\alpha}_2 < \alpha_1\left(t_{updateInt}\right)$$

Thus, it can be assumed that from an availability point of view, the outage time $t_{error} > 0$ should definitely be used on a replication system, even if a very large update interval is chosen.

Determining the Cost Neutral Update Interval

In order to decide on the length of the replication interval it makes sense to perform a comparison of the systems on a cost basis. It is assumed that outage costs $cost_e$ can be quantified. In order to perform a cost comparison, the two total cost functions are set up:

$$\gamma_{i,cost_e}\left(t_{updateInt}\right) = \gamma_i\left(t_{updateInt}, cost_e\right), i \in \{1,2\} \tag{11}$$

The maximum and minimum costs for the replication system can easily be determined by considering the limit values:

$$\gamma_{1,cost_e}^{min} := \lim_{t_{updateInt} \to \infty} \gamma_{1,400}\left(t_{updateInt}\right) \tag{12}$$

$$\gamma_{1,cost_e}^{max} := \lim_{t_{updateInt} \to 60} \gamma_{1,400}\left(t_{updateInt}\right) \tag{13}$$

The cost neutral update interval can be determined by the intersection of the two cost functions:

$$\overline{t}_{updateInt} := \gamma_{1,cost_e}\left(t_{updateInt}\right) \cap \gamma_{2,cost_e}\left(t_{updateInt}\right) \tag{14}$$

6   Evaluation

In section 3 we motivated that a quality model is needed to evaluate if a Cloud-Standby-System is useful in a given use case. In this chapter we evaluate the model by applying it to a given use case. We demonstrate how the quality model can be applied to a server deployment of 10 servers and given or experimentally determined metrics (see Table 3). It is further illustrated how the administrator of the application can be supported in his decision whether to use Cloud Standby or not.

Table 3. Input Parameter (see Table 1-3) Assumptions

Variable	Value
t_{depl}	60 min.
t_{backup}	30 min.
t_{error}	1440 min.
n_{server}	10
$cost_1$	0,68€/h/server[3]
$cost_2$	0,68€/h/server
$avail_1$	10 years
$avail_2$	10 years

For the calculation of the quality properties, it is necessary to determine the time for the deployment of the replica ($t_{replDepl}$). As the time depends on the update frequency, it must be adopted via a function. We assume that 50% of the deployment process is fixed and 50% may be affected by the update interval. The strictly monotonically increasing function should have its lowest point at an update interval of 60 and approach the limit of the time for the initial deployment t_{depl} at infinity:

$$t_{replDepl}\left(t_{updateInt}\right) = t_{depl}\left(1 - 0{,}5\ \frac{60}{t_{updateInt}}\right), t_{updateInt} \in [60, \infty]$$

This function will in our future work be determined by interpolation of data points from real experiments.

6.1   Ratio of Outage Costs to the Replication Interval

With the help of the stationary distributions π_i (see Section 4.3) and the costs in Table 3 the cost functions γ_i can now be defined depending on $t_{updateInt}$ and $cost_e$ using formula (3) with $i = 1$ (Cloud-Standby-System) and $i = 2$ (Base-System).

Representing the two functions in a graph (Fig. 4) reveals combinations where γ_1 has lower function values (total costs) and others where γ_2 is lower. The intersection of the functions establishes a curve on which both systems have the same level of costs. This function is represented in Fig. 5. Besides the combinations leading to the same costs (grey line), the combinations in which the replication system is monetarily inferior to the normal system (grey area) as well as those in which the replication system is cheaper (white area) can be identified.

---

[3] "Extra Large" Amazon EC2 instance in the availability zone EU-West or performance wise comparable instance on another vendor [5].

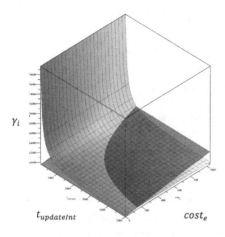

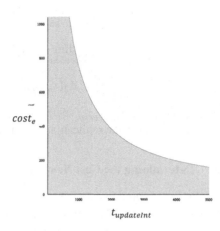

Fig. 4. Comparison of the total costs γ_1 (colored area) and γ_2(grey area) at variable $t_{updateInt}$ and $cost_e$

Fig. 5. $t_{updateInt}$ and $cost_e$ combinations in which the replication system is more expensive (grey area), costs the same (grey line) and is cheaper (white area)

The limits of the function $cost_e(t_{updateInt})$ result in the interval in which a Cloud-standby approach on the basis of total costs makes sense (see formula (5) and (6)):

$$cost_e^{min} = \lim_{t \to \infty} cost_e(t) = 6.79€/h$$

$$cost_e^{max} = \lim_{t \to 60} cost_e(t) = 8198.79€/h$$

In the case of the costs for the outage being lower than the assumed values for server costs, costs for outage times, etc. at more than 8198.79 € per hour, a replication system should be deployed in any case. However, such high costs suggest the approach of a hot standby as two systems can be operated in parallel without any further costs. Given the above-mentioned assumptions, the use of a replication system does not make sense when the outage costs are less than 6.79 € per hour. In this case no matter how large the replication interval is selected, the use of a simple, unsecured system makes more sense from a cost perspective (but not in terms of availability).

6.2   Ratio of Availability to the Replication Interval

Applying the values from Table 5, the availability functions of α_1 and α_2 can be calculated depending on $t_{updateInt}$ with formula (7).

The overall availability of the system increases according to formula (8)-(10) noticeably by introducing the replication system. The limit of the function α_1 and the value of $\overline{\alpha}_2$ are:

$$\alpha_1^{min} = \lim_{t_{updateInt} \to \infty} \alpha_1(t_{updateInt}) = 0.9999883$$

$$\alpha_1^{max} = \lim_{t_{updateInt} \to 60} \alpha_1(t_{updateInt}) = 0.9999940$$

$$\overline{\alpha}_2 = \alpha_2(t_{updateInt}) = 0.999988201$$

Since an outage time of $t_{error} > 0$ was assumed, thus it always makes sense in terms of availability to use the replication system as already presumed.

6.3   Determining the Cost Neutral Update Interval

Now the cost neutral update interval has to be defined by using formula (11), i.e. the time $\overline{t}_{updateInt}$ in which the base system and the replication system produce the same costs. Therefore, it is exemplarily assumed that the outage costs are determined: $cost_e = 400€/h$. With the help of these outage costs, the new cost functions can be set up now:

$$\gamma_{i,400}(t_{updateInt}) = \gamma_i(t_{updateInt}, 400), i \in \{1,2\}$$

Consideration of the limit value according to (12) and (13) easily depicts the minimal and maximal costs:

$$\gamma_{1,400}^{min} = \lim_{t_{updateInt} \to \infty} \gamma_{1,400}(t_{updateInt}) = 59650.34 € / \text{year}$$

$$\gamma_{1,400}^{max} = \lim_{t_{updateInt} \to 60} \gamma_{1,400}(t_{updateInt}) = 99772.07€ / \text{year}$$

The costs for the use of the system without replication can be calculated with the function $\gamma_{2,400}(t_{updateInt})$. These costs are independent of t and thus constant. It is evident that the costs of $\gamma_{1,400}$ are reduced with an increasing update interval and at some point cut with $\gamma_{2,400}$ (see formula (14)). By calculating the equation

$$\gamma_{1,400}(t_{updateInt}) = \gamma_{2,400}(t_{updateInt})$$

to $t_{updateInt}$, the update interval that can be selected without additional monetary expenses can be determined: $\overline{t}_{updateInt} = 1923.03 \; min$.

Considering the outage costs, the system assumed in the example can be made more available without higher costs at an update interval of 1923 minutes, which is a bit less than a daily update (every 1.33 days). The following changes in the availability arise from this: $\alpha_1(1923) - \alpha_2(1923) = 0.000274$. This means that the system in the given use case is within 10 years 1440 minutes or one day more available and consequently the availability class will rise from 3 to 4 with the same costs[4].

---

[4] The introduction of the Cloud-Standby-System may, however, introduce other costs that are not included herein but are subject to future work.

7   Conclusion

In this work a novel Markov chain based approach was presented that can be used to calculate the availability and long-term costs of a Cloud-Standby-System that replicates a single application from one cloud to another. It was also shown that a Cloud-Standby-System has an advantage over a base system in matters of availability even if the replication is not even performed once. It was also shown how the model can be used to configure a Cloud-Standby-System. Since it was proven that a Cloud-Standby-System provides a higher availability by design, future work is to develop a reference architecture for this kind of systems. Challenges will presumably arise with regard to the questions how the deployment of an application can be described on the different Clouds, how algorithms for the deployment and the replication look like and how they can be translated into the metric necessary for the model presented in this paper. Furthermore, future work might also concentrate on the introduction of more dynamic parameters regarding provider costs, outage costs, etc. into the model presented herein.

References

1. Hotchkiss, S.: Business continuity management in practice. BCS, the Chartered Institute for IT, Swindon, UK (2010)
2. Wood, T., et al.: Disaster recovery as a cloud service: Economic benefits & deployment challenges. In: Proc. of HotCloud, Boston (2010)
3. Mell, P., Grance, T.: The NIST definition of cloud computing (draft). NIST special publication 800, 145 (2011)
4. Klems, et al.: Automating the delivery of IT Service Continuity Management through cloud service orchestration. In: IEEE Network Operations and Management Symposium, NOMS (2010)
5. Lenk, A., et al.: What are you paying for? Performance benchmarking for infrastructure-as-a-service offerings. In: IEEE International Conference on Cloud Computing (CLOUD). IEEE (2011)
6. Gilks, W.R., Richardson, S., Spiegelhalter, D. (eds.): Markov Chain Monte Carlo in practice: interdisciplinary statistics, vol. 2. Chapman & Hall/CRC (1995)
7. Cully, B., et al.: Remus: High availability via asynchronous virtual machine replication. In: Proceedings of the 5th USENIX Symposium on Networked Systems Design and Implementation (2008)
8. Alhazmi, O., et al.: Assessing Disaster Recovery Alternatives: On-Site, Colocation or Cloud. In: 23rd IEEE International Symposium on Software Reliability Engineering Workshops (ISSREW). IEEE (2012)
9. Symantec, SMB Disaster Preparedness Survey – Global Results (January 2011)
10. Schmidt, K.: High Availability and Disaster Recovery. Concepts, Design, Implementation. Springer, Germany (2006)
11. Henderson, C.: Building Scalable Web Sites, 1st edn. O'Reilly, Sebastopol (2006)
12. Dantas, et al.: An Availibility Model for Eucalyptus Platform: An Analysis of Warm-Standby Replication Mechanism. In: IEEE International Conference on Systems, Man, and Cybernetics (2012)

Cloud4SOA: A Semantic-Interoperability PaaS Solution for Multi-cloud Platform Management and Portability

Eleni Kamateri[1,2], Nikolaos Loutas[1,2], Dimitris Zeginis[1,2], James Ahtes[3],
Francesco D'Andria[3], Stefano Bocconi[4], Panagiotis Gouvas[5], Giannis Ledakis[5],
Franco Ravagli[6], Oleksandr Lobunets[7] and Konstantinos A. Tarabanis[1,2]

[1] Centre for Research and Technology Hellas (CERTH), Thessaloniki, Greece
{ekamater,nlout,zeginis,kat}@iti.gr
[2] Information Systems Lab, University of Macedonia, Thessaloniki, Greece
{ekamater,nlout,zeginis,kat}@uom.gr
[3] ATOS Spain SA, Barcelona, Spain
{james.ahtes,francesco.dandria}@atos.net
[4] Cyntelix Corporation BV, Amersfoort, The Netherlands
sbocconi@cyntelix.com
[5] Singular Logic, Athens, Greece
{pgouvas,g.ledakis}@gmail.com
[6] Digital Enterprise Research Institute (DERI), NUI Galway, Ireland
franco.ravagli@deri.org
[7] Fraunhofer FIT, Sankt Augustin, Germany
oleksandr.lobunets@fit.fraunhofer.de

Abstract. Cloud Platform as a Service (PaaS) is a novel, rapidly growing segment in the Cloud computing market. However, the diversity and heterogeneity of today's existing PaaS offerings raises several interoperability challenges. This introduces adoption barriers due to the lock-in issues that prevent the portability of data and applications from one PaaS to another, "locking" software developers to the first provider they use. This paper introduces the Cloud4SOA solution, a scalable approach to semantically interconnect heterogeneous PaaS offerings across different Cloud providers that share the same technology. The design of the Cloud4SOA solution, extensively presented in this work, comprises of a set of interlinked collaborating software components and models to provide developers and platform providers with a number of core capabilities: matchmaking, management, monitoring and migration of applications. The paper concludes with the presentation of a proof-of-concept implementation of the Cloud4SOA system based on real-life business scenarios.

Keywords: Cloud computing, Platform as a Service (PaaS), interoperability, portability, semantics, vendor lock-in.

1 Introduction and Motivation

During the last years, Cloud computing has managed to consolidate its position in the domain of IT technologies. According to a recent survey conducted by the Open

K.-K. Lau, W. Lamersdorf, and E. Pimentel (Eds.): ESOCC 2013, LNCS 8135, pp. 64–78, 2013.
© Springer-Verlag Berlin Heidelberg 2013

Group [1], the majority of organizations currently utilize Cloud-based services and solutions, or intend to do so in the next years. Similar increase is also expected in the adoption of PaaS solutions with Gartner predicting that PaaS will increase from three percent to 43 percent of all enterprises by 2015 [2]. Furthermore, a recent Current Analysis report refers that a major shift towards PaaS is gaining momentum in 2013 [3].

PaaS is the layer that lies between the underlying system infrastructure (IaaS) and the overlaying application software (SaaS), containing all application infrastructure services including application containers (servers), application development tools, database management systems, integration middleware, portal products, business process management suites, etc. known as "*middleware*" [4]. The benefits of moving and running an ecosystem of applications on a PaaS provider vary from time- and money-saving to improved operational efficiency, performance, scalability and reliability.

However, IT managers remain sceptical of this new trend expressing considerable concerns about the possible risks that such a movement may entail. Lack of compliance, secure software development process and adequate provisions in Service Level Agreement (SLA) are some of these concerns, with vendor lock-in and interoperability often cited among the most significant challenges facing the long-term adoption of Cloud computing [1, 5].

The PaaS market segment is at its early stage and does not yet have well-established leaders, business practices or dedicated standards [4]. Most PaaS vendors such as Google App Engine and Heroku provide great functionality for developing new applications from scratch, but they do not provide answer for legacy applications, letting PaaS customers do the migration of their applications themselves and usually without adequate support. Similar problems are also experienced when PaaS customers need to migrate an application from one Cloud to another. Some PaaS vendors do not even allow software created by their customers to be moved off their platforms. But even if someone can freely move their data and applications between different Cloud platforms, the high diversity and heterogeneity of today's existing PaaS offerings act as deterrent as developers will have to re-engineer their applications to adapt them to the selected PaaS.

Even on the vendor's side, the very same "lock-in" is greatly limiting the entry of new PaaS providers with innovative offerings, due to the high switching costs that their competition's customers have.

The current state of the PaaS landscape is therefore far from a global arena open to every player. Thus, reducing the interoperability barriers present between different PaaS vendors constitutes an important step for realizing the potential of an open market global vision for Cloud computing and their platforms.

In this vein, this paper introduces an interoperable multi-PaaS Cloud solution developed by the Cloud4SOA research project, which aims to provide better accessibility and flexibility in the fragmented PaaS market. The Cloud4SOA empowers Cloud-based application developers with application portability without setting their applications and data at risk. To this end, it provides added-value capabilities that facilitate the access and lifecycle management to the PaaS offering that best matches developer's computational needs. Specifically, it supports multi-platform matchmaking, management, monitoring and migration of applications by semantically interconnecting heterogeneous PaaS offerings across different Cloud providers that share the same technology.

The rest of this paper is structured as follows. Section 2 reviews the concept of Cloud interoperability as well as the relevant initiatives dealing with this challenging issue. Section 3 presents the most representative capabilities of the Cloud4SOA system. Section 4 describes the Cloud4SOA reference architecture's layers and components. Section 5 gives an overview of the implementation process while section 6 describes the evaluation exercise conducted to assess the usefulness of the Cloud4SOA system. Finally, Section 7 concludes the paper summing up the research findings and the future work.

2   Background and Related Work

2.1   Addressing the Cloud Interoperability

In order to tackle the problem of interoperability, it is quite important to understand what interoperability is and how it can be resolved in the context of Cloud computing. Interoperability is a broad term, encompassing many different aspects related to effective collaboration of diverse resources, services and/or systems. Several attempts have been made to define, address and scope it. This section presents the varied aspects of the Cloud interoperability and a high-level picture of the most promising strategies for addressing it.

Cloud portability is highly related to Cloud interoperability and should be also considered when interoperability is analyzed. Portability refers to the ability to move and reuse applications and data from one Cloud provider to another regardless of the differences that may exist among their systems [6]. Therefore, the Cloud portability requires interoperability obstacles to have been previously resolved in order to move services among Clouds.

In addition, the Cloud interoperability is considered as a synonym of integration in this context; the ability of different Cloud services to seamlessly interoperate or work with each other targeting a common purpose. This also involves the life-cycle management of services across Cloud environments.

Trying to figure out a Cloud interoperability framework that will be adopted by current Cloud systems to resolve interoperability problems, a number of strategies have been proposed.

A common tactic to address Cloud interoperability is the use of open standards for the resources/services, security and management functions. This consensus will enable the easy integration and migration of services between heterogeneous Cloud systems. However, most of the existing Cloud solutions have not been built to comply with any established Cloud standards leading to a locked-in and fragmented Cloud market.

This deficiency can be addressed by means of interoperability techniques that will be applied to the current non-compatible Cloud systems including the creation of abstraction layers and open APIs. The main characteristic of an abstraction layer is that it is specifically conceived to hide the details of the underlying layers. Indeed, it is used to hide the differences of underlying resources/services. It can also resolve conceptualization incompatibilities arisen in the semantics of Cloud services providing an abstract view that facilitates the easy discovery and selection, customization and integration of different services. On the other hand, a standardized management interface (API) abstracts/wraps proprietary ones and resolves the arisen programmatic differences from one Cloud to another translating the commands to specific Cloud provider's management configurations.

2.2   Related Work

Cloud computing reference architectures can provide a common viewpoint of Cloud computing model and, therefore, deal with arisen interoperability issues (e.g. CSA[1], NIST[2], and recently Gartner[3] and IETF[4]). However, in real life persuading the whole community to agree on and adopt a reference architecture or a common model may sound unrealistic or at least difficult to achieve. A more flexible approach to tackle interoperability conflicts among different Cloud providers is needed such as the use of a Cloud broker that adopts the aforementioned interoperability techniques. A Cloud broker can achieve unification and connectivity among current Cloud systems, while reducing the need for reforming their establishment technology. In this section, we summarize a number of broker-based Cloud architectures derived from related EU projects that aim to address Cloud interoperability mainly in the PaaS layer as well as open and proprietary offerings targeting PaaS interoperability.

The broker-based architecture proposed in Cloud@Home [7] uses virtualization techniques to overcome compatibility problems and provide a homogeneous view of distributed resources and services.

The RESERVOIR project [8] aimed at the development of a service-oriented infrastructure that allows the interoperability of Cloud providers for the reliable delivery of services. Service providers address end-users' needs leasing computational resources from infrastructure providers which interoperate with each other creating a seamlessly infinitive pool of IT resources.

For the purposes of the Contrail project [9], a set of adapters are implemented in each Cloud provider to enable the efficient cooperation and sharing of resources coming from different Cloud providers. To this end, CONTRAIL provides a system in which resources that belong to different operators are integrated into a single homogeneous federated Cloud that users can access seamlessly.

---

[1] https://cloudsecurityalliance.org/guidance/csaguide.v3.0.pdf
[2] http://www.cloudcredential.org/images/
    pdf_files/nist%20reference%20architecture.pdf
[3] http://www.gartner.com/id=1395513
[4] http://social.technet.microsoft.com/wiki/contents/articles/
    4399.private-cloud-reference-model.aspx

The PaaSage[5] project aims at delivering an open and integrated platform to support model-based development, configuration, optimization, and deployment of existing and new applications independently of the existing Cloud infrastructures.

4CaaSt [10] introduces a broker-based architecture which decouples the development and specification of applications from their actual deployment, leaving the underlying complexity of infrastructure and platforms out of users' concerns. This platform enables the creation of a business ecosystem where services at all layers of the Cloud can be easily tailored to different users, mashed up and traded together.

The mOSAIC project [11] aims at the development of a platform that facilitates applications' deployment and portability across multiple Clouds providing a set of open APIs (independent of vendors) and a high-level abstraction of Cloud resources. In addition, mOSAIC enables developers to specify their resource requirements in terms of an ontology while the platform, using a brokering mechanism, will find best-fitting Cloud services.

The Cloud-TM project [12] aims at building an innovative middleware platform which exposes a set of APIs and abstractions for the development and administration of large scale parallel applications across a dynamic set of distributed nodes, elastically acquired from the underlying IaaS Cloud provider(s).

The goal of the Broker@Cloud [13] project is to develop a framework that will equip Cloud service intermediaries with advanced methods and mechanisms for continuous quality assurance and optimization of software-based Cloud services.

Table 1. Overview of Related Broker-based Architectures

Architecture	Layer	IaaS Inter-operability	PaaS Inter-operability	Portability	Ontology-based	Standard-ized API
Cloud@Home	IaaS	✓	✗	✗	✗	✓
RESERVOIR	IaaS	✓	✗	✗	✗	(OCCI)
Contrail	IaaS/PaaS	✓	✗	✗	✗	✓
PaaSage	IaaS/PaaS	✓	✗	✗	✓	✗
4CassSt	PaaS	✗	✓	✗	✗	✓
mOSAIC	IaaS/PaaS	✓	✗	✓	✓	✓
Cloud-TM	IaaS	✓	✗	✗	✗	✓
Broker@Cloud	IaaS/PaaS	✗	✗	✗	✗	✓
Cloud4SOA	PaaS	✗	✓	✓	✓	✓

An open API serves as a pragmatic strategy for tackling certain interoperability issues. Several open APIs and proprietary ones (such as the open DeltaCloud[6] & OpenStack[7], and the proprietary Rightscale[8] & vCloud[9]) have been proposed for the

---

[5] http://www.paasage.eu/
[6] http://deltacloud.apache.org/
[7] http://www.openstack.org/
[8] www.rightscale.com/
[9] http://www.vmware.com/products/
datacenter-virtualization/vcloud-suite/overview.html

management of IaaS services, as well as the popular OCCI[10] standard specification. As regards to the PaaS layer, early efforts have been made in the last few years. Cloudify[11] enables the deployment, management and scaling of applications on various Clouds. Compatible One[12] is an open source Cloud broker that enables to create, deploy and manage Cloud platforms. Moreover, CAMP[13], out of the OASIS group, looks to standardize basic management aspects so that PaaS providers can focus on their differentiating qualities. Furthermore, Cloud Foundry[14], developed by VMware, aims to give developers the opportunity to build Cloud Foundry PaaS implementations that will be portable across various infrastructures. OpenShift[15] is Red Hat's PaaS offering that provides developers a flexible development environment. OpenShift makes use of DeltaCloud's interoperability API to provide cross-cloud application deployment.

Table 2. Overview of Open and Proprietary PaaS Offerings

Architecture	Solution	Description	IaaS Interoperability	PaaS Interoperability
Cloudify	Open	Open PaaS	✗	✓
Compatible One	Open	Open source Cloud broker	✓	✓
CAMP	Open	Open PaaS API specification	✗	✓
Cloud Foundry	Proprietary	Open source project	✓	✗
OpenShift	Proprietary	Development environment	✓	✗

From the above analysis, we can deduce that the main role of a Cloud broker is to translate user's requirements and match them with the appropriate Cloud offerings. Semantics can enhance the matchmaking operation providing an ontology-based abstraction mechanism to support the unified representation of Cloud-based application's requirements and Cloud offerings coming from different Cloud providers enabling the ease mapping of them. Such descriptors are interpreted by the mOSAIC and 4CaaSt platforms. Furthermore, a standardized interface (API) is quite necessary to mask the programming differences of proprietary APIs and enable the seamless management of distributed resources/services as well as portability of services across platforms. As shown in Table 1, APIs are exposed by most of the platforms. Last, it has been observed that the majority of the Cloud brokers are acting in the IaaS layer, e.g. RESERVOIR, Cloud@Home, and Cloud-TM, or they are based on the personalization of the IaaS to meet user requirements at the PaaS layer such as mOSAIC and CONTRAIL. There are limited approaches exclusively focusing on PaaS interoperability and dealing with with the different data models and proprietary runtime frameworks that each application requires and each platform provider enables.

---

[10] http://occi-wg.org/
[11] http://www.cloudifysource.org/
[12] http://www.compatibleone.org/
[13] https://www.oasis-open.org/committees/tc_home.php?wg_abbrev=camp
[14] http://www.cloudfoundry.com/
[15] https://www.openshift.com/

Towards this direction, Cloud4SOA provides a broker-based solution that operates in the PaaS layer enabling interoperability and portability among different Cloud platforms (PaaS offerings). In this way, developers can select, deploy and manage their applications on a PaaS offering while they can easily switch between platforms whenever they need to without re-architecting their initial application solutions. Moreover, the ontology-based architecture introduced by the Cloud4SOA exhibits the key characteristics of an interoperable solution. Specifically, it establishes a set of abstractions among different PaaS offerings while it exposes a multi-PaaS application management standardized interface that will support the seamless deployment and management of applications across different Cloud platforms.

3   Cloud4SOA's Core Capabilities

In this section, the most representative functionalities that are implemented by the Cloud4SOA reference architecture are presented. The key core capabilities of the Cloud4SOA system have been aggregated based on the requirement analysis conducted within the first months of the Cloud4SOA project. In particular, the analysis has exposed a set of key requirements that an interoperable Cloud PaaS architecture should satisfy taking into account both current literature analysis and stakeholders' needs (for more details, see [14]).

- The **semantic matchmaking** capability resolves the semantic conflicts between diverse PaaS offerings. Specifically, it aligns the user requirements and the PaaS offerings even if they are expressed in different terms and resolves the semantic conflicts between diverse PaaS offerings in order to allow matching of concepts between different PaaS providers. The outcome is a list of PaaS offerings that satisfy developer's needs, ranked according to the number of satisfied user preferences.
- The **management** capability supports the efficient deployment and governance of applications in a PaaS-independent way. The developers can manage the life-cycle of their applications in a homogenized way, independently of the specific PaaS offering where the application is deployed. In addition, the application management capitalizes on the SLA mechanism that enables the establishment of an agreement between a PaaS offering and a developer.
- The **migration** capability allows migrating already deployed applications from one PaaS offering to another. Moving an application between PaaS offerings consists of two main steps: i) moving the application data (the application is stopped before starting to move the data) and ii) moving and re-deploying the application itself to the new PaaS offering.
- The **monitoring** capability supports a unified platform-independent mechanism, to monitor the health and performance of business-critical applications hosted on multiple Clouds environments, in order to ensure that their performance consistently meets expectations, user-defined according to their existing SLA. In order to consider the heterogeneity of different PaaS offerings, Cloud4SOA provides a monitoring functionality based on unified platform-independent metrics.

4   Cloud4SOA Reference Architecture

The main beneficiaries of the Cloud4SOA's capabilities are the Cloud-based applica-tion developer and Cloud PaaS provider. A developer may be a free-lancer or working for a company who wants to deploy their applications on a PaaS offering, a software company that wants to use a local PaaS for internal development or an Independent Software Vendor (ISV) interested in selling SaaS services on top of a hosted PaaS. On the other hand, a PaaS provider may be a small-medium enterprise (SME) or a larger industry working in the PaaS field.

Cloud4SOA combines three fundamental and complementary computing para-digms, namely Cloud computing, Service Oriented Architectures (SOA) and light-weight semantics, to propose a reference architecture and deploy fully operational prototypes optimising the initial envisioned architecture [15]. The envisioned broker-based reference architecture that exhibits these characteristics is depicted in Fig. 1 and consists of five layers, three horizontal and two vertical, outlined below.

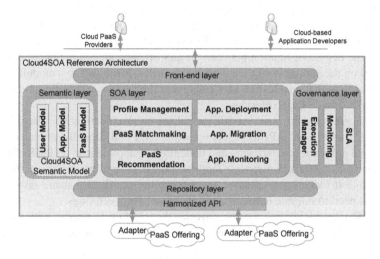

Fig. 1. Cloud4SOA Reference Architecture

4.1   Frond-end Layer

The Front-end layer supports the user-centric focus of the Cloud4SOA and the easy access of both developers and PaaS providers to Cloud4SOA's functionalities ex-posed via widgetized services which are adaptable to the user's context.

The Front-end layer makes use of a web-based interface that implements a design metaphor based on the concept of a dashboard. The choice is motivated by the fact that the user needs an overview about the performance of the application(s) deployed on different PaaS providers and a centralized point for managing applications. The dashboard offers a set of widgets which allow encapsulating functionality in a self-contained application, i.e. an application with a front-end and business logic. Widgets can be modelled to correspond to the different actions the user wants to perform on the platform, e.g. search a PaaS offering or deploy an application. At the same time, they can be grouped in different ways to allow presenting the user only with the functionalities he is likely to need in the course of a certain activity.

4.2   SOA Layer

The SOA layer acts as a mediator to the other layers' services, translating a resource centric architecture, provided by the Semantic layer with its implementation and management concepts, into the high-level architecture, letting Front-end layer access Cloud4SOA's core functionalities. The SOA layer comprises of a toolbox that is accessible through the adaptable Front-end layer including:

The *Profile Management module* capitalizes on the models provided by the Semantic layer to enable the management of the semantic profiles, namely PaaS offerings, applications and user profiles.

The *PaaS Matchmaking module* relies on the search mechanisms offered by the Repository layer and employs lightweight semantic models and techniques in order to find available, best matching (according to user requirements) PaaS offerings.

The *PaaS Recommendation module* offers suggestions for the best matches of PaaS offerings. The degree of relation between a PaaS offering and an application is computed based on the similarity of their semantic profiles. Moreover this module offers a rating mechanism that enables the user rating and the system automatic rating (based on SLA violations) of PaaS offerings.

The *Application Deployment module* capitalizes on the functionality offered by the Cloud4SOA Harmonized API to provide a set of back-end capabilities including deployment and governance (start, stop and undeploy) of applications on PaaS offerings.

The *Application Migration module* facilitates the user in migrating to another PaaS offering while it tackles the semantic interoperability conflicts that are raised when applications need to migrate between different Cloud PaaS offerings.

The *Application Monitoring module* provides the interface to interact with the monitoring functionality and to retrieve the collected data according to different parameters.

4.3   Semantic Layer and Cloud4SOA Semantic Model

The Semantic layer is the backbone of the architecture that puts in place the PaaS Semantic Interoperability Framework (PSIF) [15] and facilitates the formal representation of information (i.e. PaaS offerings, applications and user profiles). It spans the entire architecture resolving interoperability conflicts and providing a common basis for publishing and searching different PaaS offerings. Each of the three main components has a unique objective and utilizes a specific set of fundamental PaaS entities depending on its focus, implementing in this way a specific part of the adopted the Cloud4SOA Semantic Model.

The Cloud4SOA Semantic Model, depicted in Fig. 2, serves as a means for the unification and the disciplined representation of different Cloud systems. It consists of five tiers, where each tier describes a set of fundamental PaaS entities and their relations:

- The *Infrastructure tier* captures knowledge related to infrastructure modeling concepts such as hardware component, software component, programming language and QoS parameters. This tier offers a common language to describe both applications and PaaS offerings, thus enabling their matching.
- The *Platform tier* is used by PaaS providers to semantically annotate their PaaS offerings using entities to describe the platform, the infrastructure and the enterprise. It is based on the Infrastructure tier in order to operate and its main concept is the PaaS offering.
- The *Application tier* is used by developers to annotate their applications utilizing entities related to the application's requirements. It captures knowledge related to a Cloud-based Application and the central concept of this tier is the Application.
- The *User tier* facilitates the users' annotation enabling any user in the Cloud4SOA system to create a semantic profile reusing concepts coming from FOAF ontology.
- The *Enterprise tier* describes the enterprises that participate at the Cloud PaaS layer and their relations with other entities (e.g. users). This tier mainly models concepts such as of the PaaS provider and the SLA agreement.

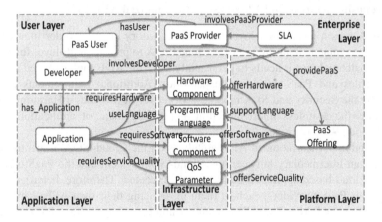

Fig. 2. Cloud4SOA Semantic Model

4.4   Governance Layer

The Governance layer implements the business-centric focus of the Cloud4SOA where developers can establish their user-defined SLA metrics to measure performance and mitigate violations. It enables the lifecycle execution and management of Cloud-based applications, taking into account monitoring information, SLAs and scalability issues. In particular:

The *Execution Management Service (EMS)* module is the key interface in everything related to the application lifecycle including deployment, un-deployment, maintenance and migration related tasks.

The *Monitoring module* is responsible for monitoring applications' and platform's health. It is based on a unified and Cloud platform-independent approach in order to consider heterogeneity of different Clouds architectures.

The *SLA module* enables the SLA management. The SLA module consists of three sub-components that interact with the Monitoring and EMS modules:

The *SLA Negotiation* allows Cloud4SOA to perform automatic negotiations on behalf of PaaS providers, based on the semantic description of offerings and the QoS requirements specified by the developer. However, in the scope of project, SLAs do not aim at representing a contractual relationship between the customers consuming virtualized Platforms and the PaaS vendors that provide them. SLAs describe the service that is delivered, the functional and non-functional properties of the resource, and the duties of each party involved.

The *SLA Enforcement* is in charge of supervising that all the agreements (SLAs guarantees) are respected.

The *SLA-Decisor* is responsible for dealing with the violations and deciding the appropriate recovery action to take (stop, migration, etc.) when a violation occurs.

4.5   Repository Layer and Cloud4SOA Harmonized API

Cloud4SOA uses a persistency layer, named Repository layer, in order to store both semantic and syntactic data. In order for Cloud4SOA to provide high-level functionalities (e.g. matchmaking) it needs to persistently store the RDF triples related to developer's profiles and PaaS providers' capabilities. Additional requirements are also imposed by the Security and SLA modules. Moreover, it provides a Harmonized API that enables the seamless interconnection and management of applications across different Cloud PaaS offerings.

The Cloud4SOA Harmonized API capitalizes on the Cloud4SOA Semantic Model and acts as an intermediary between the Cloud4SOA system and the PaaS offerings, where the Cloud-based applications are actually executed. Therefore, heterogeneity of the numerous PaaS providers, each of them introducing their own APIs, can be handled by this unified API. The API contains a number of operations that support the management of the Cloud-based applications independent of the specific API of the underlying PaaS offering. Given that each PaaS offering uses its own API, an adapter is needed as a middleware between the Cloud4SOA API and the native API of the PaaS offering. More specifically, the adapter translates the functions of the Cloud4SOA API to the PaaS offering's native API, and vice versa.

5   Implementation

During the implementation phase, all components of the Cloud4SOA platform have been implemented. The platform has been developed using JAVA technology in order to increase its portability. Specific J2EE patterns have been adopted in order to increase the flexibility during the development and the maintainability in general. The Cloud4SOA consortium tried to vertically modularize the code-organization based on the various functionalities that each component accomplishes. In addition, for a project of this scale and modularity, it was also mandatory to use build automation techniques. Maven technology uses an XML file to describe the software project being built, its dependencies on other external modules and components, the build order, directories, and required plug-ins making it ideal for the Cloud4SOA purposes. Specifically, the exploitation of MAVEN technology makes the build process easy, provides a uniform build system, provides quality project information, provides guidelines for best practices development and allows transparent migration to new features. Finally, the adoption of Spring Framework v3 simplified the collaboration between the developers thanks to the flexible instantiation methods (i.e. auto-wiring support).

Cloud4SOA is now in an invitation-only Beta phase of its release. In parallel, the project is deploying an offering focused specifically on its PaaS application/matchmaking service, hosted publically to developers. This will help gain a larger user base and provide a priority service for the fragmented nature of the PaaS market segment. The full multi-Cloud management, monitoring and migration capabilities will be rolled out by the project partners in the autumn of 2013. As an open source solution, the full release will be paired by a local implementation of the Cloud4SOA and its adapters available to download from GitHub, giving a flexible choice for developers to leverage the Cloud4SOA system between publically hosted or local versions.

6   Evaluation

The evaluation of a software product is an important phase in the development process. Cloud4SOA follows a two-fold usability evaluation approach to assert the usefulness of the Cloud4SOA system: *i)* implementation of three proof-of-concept showcases based on real-life business scenarios and *ii)* an extensive Beta program which taps the project's PaaS developer and vendor stakeholders.

Additionally, we designed and conducted system performance studies to estimate capacity of the existing closed beta deployment and learn the ways of scaling Cloud4SOA's services for higher demands.

6.1   Internal Evaluation via Industry Showcases

In showcase #1, Portugal Telecom Inovação (PTIN)[16], the research and development part of Portugal Telecom Group (PT), has developed the business intelligence showcase. PTIN has created a context-aware multimedia framework. Within the framework, a XMPP server has an active role in the processes performed by 3 service enablers that have been re-designed based on SOA concepts. Following this development, PTIN has ported, through Cloud4SOA, these services from the framework to several PaaS providers recommend and supported by Cloud4SOA. The deployment and on-demand migration of context-aware multimedia services to different PaaS providers has enabled the seamless integration with services deployed in the same or different Clouds and with profiling and location tracking services exposed from the PTIN's infrastructure, offering to the mobile end-users high capacity value-added services.

---

[16] http://www.ptinovacao.pt/

In showcase #2, the Fraunhofer Institute for Applied Information Technology (FIT)[17] has implemented the industrial business collaboration showcase. Specifically, FIT has adapted the existing Basic Support for Cooperative Work (BSCW)[18] application to be deployed via the Cloud4SOA system as a Cloud-enabled service on a PaaS platform with the final goal of an efficient execution and effective governance of the BSCW service on a PaaS platform. The interoperability of different BSCW servers would be enabled on a back-end and file store level reducing administration overhead and providing users who work on different servers a seamless cooperation environment.

ROMTELECOM[19] has implemented the existing VPN Portal as the network-monitoring showcase in the Cloud4SOA project. Virtual Private Network (VPN) Portal is a customer-facing portal that presents to the customers information and reports available in several internal systems and allows to view and manage incident tickets. Parts of the VPN Portal have been ported on a PaaS in order to be easily integrated with other portals. The showcase has developed and tested the effectiveness of the portability of the customer-facing interfaces in the Cloud, the separation of the presentation interfaces from the computational-intensive algorithms and from the internal databases, and the ad-hoc migration of parts of the application among different Cloud infrastructures, in the same time testing the effectiveness of using a proprietary database in "cloudified" applications.

A valuable continuous feedback has been provided during all the phases of the system development helping to resolve inconsistencies between designers' and users' mental models, and adjust the system architecture. The aspects touched by this early feedback include but are not limited by PaaS adapters' architecture design and development, application deployment flows (e.g. Git-based deployment implementation), design of UI (e.g. GUI or CLI), design of the monitoring subsystem.

6.2   Performance Studies

An important aspect of the Cloud4SOA evaluation is performance evaluation that aims to collect and disseminate the data related to system performance under a real-life workload. This step has been performed before the launch of the external Beta program in order to avoid hitting the performance issues after opening the system to a wider sample of Cloud4SOA stakeholders.

The performance studies follow a common design similar to every web-based application. First, a workload model is created and expressed in terms of use-cases of using the Cloud4SOA web-based GUI by an end-user. The workload model includes parameters to define the number of simultaneous end-users working with the Cloud4SOA system, user-thinking time between the subsequence requests and full load ramp-up period.

The performance studies help us to learn more about the limits of the current deployment of the Cloud4SOA and the possible ways of scaling different components of the system.

---

[17] http://www.fit.fraunhofer.de/en.html
[18] https://public.bscw.de/pub/
[19] http://www.romtelecom.ro/

6.3   Cloud4SOA Stakeholder Beta Program

The goal of the final external evaluation is to assert Cloud4SOA added-value services usefulness on a significant sample of end-users invited to an early beta access to the system.

Through a campaign of industry events, developer conferences and workshops, the project has already begun to gather direct feedback based on its Beta release. One such set of comments that has influenced the initial Cloud4SOA deployment model is based on developer priorities of today compared to an evolving PaaS market that will mature in the next few years. For example, the Cloud4SOA application-to-provider matchmaking capability has received much more interest than anticipated, especially for a project focused more on the actual alleviation of vendor lock-in (i.e. the Cloud4SOA's migration capability). As such, Cloud4SOA is releasing a standalone platform matchmaking service in order to offer an immediate added-value for developers in the fragmented PaaS market of today, which is helping build momentum and user-base for the full post-Beta release of the Cloud4SOA later in 2013 with the more advanced multi-PaaS management and migration capabilities.

This combination of an extensive invitation-only current Beta (representing the full matchmaking, management, monitoring and migration capabilities) and the fully public platform matchmaking standalone, Cloud4SOA is currently receiving a broad external evaluation for its release schedule, feature set rollout and future market deployment.

7   Conclusion and Next Steps

Cloud4SOA is expected to push towards a more open, competitive and dynamic market segment for rising PaaS providers and their potential developers. In particular, it addresses key PaaS-oriented adoption barriers in Cloud computing, such as the segment's fragmented presentation of platform offerings and the vendor lock-in risk that remains a key concern for small and large companies alike.

Moreover, Cloud4SOA has just recently begun contributing to OASIS's new CAMP working group, an industry-backed standard specification that provides a basic platform management API. The working group's progress and first specification helps validate the project's objectives, and could allow the Cloud4SOA system to act as a bridge between CAMP compliant and non-compliant platforms, as well as other multi-Cloud ecosystem scenarios.

Acknowledgments. This work is partially funded by the European Commission within the 7th Framework Programme in the context of the ICT project Cloud4SOA (http://www.cloud4soa.eu/) under grand agreement No. 257953. The authors would like to thank the entire Cloud4SOA consortium that participated in the collaborative development of the Cloud4SOA system and are not listed as authors of this paper.

References

1. The Open Group Cloud Computing Work Group: Cloud ROI Survey Results Comparison 2011 & 2012 (2012), http://www.opengroup.org/getinvolved/workgroups/cloudcomputing
2. Platt, B.: People want PaaS: Nearly 60 percent of companies say they will deploy PaaS soon (2012), http://venturebeat.com/2012/11/29/paas-engine-yard/
3. Singh, A.: Current Analysis: PaaS to Play a Critical Role in Enterprise Development (2012), http://www.currentanalysis.com/news/2012/pr-paas-platform.asp
4. Pettey, C., Goasduff, L.: Gartner Says Platform as a Service Is On the Cusp of Several Years of Strategic Growth (2012), http://www.gartner.com/newsroom/id/1911014
5. The Open Web Application Security Project (OWASP): Cloud - Top 5 Risks with PAAS (2011), https://www.owasp.org/index.php/Cloud_-_Top_5_Risks_with_PAAS
6. Oberle, K., Fisher, M.: ETSI CLOUD – initial standardization requirements for cloud services. In: Altmann, J., Rana, O.F. (eds.) GECON 2010. LNCS, vol. 6296, pp. 105–115. Springer, Heidelberg (2010)
7. Cunsolo, V.D., Distefano, S., Puliafito, A., Scarpa, M.: Cloud@Home: Bridging the gap between volunteer and cloud computing. In: Huang, D.-S., Jo, K.-H., Lee, H.-H., Kang, H.-J., Bevilacqua, V. (eds.) ICIC 2009. LNCS, vol. 5754, pp. 423–432. Springer, Heidelberg (2009)
8. Rochwerger, B., et al.: The reservoir model and architecture for open federated cloud computing. IBM Journal of Research and Development 53(4), 4–1 (2009)
9. Harsh, P., Jegou, Y., Cascella, R.G., Morin, C.: Contrail virtual execution platform challenges in being part of a cloud federation. In: Abramowicz, W., Llorente, I.M., Surridge, M., Zisman, A., Vayssière, J., et al. (eds.) ServiceWave 2011. LNCS, vol. 6994, pp. 50–61. Springer, Heidelberg (2011)
10. Garcia-Gomez, S., et al.: Challenges for the comprehensive management of Cloud Services in a PaaS framework. Scalable Computing: Practice and Experience 13(3) (2012)
11. Petcu, D., et al.: Portable Cloud applications-From theory to practice. Future Generation Computer Systems (2012) (in press)
12. Romano, P., et al.: Cloud-TM: harnessing the cloud with distributed transactional memories. ACM SIGOPS Operating Systems Review 44(2), 1–6 (2010)
13. Grivas, S.G., et al.: Cloud broker: Bringing intelligence into the cloud. In: IEEE 3rd International Conference on Cloud Computing (CLOUD), pp. 544–545. IEEE (2010)
14. Loutas, N., et al.: D1.1 Requirements Analysis Report. Cloud4SOA Project Deliverable (2011), http://www.cloud4soa.eu/sites/default/files/Cloud4SOA%20D1.1%20Requirements%20Analysis.pdf
15. Loutas, N., et al.: Towards a Reference Architecture for Semantically Interoperable Clouds. In: IEEE 2nd International Conference on Cloud Computing Technology and Science, pp. 143–150. IEEE (2010)
16. Loutas, N., et al.: A Semantic Interoperability Framework for Cloud Platform as a Service. In: IEEE 3rd International Conference on Cloud Computing Technology and Science, pp. 280–287. IEEE (2011)

Implementation and Evaluation
of a Multi-tenant Open-Source ESB

Steve Strauch, Vasilios Andrikopoulos, Santiago Gómez Sáez,
and Frank Leymann

Institute of Architecture of Application Systems, University of Stuttgart, Germany
Universitätsstraße 38, 70569 Stuttgart, Germany
lastname@iaas.uni-stuttgart.de

Abstract Offering applications as a service in the Cloud builds on the
notion of application multi-tenancy. Multi-tenancy, the sharing of application instances and their underlying resources between users from
different organizational domains, allows service providers to maximize
resource utilization and reduce servicing costs per user. Realizing application multi-tenancy however requires suitable enabling mechanisms
offered by their supporting middleware. Furthermore, the middleware itself can be multi-tenant in a similar fashion. In this work we focus on
enabling multi-tenancy for one of the most important components in
service-oriented middleware, the Enterprise Service Bus (ESB). In particular, we discuss the prototype realization of a multi-tenant aware ESB,
using an open source solution as the basis. We then evaluate the performance of our proposed solution by an ESB-specific benchmark that we
extended for multi-tenancy purposes.

Keywords: Multi-tenancy, Enterprise Service Bus (ESB), ESB benchmarking, JBI specification, Platform as a Service.

1 Introduction

The Enterprise Service Bus (ESB) technology addresses the fundamental need
for application integration by acting as the messaging hub between applications.
As such, in the last years it has become ubiquitous in service-oriented enterprise
computing environments. ESBs control the message handling during service invocations and are at the core of each Service-Oriented Architecture (SOA) [12].
Given the fact that the Cloud computing paradigm [16] is discussed in terms
of the creation, delivery and consumption of services [5], it is therefore essential
to investigate into how the ESB technology can be used efficiently in a Cloud-
oriented environment.

For this purpose, in our previous work we focused on investigating how to
make ESBs *multi-tenant aware* [21]. In this context, making an ESB multi-
tenant aware means that the ESB is able to manage and identify multiple tenants
(groups like companies, organizations or departments sharing the application)
and their users, providing tenant-based identification and hierarchical access

K.-K. Lau, W. Lamersdorf, and E. Pimentel (Eds.): ESOCC 2013, LNCS 8135, pp. 79–93, 2013.
© Springer-Verlag Berlin Heidelberg 2013

control to them. In other words, the ESB should provide the appropriate mechanisms that allow (multi-)tenant applications to seamlessly interact with it while sharing one (logical) instance of the ESB. Given the role of the ESB middleware in the technological stack, there are two fundamental aspects of multi-tenancy awareness: communication (i.e. supporting message exchanges isolated per tenant and application), and administration and management (i.e. allowing each tenant to configure and manage individually their communication endpoints at the ESB).

Multi-tenancy has been previously defined in different ways in the literature for SOA and middleware, see for example [10], [17], [14], [23]. Such definitions however do not address the whole technological stack behind the different Cloud service models as defined in [16] (i. e. IaaS — Infrastructure as a Service, PaaS — Platform as a Service, SaaS — Software as a Service). For these reasons in [21] we define multi-tenancy as *the sharing of the whole technological stack (hardware, operating system, middleware and application instances) at the same time by different tenants and their users.*

Multi-tenancy is one of the key enablers that allow Cloud computing solutions to serve multiple customers from a single system instance (the other being virtualization of the application stack). Using these techniques, Cloud service providers maximize the utilization of their infrastructure, and therefore increase their return on infrastructure investment, while reducing the costs of servicing each customer. On the Cloud service consumer side, the fundamental assumption in using multi-tenant applications is that tenants are well isolated from each other, both in terms of data and computational resources. This ensures that the operation of one tenant does not have any discernible effect on the efficacy and efficiency of the operation of the other tenants. Ensuring tenant isolation in Cloud solutions however is a notoriously difficult problem and remains largely an open research question, see for example [10] and [14].

Towards this direction, in this work we investigate the performance of a multi-tenant aware ESB implementation from both perspectives, i.e. service providers and consumers. For this purpose we first present in detail the realization of the ESB^{MT} architectural framework [21] based on the Java Business Integration (JBI) specification [11] into a multi-tenant aware ESB solution. We then evaluate the performance of our solution in terms of response time as experienced by the service consumer (i.e. the application tenant), and CPU and memory utilization (that are of particular interest to the service provider). For this purpose we extend and modify an industry benchmark for ESBs in order to make it suitable for driving multi-tenant, in addition to non multi-tenant, interactions. Our contributions can be summarized as follows:

- A detailed presentation of the realization of a multi-tenant aware ESB solution implementing the ESB^{MT} framework [21] by extending the open source Apache ServiceMix solution [3].
- The creation of an ESB benchmark which allows evaluating the performance and utilization of multi-tenant aware solutions by extending an existing benchmark [2].

– An analysis of the performance and utilization characteristics of our proposed implementation compared against a baseline, non multi-tenant aware ESB solution (Apache ServiceMix).

The remaining of the paper is structured as follows: Section 2 briefly summarizes the JBI specification and the ESB^{MT} framework which is based on JBI. Section 3 discusses the realization of this framework using Apache ServiceMix as a proof-of-concept implementation for our proposal, together with the technologies involved. Section 4 introduces the benchmarking tool that we developed as part of this work, discusses the benchmarking environment, and presents the results of this evaluation. Section 5 discusses the key findings of our evaluation. The paper closes with Section 6 and Section 7 summarizing related work, and concluding with some future work, respectively.

2 Background

Java Business Integration Environment. The Java Business Integration (JBI) specification defines a standards-based environment for integration solutions by specifying the interaction of JBI components installed in a JBI container [11]. A number of middleware technologies like ESBs (e.g. Open ESB[1], Apache ServiceMix [3]) and application servers (like GlassFish[2]) implement the JBI specification. By basing our approach on the JBI specification we therefore ensure that we produce a generic and reusable solution that can be replicated across different ESB solutions (and other technologies that implement the JBI specification).

Figure 1 provides an overview of the JBI environment, based on [11]. JBI-compliant components are deployed in the container and interact through a *Normalized Message Router* (NMR). The components consume or provide services described in WSDL 2.0[3]. Two types of JBI components are specified: *Binding Components* (BCs), providing connectivity to external services and mediating between external protocols and the NMR, and *Service Engines* (SEs), offering business logic and message transformation services inside the JBI container. Configuration of the components is achieved by a management framework based on Java Management Extensions (JMX). The framework allows the installation of JBI components, deployment and configuration of service artifacts called *Service Units* (SUs), and controlling the state of both individual SUs and the JBI container. Different SUs are usually packaged in *Service Assemblies* (SAs), as shown in Fig. 1, in order to solve larger integration problems.

ESB^{MT}: A Multi-tenant ESB Architecture. In our previous work [21] we identified the requirements for enabling multi-tenancy in ESB solutions and categorized them into *functional* and *non-functional* requirements. Functional

---

[1] Open ESB: http://openesb-dev.org
[2] GlassFish: http://glassfish.java.net
[3] WSDL 2.0 Specification: http://www.w3.org/TR/wsdl20/

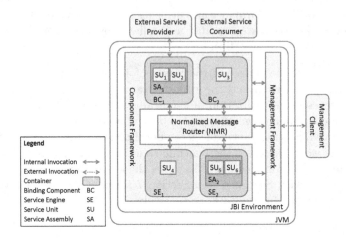

Fig. 1. Overview of the JBI environment

requirements can be further classified as *tenant-related* and *integration-related*. Tenant-related requirements ensure the fine-grained management of both tenants and their corresponding users. In addition, the functionality of the ESB should be provided for each tenant in a transparent manner, without integration effort on behalf of the tenants. Integration-related requirements ensure that other PaaS components or external applications that might not be multi-tenant can also interact with the system in order to share, e.g. the tenant or service registry maintained by the ESB. Non-functional requirements ensure *tenant isolation* and *security* as well *reusability* and *extensibility*. Tenant isolation requirements include data (preventing tenants to access data belonging to other tenants) and performance isolation (ensuring tenants have access only to their assigned computational resources). Security requirements describe the need for appropriate mechanisms for authorization, authentication, integrity, and confidentiality to be in place. Finally, reusability and extensibility requirements define the technology- and solution-independence of the proposed architecture.

Based on these requirements, in [21] we proposed ESB^{MT}, a JBI-based ESB architecture that satisfies these requirements. Figure 2 provides an overview of ESB^{MT}. The three layer architecture consists of a *Presentation* layer, a *Business Logic* layer, and a *Resources* layer. The purpose, contents, and implementation of each layer is discussed in the following.

3   Implementation

For purposes of implementing ESB^{MT} we extended the open source ESB Apache ServiceMix version 4.3.0 [3], hereafter referred to simply as ServiceMix. All artifacts required to install and setup the ESB^{MT} realization including a manual are publicly available at http://tiny.cc/ESB-MT-install. The presentation

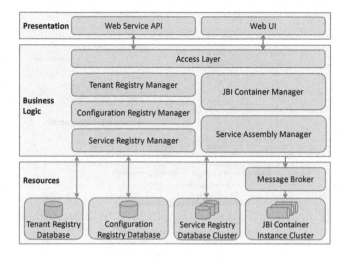

Fig. 2. Overview of ESB^{MT}

of the implementation follows the ESB^{MT} architecture as illustrated in Fig. 2. More specifically:

Resources Layer. The Resources layer consists of a *JBI Container Instance Cluster* and a set of registries. The JBI Container Instance Cluster bundles together multiple JBI containers (in the sense of Fig. 1). Each one of these instances performs the tasks usually associated with traditional ESB solutions, that is, message routing and transformation. For purposes of performance, instances are organized in clusters, using an appropriate mechanism like the one offered by ServiceMix. Realizing multi-tenancy on this level means that both BCs and SEs are able to:

- handle service units and service assemblies containing tenant and user specific configuration information, and
- process such deployment artifacts accordingly in a multi-tenant manner. For example, a new tenant-specific endpoint has to be created whenever a service assembly is deployed to this JBI component in order to ensure data isolation between tenants.

The installation/uninstallation and configuration of BCs and SEs in a JBI Container Instance is performed through a set of standardized interfaces that also allow for backward compatibility with non multi-tenant aware components.

In terms of implementation technologies, ServiceMix is based on the OSGi Framework[4]. OSGi bundles realize the ESB functionality complying to the JBI specification. The original ServiceMix BC for HTTP version 2011.01 and the original Apache Camel SE version 2011.01 are extended in our prototype in order to support multi-tenant aware messaging. These components are able to marshal,

---

[4] OSGi Version 4.3: http://www.osgi.org/Download/Release4V43/

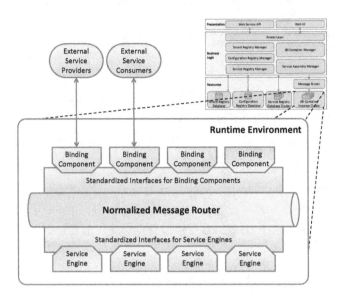

Fig. 3. Architecture of an ESB Instance

demarshal, and process messages with the tenantID and userID included as part of their SOAP header. Our ServiceMix extension also implements an OSGi-based management service which listens to a JMS topic for incoming management messages sent by the Web application.

The Resources layer also contains three different types of registries (Fig. 2): the *Service Registry* stores the services registered with the JBI environment, as well as the service assemblies required for the configuration of the BCs and SEs installed in each JBI Container Instance in the JBI Container Instance Cluster in a tenant-isolated manner [7]; the *Tenant Registry* records the set of users for each tenant, the corresponding unique identifiers to identify them, as well all necessary information to authenticate them; finally, the *Configuration Registry* stores all configuration data created by tenants and the corresponding users, except from the service registrations and configurations that are stored in the Service Registry. Due to the fact that tenant or user actions affect more than one registries at the time, all operations and modifications on the underlying resources are implemented as distributed transactions based on a two-phase commit protocol [9] to ensure consistency. The *ServiceRegistry, TenantRegistry*, and *ConfigurationRegistry* components are realized based on PostgreSQL version 9.1.1 [19]. Figure 4 shows the entity-relationship diagram of the information stored in the Configuration Registry.

Business Logic Layer. The Business Logic layer contains an *Access Layer* component, which acts as a multi-tenancy enablement layer [10] based on role-based access control [20]. Different categories of roles can be defined based on their interaction with the system: system-level roles like administrators, and tenant-level roles like operators. The system administrator configures the whole

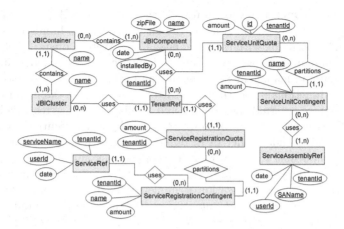

Fig. 4. ER diagram of JBI components in the Configuration Registry using (Min,Max) notation

system and assigns quotas of resource usage. The tenant users consume the quotas of resource usage to deploy service assemblies or to register services. This information is stored in the Configuration Registry (see quota and contingent entities in Fig. 4). A tenant administrator can partition the quota of resource usage obtained from the system administrator. It is important that the system administrator assigns a default tenant administrator role to at least one tenant user to enable the corresponding tenant to perform actions. This default tenant administrator can then appoint other tenant administrators or assign tenant operator roles to tenant users. The tenants and their corresponding users have to be identified and authenticated once when the interaction with the JBI environment is initiated. Afterwards, the authorized access is managed by the Access Layer transparently. The identification of tenants and users is performed based on unique *tenantID* and *userID* keys assigned to them by the Access Layer.

The various *Managers* in this layer (Fig. 2) encapsulate the business logic required to manage and interact with the underlying components in the Resources layer: *Tenant Registry*, *Configuration Registry*, and *Service Registry Managers* for the corresponding registries, *JBI Container Manager* to install and uninstall BCs and SEs in JBI Containers in the cluster, and *Service Assembly Manager* for their configuration through deploying and undeploying appropriate service artifacts.

The Business Logic layer of the proposed architecture is implemented as a Web application. In order to ensure consistency, the application is running in the Java EE 5 application server JOnAS version 5.2.2 [18], which can manage distributed transactions. As the management components of the underlying resources are implemented as EJB components, we use container-managed transaction demarcation, which allows the definition of transaction attributes for whole business methods, including all resource changes.

Presentation Layer. The Presentation layer contains the *Web UI* and the *Web service API* components which allow the customization, administration, management, and interaction with the other layers. The Web UI offers a customizable interface for human and application interaction with the system, allowing for the administration and management of tenants and users. The Web service API offers the same functionality as the Web UI, but also enables the integration and communication of external components and applications. It is realized based on the JAX-WS version 2.0[5]. For both interface mechanisms, security aspects such as integrity and confidentiality of incoming messages must be ensured by appropriate mechanisms, e.g. Secure HTTP connections and WS-Security[6]. As a result, signing and encryption of SOAP messages is supported by the implementation. Furthermore, authentication is implemented by using a custom SOAP header element named TenantContext. The Tenant Context contains the tenantID and userID both represented as UUIDs, and the password of the user. This header element is encrypted and signed. Thus, users of other tenants are prevented to act on behalf of the sending user.

4   Evaluation

As discussed in the opening of this paper, multi-tenancy of Cloud solutions can be decomposed into two perspectives: *performance*, as experienced by the ESB users, and *resource utilization*, of primary concern to the ESB provider. These two perspectives are the focus of our evaluation of the ESB^{MT} implementation. In order to provide a baseline against which we evaluate our proposal we use the backward compatibility feature of ESB^{MT} as non multi-tenant aware version of the ESB, because the functionality in this case is the same as of the original non multi-tenant ServiceMix that we based our implementation on. The following sections discuss the method, workload, experimental setup and results towards this goal.

4.1   Method

Our investigation showed that there is no commonly agreed benchmark for ESBs, see for example [23]. For this reason we chose to use the industrial ESB benchmark by AdroitLogic [2] as a basis. This benchmark has been in development since 2007, and a number of open source ESB solutions have been evaluated in six rounds, with the latest round results coming out in August 2012. All information about the benchmark, as well as the results of each evaluation round are publicly available at [2].

   We had to deal with two major obstacles in adopting this benchmark. Firstly, ServiceMix version 4.3.0 failed to pass smoke testing by AdroitLogic for one of the benchmarking scenarios and as a result ServiceMix has not been included in their evaluation. By using one of the other benchmarking scenarios, however,

---

[5] http://jcp.org/aboutJava/communityprocess/final/jsr224/
[6] http://www.oasis-open.org/committees/tc_home.php?wg_abbrev=wss

we were able to execute the benchmark normally. Secondly, this benchmark was not designed for multi-tenancy, using only one communication endpoint with multiple users of the same tenant sending concurrent requests. Thus, we had to adapt the AdroitLogic Benchmark Driver accordingly, as described in the following sections.

4.2 Workload

For purposes of evaluation we derived three test scenarios from the Direct Proxy Service scenario in AdroitLogic's benchmark [2]. The Direct Proxy Service scenario demonstrates the ability of an ESB to act as a virtualization layer for back-end Web services, operating as a proxy between a client (the AdroitLogic Benchmark Driver) and a simple echo service on the provider side. Starting from this point, we defined the following scenarios:

1. a non multi-tenant ESB deployment (backward compatibility feature of ESB^{MT}) on one Virtual Machine (VM) image, acting as the baseline for comparisons;
2. the same non multi-tenant ESB deployed across 2 VMs, in order to simulate the effect of *horizontal scaling* [22], i.e. adding another application VM when more computational resources are required; and,
3. our ESB^{MT} implementation deployed on 1 VM.

Following the test parameters set by the benchmark we configured in each ESB deployment with $1, 2, 4$, and 10 endpoints per scenario. The message size used by the Benchmark Driver is fixed to 1KB, composed out of random characters. The original Benchmark Driver steadily increases the number of concurrent users of the ESB ($2000, 4000, 8000, 16000, 64000$, and 128.000) and sends a fixed number of requests per user for each round of the benchmark. Since in our case we have multiple endpoints and tenants, we distribute these requests between the different endpoints (or tenants in the third scenario) and we send them concurrently across each endpoint. In the first round of the benchmark for example, and for 4 endpoints/tenants, we send $2000/4 = 500$ requests per endpoint or tenant for a total of 2000 requests; in the next round we send $4000/4 = 1000$ requests, and so on. Each endpoint or tenant receives in any case 10K messages as a warm-up before any measurements.

4.3 Experimental Setup

Figure 5 provides an overview of the experimental setup realizing our adaptation of the Direct Proxy Service Scenario including message flow, control, and measurement points. The test cases were run on Flexiscale[7] and three Virtual Machines: VM0 (6GB RAM, 3 CPUs), VM1 (4GB RAM, 2 CPUs), and VM2 (4GB RAM, 2 CPUs). All three VMs run Ubuntu 10.04 Linux OS and every CPU is an AMD Opteron Processor with 2GHz and 512KB cache. In VM0,

---

[7] Flexiant Flexiscale: http://www.flexiscale.com/

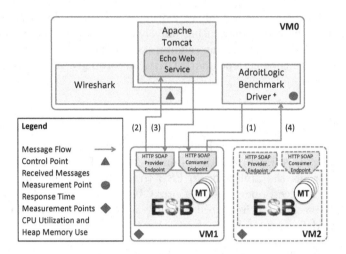

Fig. 5. Overview of the Experimental Setup

an Apache Tomcat 7.0.23 instance was deployed with the Echo Web service, the adapted AdroitLogic Benchmark Driver, and Wireshark 1.2.7 for monitoring HTTP requests and responses. In VM1 and VM2, the ESB^{MT} implementation is deployed, which required also the deployment of PostgreSQL 9.1.1 database (for the registries), and Jonas 5.2.2 server for the Web application implementing the Business Logic layer. The endpoints deployed in ServiceMix are using HTTP-SOAP, see Fig. 5. Scenarios 1 and 2 are using the backward compatibility feature of ESB^{MT} for non multi-tenant operation.

The total time in receiving the receipt acknowledgment by the Echo Web service for each message was measured at the AdroitLogic Benchmark Driver, in order to calculate latency. The CPU utilization for the ServiceMix process and the Java Virtual Machine (JVM) heap memory use was measured directly in VM1 and VM2. The maximum JVM heap memory size was set to 512MB before the warm-up phase for both VM1 and VM2.

4.4   Experimental Results

Performance: Figure 6 summarizes and presents the latency recorded for all scenarios and work loads. The baseline for the presentation is the non multi-tenant aware implementation of the ESB on one VM (1VM-NonMT-* Endpoints in Fig. 6). As shown in the figure, our proposed multi-tenant aware implementation of the ESB exhibits a performance decline of around 30% across the different cases when comparing the same number of endpoints and tenants in the other scenarios. The same load across 2 tenants instead of 2 endpoints, for example, results in 23, 57% more latency on average (Fig. 6b), 24, 68% more for 4 tenants/endpoints (Fig. 6c) and 39, 44% increase for 10 tenants/endpoints (Fig. 6d).

When comparing 1 tenant against 1 endpoint (Fig. 6a) an 50% reduction of response time is observed, showing that the performance decrease is actually

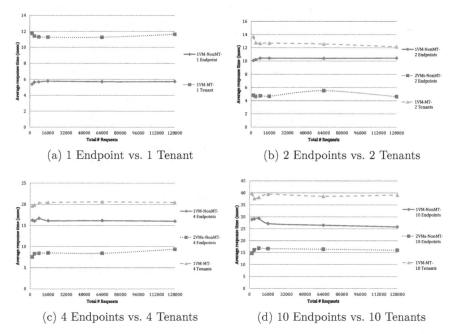

Fig. 6. Average response time (latency) for 1KB size messages

ameliorated when more tenants/endpoints are added. Also of particular interest is the fact that adding a VM and distributing the requests between those VMs — essentially reducing the number of active endpoints by half — improves response time by 50% *only for 2 endpoints* (53, 07%), degrading from there with the number of endpoints (48, 10% for 4, and 42% for 10).

Utilization: The measurements for CPU and memory utilization for the same loads are summarized by Table 1. The reported CPU utilization is normalized over the number of CPUs of the VMs containing the ESB implementation (Fig. 5). Memory utilization is presented as a percentage of the maximum heap size for the JVM containing the ESB (approximately 455MB). In both cases, the figures for the 2VMs scenario are calculated as the average of the utilization of each VM.

As shown in Table 1, the overall utilization of system resources increases with the introduction of multi-tenancy. The additional computation required for processing the tenant and user information, and routing the messages accordingly, translates into more than 300% increase in CPU utilization compared to the baseline, non multi-tenant aware implementation. With respect to the same scenario, standard deviation σ is increasing with the number of tenants introduced. However, given the proximity of the average and median values to the maximum CPU utilization in all cases, this can be interpreted as a distribution heavily concentrated towards the maximum utilization. With respect to memory utilization, Table 1 shows also an overall increase of around 100% across the three cases of ESB^{MT} (2, 4 and 10 tenants). The low standard deviation, and the small

Table 1. CPU and Memory utilization

		1/2E	2/2E	1/2T	1/4E	2/4E	1/4T	1/10E	2/10E	1/10T
CPU (%)	Average	10,77	8,55	47,01	11,71	8,46	54,42	14,99	9,69	66,33
	Median	11,00	9,42	50,00	12,00	10,00	58,33	16,33	11,83	76,00
	Max	12,00	16,33	51,67	13,00	10,67	60,33	19,00	12,67	78,33
	σ	1,63	3,21	9,03	2,07	3,14	11,38	3,72	4,09	21,39
Memory (%)	Average	18,47	15,99	37,67	23,90	15,22	42,93	20,54	13,26	47,06
	Median	17,71	15,66	36,09	23,37	15,47	43,57	20,70	13,36	46,51
	Max	35,43	22,98	67,31	36,09	20,00	70,50	29,06	18,34	80,78
	σ	0,05	0,05	0,13	0,05	0,02	0,14	0,04	0,02	0,15

Legend:	*1/iE*: 1 VM, non multi-tenant, *i* endpoints;
	2/jE: 2 VMs, non multi-tenant, *j* endpoints in total;
	1/kT: 1 VM, multi-tenant aware, *k* tenants

differences between average and median values show that memory consumption is relatively steady over all work loads. Similar behavior is observed also for the other two (non multi-tenant) scenarios.

5 Discussion

The results presented in the previous section show that performance reduction in our implementation is significant (one third of the baseline performance) w.r.t. to system latency. However, it has to be noted that we have not introduced any optimization techniques in our multi-tenant aware ESB solution, or tried to implement performance isolation between tenants. As such, there is much space for improvement in this respect. CPU utilization on the other hand increases more than threefold and remains high for the most part of the benchmark, while memory utilization doubles but remains well below the 50% of the maximum allowed size on average. Our ESB^{MT} therefore has a relatively small impact on memory requirements, but incurs high computation resource demands. Computational resources are relatively cheap (compared, e.g., to storage space) and continue to grow cheaper over time [4]. The actual cost of using our approach must therefore be evaluated against the possibilities opened by the fine granularity of administration and management on the level of both tenants and users.

Horizontal scaling the ESB produces the desired results, i.e. 50% improvement for adding one VM, only for 2 endpoints distributed between the 2 VMs. Adding another VM produces diminishing returns as the number of endpoints (representing applications using the same ESB) increases. This needs to be weighed against the cost of deploying and operating multiple VMs. Furthermore, the measurements presented in Section 4 for the horizontal scaling scenario assume that the requests are evenly distributed between the two VMs, emulating the effect of a load balancer operating on the front end of the ESB. Actually implementing such a solution will incur additional development and operating costs that need to be considered. In principle therefore we can conclude that the realization of our proposal achieves its envisioned goal as far as service providers are concerned, i.e. increasing CPU utilization, while imposing a relatively small memory footprint. Performance on the service consumer side however is impacted negatively and further work towards the direction of ameliorating this effect is necessary.

6 Related Work

Existing approaches on enabling multi-tenancy for middleware typically focus on different types of isolation in multi-tenant applications for the SaaS delivery model, see for example [10]. As discussed also in [23] however, only few PaaS solutions offer multi-tenancy awareness allowing for the development of multi-tenant applications on top of them. The work of Walraven et al. [23] follows a similar approach to ours; our work however proposes a more generic approach built around any ESB technology that complies with the JBI specification, and does not require the implementation of a dedicated support layer for these purposes.

Focusing on ESB solutions, in [1] we surveyed a number of existing ESB solutions and evaluated their multi-tenancy readiness. Our investigation showed that the surveyed solutions in general lack in support of multi-tenancy. Even in the case of products like IBM WebSphere ESB[8] and WSO2 ESB[9] where multi-tenancy is part of their offerings, multi-tenancy support is implemented either based on proprietary technologies like the Tivoli Access Manager (in the former case), or by mitigating the tenant communication and administration on the level of the message container (Apache Axis 2[10] in the latter case). In either case, the used method can not be applied to other ESB solutions and as a result no direct comparison of the applied multi-tenancy enabling mechanisms can be performed. The presented approach differs from existing approaches by integrating multi-tenancy independently from the implementation specifics of the ESB.

The different benchmarks and metrics developed in the domain of Cloud computing in the recent years focus on a particular type of Cloud services such as databases [8], on Cloud-related features such as elasticity [6] and performance isolation [13], or on virtualization technology [15]. To the extent of our knowledge, there is no commonly agreed approach and benchmark for the evaluation of the performance of multi-tenant PaaS middleware components such as an ESB. AdroitLogic completed in August 2012 [2] the 6th round of public ESB performance benchmarking since June 2007. This round included eight free and open source ESBs including Apache ServiceMix version 4.3.0 — for which however they were not able to execute for all defined scenarios. Our ESB performance evaluation approach reuses, but adapts and extends, the AdroitLogic Benchmark Driver and our test scenarios are derived from the Direct Proxy scenario, but extended in order to consider multi-tenancy.

---

[8] IBM WebSphere ESB: http://tiny.cc/IBMWebSphereESB

[9] WSO2 ESB: http://wso2.com/products/enterprise-service-bus/

[10] Apache Axis: http://axis.apache.org/axis2/java/core/

7   Conclusions and Future Work

Multi-tenancy allows Cloud providers to serve multiple consumers from a single system instance, reducing costs and increasing their return of investment by maximizing system utilization. Making therefore ESB solutions, a critical piece of middleware for the service-oriented enterprise environment, multi-tenant aware is essential. Multi-tenancy awareness manifests as the ability to manage and identify multiple tenants (organizational domains) and their users, and allow their applications to interact seamlessly with the ESB. Allowing multiple tenants however to use the same ESB instance requires to ensure that they are isolated from each other. There is therefore a trade-off between the benefits for the ESB provider in terms of utilization and their impact on the performance of applications using the ESB that needs to be investigated.

Toward this goal, in the previous sections we present the realization of our proposal for a generic ESB architecture that enables multi-tenancy awareness based on the JBI specification. We first provide the necessary background and explain our proposed architecture across three layers based on previous work. We then discuss in detail the realization of this architecture by extending the open source Apache ServiceMix ESB solution. In the next step we adapt the ESB benchmark developed by AdroitLogic to accommodate multi-tenancy and we use it to measure the performance and resource utilization of our ESB solution.

Our analysis shows that our current, not optimized in any manner implementation of a multi-tenant aware ESB solution succeeds in increasing the CPU utilization while having a relatively small impact on the memory footprint. In this sense it succeeds as far as the ESB provider is concerned. On the other hand, there is a significant reduction in performance experienced by the ESB consumers which needs to be ameliorated by re-engineering and fine-tuning our implementation accordingly. Techniques for performance isolation have also to be brought into play [14]. In the scope of this work, this is a direction that we want to investigate in the future. We also plan to take advantage of using the JBI specification as the basis of our architectural framework and apply the same techniques and architectural solutions to other ESB solutions, as well as non-ESB solutions, like for example application servers, that comply with this specification.

Acknowledgments. The research leading to these results has received funding from projects 4CaaSt (grant agreement no. 258862) and Allow Ensembles (grant agreement no. 600792) part of the European Union's Seventh Framework Programme (FP7/2007-2013).

References

1. 4CaaSt Consortium: D7.1.1 – Immigrant PaaS Technologies: Scientific and Technical Report. Deliverable (July 2011), http://www.4caast.eu/wp-content/uploads/2011/09/4CaaSt_D7.1.1_Scientific_and_Technical_Report.pdf
2. AdroitLogic Private Ltd.: Performance Framework and ESB Performance Benchmarking, http://www.esbperformance.org

3. Apache Software Foundation: Apache ServiceMix,
   `http://servicemix.apache.org`
4. Armbrust, M., et al.: Above the Clouds: A Berkeley View of Cloud Computing. Tech. Rep. UCB/EECS-2009-28, EECS Department, University of California, Berkeley (2009)
5. Behrendt, M., et al.: Introduction and Architecture Overview IBM Cloud Computing Reference Architecture 2.0 (February 2011), `http://www.opengroup.org/cloudcomputing/uploads/40/23840/CCRA.IBMSubmission.02282011.doc`
6. Brebner, P.: Is your Cloud Elastic Enough?: Performance Modelling the Elasticity of Infrastructure as a Service (IaaS) Cloud Applications. In: Proceedings of ICPE 2012, pp. 263–266 (2012)
7. Chong, F., Carraro, G., Wolter, R.: Multi-Tenant Data Architecture. MSDN (2006), `http://msdn.microsoft.com/en-us/library/aa479086.aspx`
8. Cooper, B.F., et al.: Benchmarking Cloud Serving Systems with YCSB. In: Proceedings of the 1st ACM Symposium on Cloud Computing, pp. 143–154. ACM (2010)
9. Coulouris, G., Dollimore, J., Kindberg, T.: Distributed Systems: Concepts and Design. Addison Wesley (June 2005)
10. Guo, C., et al.: A Framework for Native Multi-Tenancy Application Development and Management. In: Proceedings of CEC/EEE 2007, pp. 551–558. IEEE (2007)
11. Java Community Process: Java Business Integration (JBI) 1.0, Final Release (2005), `http://jcp.org/aboutJava/communityprocess/final/jsr208/`
12. Josuttis, N.: SOA in Practice. O'Reilly Media, Inc. (2007)
13. Krebs, R., Momm, C., Kounev, S.: Metrics and Techniques for Quantifying Performance Isolation in Cloud Environments. In: Proceedings of the 8th International ACM SIGSOFT Conference on Quality of Software Architectures, pp. 91–100. ACM (2012)
14. Krebs, R., Momm, C., Kounev, S.: Architectural Concerns in Multi-Tenant SaaS Applications. In: Proceedings of CLOSER 2012. SciTePress (2012)
15. Makhija, V., et al.: VMmark: A Scalable Benchmark for Virtualized Systems. Tech. Rep. VMware-TR-2006-002, VMware, Inc. (2006)
16. Mell, P., Grance, T.: The NIST Definition of Cloud Computing (September 2011), `http://www.nist.gov/customcf/get_pdf.cfm?pub_id=909616`
17. Mietzner, R., Unger, T., Titze, R., Leymann, F.: Combining Different Multi-Tenancy Patterns in Service-Oriented Applications. In: Proceedings of EDOC 2009, pp. 131–140. IEEE (2009)
18. OW2 Consortium: JOnAS: Java Open Application Server,
    `http://wiki.jonas.ow2.org`
19. PostgreSQL Gobal Development Group: PostgreSQL,
    `http://www.postgresql.org`
20. Sandhu, R.S., et al.: Role-based Access Control Models. Computer 29, 38–47 (1996)
21. Strauch, S., Andrikopoulos, V., Leymann, F., Muhler, D.: ESB^{MT}: Enabling Multi-Tenancy in Enterprise Service Buses. In: Proceedings of CloudCom 2012, pp. 456–463. IEEE (2012)
22. Vaquero, L., Rodero-Merino, L., Buyya, R.: Dynamically Scaling Applications in the Cloud. ACM SIGCOMM Computer Communication Review 41(1), 45–52 (2011)
23. Walraven, S., Truyen, E., Joosen, W.: A Middleware Layer for Flexible and Cost-Efficient Multi-Tenant Applications. In: Kon, F., Kermarrec, A.-M. (eds.) Middleware 2011. LNCS, vol. 7049, pp. 370–389. Springer, Heidelberg (2011)

Putting the Customer Back in the Center of SOA with Service Design and User-Centered Design

Arnita Saini, Benjamin Nanchen, and Florian Evequoz

University of Applied Sciences Western Switzerland (HES–SO), Sierre, Switzerland
arnita.04@gmail.com, {benjamin.nanchen,florian.evequoz}@hevs.ch
http://iig.hevs.ch

Abstract. This article introduces a methodology used for designing the online presence of a Swiss SME providing Cloud Services. The Web application used for the purchasing and administration, backed by a Service-Oriented Architecture (SOA), has been designed to be customer-centric using a combination of different techniques borrowed from the fields of ethnomethodology, service design and user-centered design. The tools employed include service blueprint design and affinity diagram analysis followed by prototyping and subsequent usability evaluation. This collaborative methodology explained with the help of the applied research project use case is seen to yield excellent results in terms of customer-orientation.

Keywords: Service Design, User-Centered Design, Service Oriented Architecture.

1   Introduction

The concept of service has two distinct meanings [6]. On the business front, it represents the business service exposed to the customer. On the technological front, a (software) service represents a small software component encapsulating specific functionalities, and is the basis of a Service-Oriented Architecture (SOA).

SOA is the method of choice for structuring large software systems into discrete business components (i.e. individual services). It helps adapt software to changes in business processes and thus provides an excellent way to develop applications for supporting business processes [4, 17, 19]. However, use of this model alone does not ensure customer friendliness to an application developed with the help of the SOA. Indeed, the approaches for engineering an SOA and align the business with IT do not typically include the customers themselves. They start downstream after the definition of business services. Therefore the link between the customer needs and the individual software services is generally not explicit [6, 9].

To overcome this shortcoming, we propose to employ an interdisciplinary methodology combining user-centered design [12, 15] and service design [8]. Those approaches have been found to help manage the complexity of software [21], ease their use [7, 14] and improve the satisfaction of the customer [8]. Therefore our goal is to combine those methods to design an SOA-based application exposed to the final customer with explicit links between the customer needs and the related software services.

K.-K. Lau, W. Lamersdorf, and E. Pimentel (Eds.): ESOCC 2013, LNCS 8135, pp. 94–103, 2013.
© Springer-Verlag Berlin Heidelberg 2013

User-centric principles were already applied in the context of SOA by previous research [5, 18]. However, the intent was to facilitate the re-use of software services by the developer calling the services, and not to improve the quality of the service delivered to the final customer as in our case. Therefore, the originality of our work is the mix of user-centered design and service design to explicitly align the needs of the customer with the SOA.

This article presents our methodology in the context of a use case conducted with a Swiss Cloud Services provider. We start by presenting the situation at the beginning of the project and the goals. We present next the methodology, starting from the data collection, moving to the interpretation and recommendations for the design. Lastly, we discuss the methodology and results.

2   Initial Situation and Project Goal

Krios is a ten-year old Swiss company active in the Cloud Computing business. It offers mainly PaaS, DaaS and SaaS services to SMEs in Switzerland. As the products portfolio of Krios has grown organically along the years without a clear overall structure, it became extremely challenging to manage the settings of each particular product that was technically organized as an independent silo with an ad hoc administration interface. In case of changes, this leaded to problems like lack of traceability of processes, too many ad hoc administration consoles or increased risk of manual errors. To overcome those problems, an important redesign project was launched. The goal of this project was twofold: first, tackle the backend complexity by adopting a Service-Oriented Architectural framework to allow the integration of the different software silos; second, reduce the frontend complexity through the design of a web application, called INFOPLACE, that must be built on top of the SOA and presented to the final customer. The INFOPLACE will allow the customer to purchase and administrate the different services Krios offers. The focus of this paper is on the design of the INFOPLACE and its link to the SOA.

3   Methodology at a Glance

Consistent with previous research [11], the project team consisted of members belonging to a variety of backgrounds including service design, business process management, computer science and interaction design. The methodology chosen reflects those various backgrounds by borrowing mainly from the fields of service design and user-centered design. It consists of 9 steps distributed in 4 phases, as depicted in Fig.1. First, data gathering is done in three stages. Then the results are consolidated in the data interpretation phase that provides the material for the main phase "Design from insights". This phase introduces the service blueprint that links the SOA with the customer needs. The service blueprint then provides the basis for the wireframing and information architecture of the final application. The application is finally prototyped and evaluated in a last phase. In the following sections, we describe the methodology in greater details.

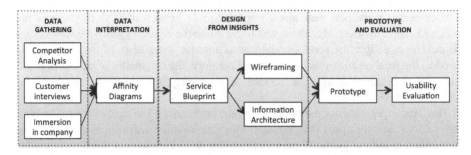

Fig. 1. Phases and steps of the methodology

4   Data Gathering through Ethnomethodology

Considering services are based on human factors (expertise, experience, empathy and other non-quantifiable qualities), quantitative techniques are insufficient to study and evaluate the status of a service. Ethnomethodology is a powerful tool for studying contexts, behaviors and activities that the service environment is comprised of [13]. Ethnomethodology could be conducted "through site visits, immersion work, and contextual semi-directed interviews with service providers and service consumers in order to identify the salient attributes of a given service experience" [10]. In context of the current project, ethnomethodology was done in three phases:

4.1   Phase 1: Competitor Interface Analysis

An assessment of user interfaces of the competition faced by Krios was done first. The competitors chosen were Amazon, Office 365 due to their worldwide reputation, Swisscom, a Swiss IT services company and Infomaniak, a direct competitor of Krios. The goal was to gain understanding of how these competitors provided their services through their respective user interfaces. The assessment followed a simple protocol of visiting the home page, purchasing and customizing a service. This was supplemented with Heuristic Evaluation [16] to identify the usability strengths and weaknesses of three of the service vendor interfaces i.e. Swisscom, Office 365 and Amazon. For this evaluation, the evaluator spent around one hour with each of the interfaces. This phase provides us with a list of best practices in the domain.

4.2   Phase 2: Semi-Structured Interviews with Customers

Following a semi-structured interview protocol, a total of 8 participants, including 5 customers, 1 collaborator of Krios and the 2 managers of Krios were interviewed. All interviews were conducted contextually. Two to three members of the team would conduct the interviews. Field notes were made of observations and important user statements. The topics addressed were divided into mainly four parts, General context of work, Experience of Krios services, Quality of service and other category-relevant general questions. This phase provides us with the customer's expectations.

4.3   Phase 3: Immersion Work at Krios

Three team members visited Krios during working days and focused on understanding the physical, organizational and technical environment to identify the underlying performance drivers. A detailed task analysis session [12, 20] was conducted to understand the existing system and the information flows that are important and need to be incorporated into INFOPLACE. It was videotaped and reviewed for interpretation. Moreover, Krios provided us with a detailed list of their current Information Systems and their dependencies to the business services. This phase provides us with the back office's constraints.

5   Data Interpretation

On retrospective analysis of the interview transcripts and videos, extensive notes were made about the key observations, user statements, breakdowns and design ideas. Notes made during this interpretation session were then used in doing a user-centric analysis using the Affinity diagram tool. An effective data consolidation technique [2], this helped map the issues and insights into a hierarchical diagram and summarize details, prioritize issues and find patterns and insights in interpreted data. The main outcomes of interpretation sessions were as follows:

1. Simplicity in design emerged as an important factor. By comparison to the former Krios administration interface and intelligent borrowing from competitor interface analysis, recommendations for design emerged.
2. The customer's main requests were identified as: changing user data, account creation or removal, permission change and service purchase.
3. Since INFOPLACE was intended to be an online customer service offered by Krios to assist in purchasing and consuming their services, it was considered post-interpretation sessions by the Krios management that assistance for purchase should be provided through implementation of wizards. Focus was given to design work on "service purchase" in accordance with Krios
4. The services provided by Krios can be roughly divided into three categories: hosting, SaaS and customer service. INFOPLACE belongs to the customer service category.
5. Based on the insights gained after interpretation, it was understood that as a service consumer, every user assumes at any given point one of the two roles on INFOPLACE defined as follows: (a) Master User (while performing enterprise transactions with Krios and managing employees and accounts, role imparted as the point of contact of an client enterprise of Krios); (b) Base User (while consuming service and using products, the role of end-users). Differing INFOPLACE needs were found to belong to two categories based on functions and tasks to be done. These roles help define a user's access on INFOPLACE so that appropriate features and components of service can be availed based on the roles.

6   Designing from Insights

6.1   Service Blueprint

The technique of Service Blueprint is particularly well suited to "capture the entire customer service experience from the customer's point of view". Its goal is to improve the perceived quality of service by identification of failure points in a service operation [3].

The technique helps in distinguishing visible activities (onstage) from support activities (backstage) from the customer's point of view. Five elements compose the Service Blueprint: Customer actions, Onstage/Visible Contact Employee Actions, Backstage/Invisible Contact Employee Actions, Support Processes and Physical Evidence. The Physical Evidence is the concrete result presented to the customer in response to their action. Based on this physical evidence, the customer evaluates the quality of service. The Support Processes indicate the role of the underlying IT systems, thus providing a direct link between the needs of the customer and the SOA. This is the main input of our interdisciplinary approach applying a combination of user-centered design and service design.

Different steps are needed to build a Service Blueprint: (1) clearly articulate service process, specify which segment of customers is the focus of the Blueprint, (2) delineate the actions of customers, (2) delineate the contact employee actions, both onstage and backstage, (3) delineate the support processes, (4) add links that connect the customer to contact employee activities and to needed support functions, (5) add the physical evidences [3].

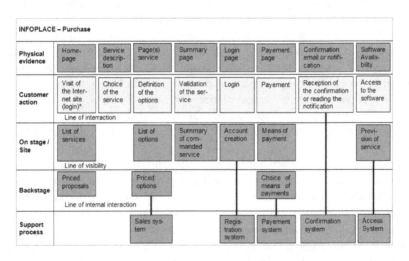

Fig. 2. Service blueprint for Purchase of service

Fig.2 presents the Service Blueprint corresponding to the purchase of a service that was identified as a critical function of INFOPLACE. To build this Service Blueprint, we used the outcomes of the competitors' analysis (best practices) and of customer's interviews (customer expectations) consolidated in the affinity analysis phase. First, the customer's actions needed to buy a service were identified, and then the necessary steps needed by Krios (backstage). Those were then linked with the underlying SOA (support process). In parallel, the information that INFOPLACE must provide to the customer (onstage) was added. At the end, the physical evidence was included.

In this context, the Service Blueprinting technique helps outline the various processes that must take place onstage or backstage. Based on these processes, calls to the SOA for the respective service/business function is identified (Support Process shows the called systems) and directly related to the customer actions.

6.2   Wireframing

Based on the service blueprint designed for purchase of service, we designed wireframes for service purchase using the customer actions and on-stage features identified. Wireframing helps in designing the layout and positioning of features related to the task. Also, navigation from one screen to another for accomplishing the task is designed. The first two screen views of the "purchase service wizard" are shown in Fig.3.

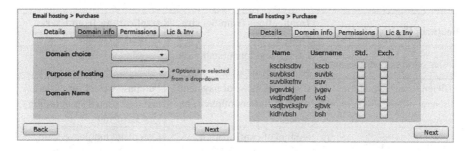

Fig. 3. Wireframes of the Purchase wizard for email-hosting service purchase

6.3   Information Architecture

In coherence with Service Blueprint and related task screens, the information architecture of Infoplace was built. Such architecture decides the content and hierarchy of screens, based on tasks (customer's actions of service blueprint) and functions (support process of service blueprint) to be performed, taking into consideration user's navigational paths (physical evidences of service blueprint) and structures the information to be delivered. For example, at the first level of architecture, the home screen would have an option for purchasing a particular service, say E-mail hosting. On clicking this, the user is displayed a screen with information about service followed by a wizard of service purchase in the third level. Post completion of this wizard, the user is displayed the relevant information of licensing, invoices and finally informed of purchase after which he returns back to level one of architecture, the home screen. In this way, the information architecture structures the information within the INFOPLACE.

Similar to the above described service purchase scenario, various features and functions were designed using service blueprint and wireframing techniques and incorporated into the architecture. Some of the features that materialized into design have been mentioned below in Table 1. Design implications for these features coming from domains of service design and user-centered design are mentioned. Second and third columns of the table ascertain how the features are implemented using knowledge from the corresponding domains. For example (see last row of Table 1), letting the customers give their feedback to the site administrators in case of problems was identified as a desirable feature of INFOPLACE. For helping customers who are facing problems, a complaint lodging system was designed. Complaints are then notified to the Admin who addresses the complaints and users are then notified about rectification of the problem. The Admin can also provide additional information to customers. These were the implications of user-centered design. For such complaint lodging and addressing to take place, the system of confirmation process enables notification of messages to the Admin and customers. This is the implication of Service design.

Table 1. Sample of the features desired and their design implications

Features Desired	Implications from Service Design	Implications from User-Centered Design
Easier setting of permissions	Centralized functionality for setting permissions	Permissions categorized based on employees, products
Efficient management of purchase orders, invoices and licenses	Choice of mode of payment through System of payment process	Purchase wizard for easier and user friendly purchasing and invoicing
Information about problems faced, address complaints	System of confirmation process enables notification, reception of messages	Complaint lodging system, notifications sent about the problems and what is done

7   Prototype Implementation and Usability Evaluation

Once the initial design was finalized, the visual design proposed was combined with the layout of Krios website in order to retain consistency. The final screens can be seen in Fig.4. In order to further improve the quality of the interface design, the INFOPLACE prototype was evaluated by five usability experts using Nielsen's heuristics [16]. Suggestions for solving the usability problems found were then given from perspectives of design as well as development. The most severe problems will be corrected prior to release of INFOPLACE.

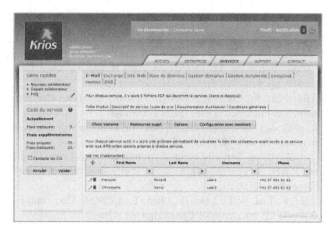

Fig. 4. A prototype screen of INFOPLACE

8   Discussion and Conclusions

The service-oriented architecture (SOA) facilitates scalability, availability and performance of service. However, along with this, it is necessary that service-orientation must be aware of the desires and needs of its users. User centered design (UCD) methods help in bridging this gap. We have proposed in this article an interdisciplinary methodology combining a customer-oriented focus given by the Ethnomethodology and the Service Design, with UCD methods from Interaction Design perspective. Needs and goals of customers and users were identified using a combination of competitor interface analysis and interviews as part of ethnomethodology. Service design blueprint increased the understanding of customer-oriented business processes and their links to the underlying systems. Such an interdisciplinary approach facilitated participation among team members and led to a dynamic process of work by drawing inputs from the different skills and expertise within the team. An important side effect of the project is that the findings have motivated Krios management in simplifying their products portfolio, for example, reducing their products list, providing pre-configured packages with appropriate pricing, hiding details of parameterization of services i.e. providing less complexity to the user. Also, a follow up study is planned to evaluate the acceptance of the new system amongst the customers. Thus, it can be said that, thanks to this project, Krios has progressed onto higher rungs of the usability maturity ladder, moving on from "Unrecognized" or ignorant to the "Implemented" or the enlightened stage [1]. In line with this, it was observed that commitment by top-level management of Krios proved to be a tremendous drive in the effective and timely realization of this project.

Lastly, the authors are convinced of the value of such collaborative work in gaining customer satisfaction by moving from workflows over SOA to customer experience focused design using collaboration between UCD and Service Design.

References

1. Ashley, J., Desmond, K.: Usability Maturity: A Case Study in Planning and Designing an Enterprise Application Suite. In: Kurosu, M. (ed.) Human Centered Design, HCII 2009. LNCS, vol. 5619, pp. 579–584. Springer, Heidelberg (2009)
2. Beyer, H., Holtzblatt, K.: Contextual Design: Defining Customer-Centered Systems. Morgan Kaufmann, San Francisco (1998) ISBN 1-55860-411-1
3. Bitner, M.J., et al.: Service blueprinting: A practical technique for service innovation. California Management Review 50(3), 66–94 (2008)
4. Brown, A., et al.: Using Service-Oriented Architecture and Component-Based Development to Build Web Service Applications. A Rational Software White paper, Rational Software Corporation (2002)
5. Chang, M., He, J., Tsai, W.T., Xiao, B., Chen, Y.: UCSOA: User-centric service-oriented architecture. In: IEEE International Conference on e-Business Engineering, ICEBE 2006, pp. 248–255. IEEE (2006)
6. Chen, H.M.: Towards service engineering: service orientation and business-IT alignment. In: Proceedings of the 41st Annual Hawaii International Conference on System Sciences. IEEE (2008)
7. Cloyd, M.H.: Designing User-Centered Web Applications in Web Time. IEEE Software 18, 62–69 (2001)
8. Elizabeth, B., Sanders, N.: From User-Centered to Participatory Design Approaches. In: Frascara, J. (ed.) Design and the Social Sciences. Taylor & Francis Books Limited (2002)
9. Engels, G., Hess, A., Humm, B., Juwig, O., Lohmann, M., Richter, J.P., ... Willkomm, J.: A method for engineering a true service-oriented architecture. To appear: Proceedings of the 10th International Conference on Enterprise Information Systems, Barcelona, Spain (2008)
10. Fragnière, E., Nanchen, B., Sitten, M.: Performing Service Design Experiments Using Ethnomethodology and Theatre-Based Reenactment: A Swiss Ski Resort Case Study. Service Science 4(2), 89–100 (2012)
11. Khambete, P.: A Pattern Language for Touch Point Ecosystem User Experience: A Proposal. In: Proceedings of the 3rd International Conference on Human Computer Interaction, India HCI, pp. 68–74 (2011) ISBN: 978-1-4503-0729-1
12. Maguire, M.: Methods to support human-centred design. Int. J. Human-Computer Studies 55, 587–634 (2001)
13. Makino, Y., Furuta, K., Kanno, T., Yoshihara, S., Mase, T.: Interactive method for service design using computer simulation. Service Sci. 1(2), 121–134 (2009)
14. Moallem, A.: Excellence in Ease of Use with Rich Functionality. In: Jacko, J. (ed.) Human-Computer Interaction, Part IV, HCII 2007, LNCS, vol. 4553, pp. 672–681. Springer, Heidelberg (2007)
15. Murugesan, S., Deshpande, Y., Hansen, S., Ginige, A.: Web Engineering: A New Discipline for Development of Web-Based Systems. In: Murugesan, S., Desphande, Y. (eds.) Web Engineering 2000. LNCS, vol. 2016, pp. 3–13. Springer, Heidelberg (2001)
16. Nielsen, J., Molich, R.: Heuristic evaluation of user interfaces. In: Proceedings of the SIGCHI Conference on Human Factors in Computing Systems, CHI, pp. 249–256 (1990)
17. Patig, S., Wesenberg, H.: Role of Process Modeling in Software Service Design. In: Baresi, L., Chi, C.-H., Suzuki, J. (eds.) ICSOC-ServiceWave 2009. LNCS, vol. 5900, pp. 420–428. Springer, Heidelberg (2009)

18. Soriano, J., Lizcano, D., Hierro, J.J., Reyes, M., Schroth, C., Janner, T.: Enhancing user-service interaction through a global user-centric approach to SOA. In: Fourth International Conference on Networking and Services, ICNS 2008, pp. 194–203. IEEE (2008)
19. Stojanovic, Z., et al.: Modeling and Design of Service-Oriented Architecture. In: IEEE International Conference on Systems, Man and Cybernetics (2004)
20. Task Analysis methods, http://www.usabilitynet.org/tools/taskan alysis.htm (accessed on June 15, 2012)
21. Uflacker, M., Busse, D.: Complexity in Enterprise Applications vs. Simplicity in User Experience. In: Jacko, J. (ed.) Human-Computer Interaction, Part IV HCII 2011. LNCS, vol. 4553, pp. 778–787. Springer, Heidelberg (2007)

RAFT-REST - A Client-Side Framework for Reliable, Adaptive and Fault-Tolerant RESTful Service Consumption

Josef Spillner, Anna Utlik, Thomas Springer, and Alexander Schill

Technische Universität Dresden,
Faculty of Computer Science,
01062 Dresden, Germany
{josef.spillner,thomas.springer,alexander.schill}@tu-dresden.de,
anna.utlik@mailbox.tu-dresden.de

Abstract. The client/server paradigm in distributed systems leads to multi-stakeholder architectures with messages exchanged over connections between client applications and services. In practice, there are many hidden obstacles for client developers caused by unstable network connections, unavailable or faulty services or limited connectivity. Even if many frameworks and middleware solutions have already been suggested as corrective, the rapid development of clients to (almost) RESTful services remains challenging, especially when mobile devices and wireless telecommunications are involved. In this paper we introduce RAFT-REST, a conceptual framework aimed at engineers of clients to RESTful services. RAFT-REST reduces the effort to achieve reliable, adaptive and fault-tolerant service consumption. The framework is applied and validated with ReSup, a fully implemented flavour for Java clients which run on the desktop and on Android mobile devices. We show that by using the framework, message loss can be reduced significantly with tolerable delay, which contributes to a higher quality of experience.

1 Introduction

As the World Wide Web and the Internet of Services become more enriched with different kinds of information and functionality, private and commercial participants in these networks find new ways to expose their internal data, applications and even hardware resources. From the user's point of view, the interaction with such services is not restricted anymore to read-only access to information, but also includes utilisation and modification of data resources for creating complex applications and systems. Web services following the paradigm of Representational State Transfer, or simply RESTful web services, are attracting the attention of an increasing number of individual developers and service-driven companies as an easy and scalable way to provide an interface to different user groups. This has led to an enormous growth of the adoption of distributed RESTful applications. Many popular Internet-scale services like Facebook, Twitter, Dropbox, Flickr and Amazon S3 rely on the RESTful service paradigm.

K.-K. Lau, W. Lamersdorf, and E. Pimentel (Eds.): ESOCC 2013, LNCS 8135, pp. 104–118, 2013.
© Springer-Verlag Berlin Heidelberg 2013

This development is a result of major advantages RESTful services offer. Based on HTTP for resource access and service invocation in almost all practical realisations of the RESTful approach, overhead with auxiliary data otherwise used for encapsulating messages in envelopes and expressing operations [1] is reduced. Compared with SOAP-formatted and other procedural service protocols [10], RESTful services are easier to develop and use and fit more naturally the underlying stateful entity model like databases and hardware resources. Additionally due to the absence of the auxiliary data and the predictable nature of their requests they typically offer better performance. The latter property allows these services to be consumed with less restrictions on devices with limited computational power, such as mobile phones, tablets and embedded systems. Thus, with the simultaneous increase of radio communication and wireless network covered areas, RESTful services give their consumers a possibility to access and store valuable information in any place, at any time, and from the most comfortable terminal.

The other side of the coin is a high dependency on a stable and continuously available network connection, which raises a set of challenges for the development of RESTful service clients, especially when mobile devices and wireless telecommunications are involved. The addressed statelessness prevents services from keeping any information about clients on the service side, thus making the client responsible for maintaining the session integrity and handling its interruption due to network volatility and service failures. Mitigating this issue implies writing fault-handling code that is individual to every service. Additionally, a high dependency on external services makes mobile applications and other clients consuming RESTful services unusable during a network downtime, as no data which would be necessary for these applications can be received. It is left to the client developer if caching of data and its further reuse from a cache storage should be implemented in the application or not. However, the RESTful paradigm encourages caching and provides sufficient means to benefit from this technique.

As another drawback, the wild growth of services and client programming techniques for them has led to the lack of standardisation and formalised service description and engineering methodologies. Although the basic principles of REST are well known [4] and a lot of best practices and recommendations have been published in developer-oriented literature [11,9,14] to determine one good way of designing RESTful services, many implementations bypass some or even all those rules and hence require treatment of *almost-REST* anomalies.

The current approach to develop RESTful service clients is to use a service-specific framework offered by service providers. These frameworks provide a high-level API which might be the most convenient and appropriate solution if a client for a particular service should be implemented. As soon as a RESTful service client should consume services provided by different vendors service-specific frameworks are not appropriate. In addition, as we will discuss in the related work section, these frameworks only have a very limited support for fault-handling, disconnection support and configurability. Altenative approaches use low-level network programming based on HTTP or support access to RESTful services at message or service level. While these approaches are more general, flexibile, configurable and reusable, implementation effort is also significantly higher. Especially, advanced mechanisms for fault-handling, configuration, caching and adaptivity have to be implemented by the developer. Thus, development of RESTful service clients, especially for mobile devices, is currently a challenging, costly and time consuming task.

In this paper we therefore introduce RAFT-REST, a conceptual framework for reliable, adaptive and fault-tolerant access to RESTful services. Any implementation of it is targeted to the provision of service handling support on the client side in the context of unreliable network conditions combined with often sloppy almost-RESTful service interfaces. The conceptual framework proposes a novel way of accessing and consuming RESTful services from applications which cannot assume high-quality networks and service behaviour.

The contribution of the paper is threefold. Firstly, we describe the results of an analysis of 12 highly popular RESTful services and a set of fault-tolerant consumption frameworks with respect to support for the aforementioned problems. This analysis underpins the current state of service-specific frameworks as stated before. Secondly, we introduce the concepts of RAFT-REST as a conceptual, generic and portable client-side framework for rapid and cost efficient development of reliable, fault-tolerant and adaptive RESTful service clients. Thirdly, we describe ReSup, a concret implementation of the RAFT-REST concepts for Java clients running on a desktop or Android device. We especially present and evaluation of fault-handling, configurability and performance for the use case of reliable mobile service consumption.

The remainder of the paper is organized as follows: In Section 2 we present and compare related client-side service integration approaches. Then, we introduce RAFT-REST as a concept and an architecture for reliable service consumption in Section 3. Through a reference implementation on Android, RAFT-REST is then evaluated for the use case of reliable mobile service consumption in Section 4. Finally, the performed work and its results are summarised and directions for future research towards more failure-aware service-oriented architectures are explained.

2   Related Work: SDKs and Fault-Tolerant Frameworks

Developers of clients for RESTful service interfaces have a choice in the level of assistance which coincides with the level of restriction to certain libraries, toolkits and providers. The following methodologies exist:

- Low-level network programming through APIs such as `socket` or, slightly more comfortable, on the HTTP level, such as `HttpUrlConnection`, `HttpClient` and `curl`. These libraries partially offer functions to overcome communication issues, but do not understand service response semantics.

– Message-level programming where each message is represented as a data structure. The data types are generated from message and interaction descriptions such as RPC IDL, Protocol Buffers, ggzcommgen or XML Schema. In this methodology, the message transport (e.g. HTTP or message buses) needs to be selected but not explicitly handled by the client developer.
– Service-level programming where messages descriptions are complemented by interfaces and endpoints, metadata about the provider and service context, as well as quantitative non-functional properties describing for instance the cost of a single invocation [8]. In this methodology, the most suitable message transport is selected automatically.
– Provider-level programming by using a provider-specific software development kit (SDK). This methodology trades the ability to switch flexibly between providers for a simplified programming model, in particular avoiding the need to configure endpoints within the application. Sometimes, the SDKs even offer graphical elements aimed at instant service consumption by humans.

None of these practical methodologies are well-suited for imperfect network conditions and generic service faults. Researchers have found several API and SDK shortcomings and proposed improvements. We will summarise the findings and extend them with our own observations. Additionally, we will highlight some proposed service consumption concepts which focus on reliability and fault-tolerance, and explain why they don't fully match the needs of developers of applications in imperfect networks.

2.1 Conventional Consumption Frameworks

RESTful services and programmable web APIs are expected to follow certain established guidelines and best practices. Among them are (1) well-designed URIs as resource identifiers, (2) well-projected request semantics on top of the method semantics which the transport channel provides, (3) appropriate status codes, (4) conscious use of metadata along with each request and response, and (5) correspondence between content types and well-formed messages.

Vendors of services typically offer SDKs for a variety of programming languages, frameworks and platforms. These SDKs are almost always restricted to a single service endpoint. Furthermore, they mirror all design weaknesses which violate the guidelines for service design.

As a complement to previous API and SDK analysis work [11,14,2], we have performed an up-to-date analysis of 12 currently highly popular RESTful services which confirms the view that more robust and reliable integration and consumption techniques are needed. The analyis encompasses social interaction (Shuffler.fm and Facebook), data storage (Dropbox and Amazon S3), images (Flickr and Daisy), audio (SoundCloud) and video (Vimeo), open data (Open 311) and security and management of resources (CloudPassage and Sun Cloud). These services differ not only in their domains, but also in technical characteristics including the data model, message body formats, CRUD operations (Create/Read/Update/Delete),

HTTP headers and HTTP response codes. Further differences exist in their adaptivity, security, internationality and documentation.

Guideline violations among this set of APIs are plentyful, hence we can only briefly mention some notable examples. In the Facebook Graph API, POST is used for both creations and updates, while PUT is not used. In Flickr, the semantic difference between POST and GET is expressed with a GET parameter. Amazon S3 transmits only stock response codes in the headers and delivers meaningful error symbols in the body, and Flickr omits the codes altogether.

Table 1 summarises the SDK characteristics for services whose SDK offers at least some fault tolerance or caching.

Table 1. Result of client libraries evaluation

	Facebook	Dropbox	Amazon S3	Flickr	Sound-Cloud
Representation of resource data model as API types	+	+	+	+	−
Wrapping of received exceptions into verbose error messages	+	+	+	−	+
Request retry techniques	−	−	+	−	−
Handling of connection or read timeouts	−	+	+	-	−
Data integrity checking	−	−	+	−	−
Caching of successful responses	+	+	−	−	−

2.2 Fault-Tolerant Consumption Frameworks

Researchers have found existing SDKs to be essential for a quick adoption of new services among application developers, and yet insufficient due to their restriction to one service, mirroring of service design weaknesses, and assumption of perfect networks [7,3]. In this section, four proposals with partially existing framework or code implementations will be presented and compared: iTX, FTWeb, DR-OSGi and FT-REST.

The issue of maintaining a stable Internet connection in wireless networks is a well known problem of mobile devices. Modern distributed applications, typically developed on web services, often rely on mobile components, which heavily depend on different types of wireless connection (WIFI, GPRS, UMTS, Wi-Max, etc.). Apart from instability of applications, for mobile devices individually such network problems can cause performance and monetary costs. Many research efforts have been started in this area in order to achieve resilience of such application against network volatility.

The authors of the mobile recovery concept [15] describe the problem of mobile client state recovery after the network disconnection and reconnection. The goal of this work is to reduce the costs of recovery if a user was involved in a long-lasting network transaction which was interrupted. The notion of Internet transaction (iTX), as used in this work, has been taken from the familiar concept of database transactions and describes the user interaction with one or more network resources for achieving one or more objectives. The proposed solution involves logging of user state for each step of iTX. As initial steps in transaction can branch into several parallel and independent subtransactions, it is necessary to track in which subtransaction the user is at any given moment, and evaluate which actions should and can be recovered. Therefore, the proposed solution allows to reuse the current state from the log and does not repeat the steps of transactions again, thus saving network traffic. However, the algorithm of the given solution requires continuous computation and updating of an action graph, as well as persistent storage for user states. This is why mobile devices, due to limited battery, memory and processing power, are a bad choice for placement of this solution.

The authors of the FTWeb project [13] and the Fault Tolerant Web Service Framework [12] both provide a fault tolerant layer for unreliable web services. The model proposed in FT-Web provides a software layer that acts as proxy between client requests and service responses. This proxy ensures transparent fault handling for client by usage of active replication. The given approach addresses requirements of high service availability and reliability for distributed systems. In contrast, the Fault Tolerant Web Service Framework project proposes customisable fault-tolerance connectors between client and service. Each such connector is a software component which captures web service interactions and partially performs built-in fault tolerance actions. It encapsulates pre-processing and post-processing of requests, and recovery actions which can be parameterised by user. Connectors reside on a third-party infrastructure between service providers and consumers. An infrastructure assumption on which the given approach relies is redundant services. This is used by recovery strategies which implement passive and active replication of request between equivalent services. Both of these approaches are targeted at SOAP web services, and involve third party components between clients and services.

The bundle-oriented DR-OSGi [6] proposes a systematic handling of network outages in distributed system in a consistent and reusable way by implementing fault tolerant strategies as reusable components. This solution is targeting service-oriented applications implemented on top of the OSGi platform. Hardening strategies for network volatility resilience, such as caching, hoarding, replication, etc., are provided as OSGi bundles, and could be added to existing applications transparently. Although the presented benchmarks are showing improved results with DR-OSGi when network becomes unavailable in exchange for a small performance overhead, this solution affords needless system resources consumption. This circumstance prevents it from being widely used on mobile devices. Also, the underlying OSGi framework restricts the usage of DR-OSGi on platforms where OSGi is not supported, or must be pre-installed manually, for instance on Android.

The work in FT-REST [3] presents an approach to fault handling in client RESTful applications. This proposal consists of a domain-specific Fault Tolerance Description Language (FTDL) and client-side library. FTDL is used to specify fault tolerance policies for RESTful application which are compiled afterwards by FT-REST framework into platform specific code. This code module can be added to the business logic of applications and acts as a fault-tolerant layer between the application and a RESTful service. The authors claim that this concepts brings benefits in programmability – by separating the fault tolerance concern from the underlying logic, the programmer can fully focus on implementing the core of application; reusability – by reusing the XML-structured FTDL specification of a service between different applications and across platforms; and extensibility – by robust extension of FTDL fault-tolerant strategies instead of writing fault-tolerant code. FT-REST encapsulates the following fault tolerance strategies: retry (reattempting a service endpoint), sequential (iteration through the set of equivalent endpoints), parallel (simultaneous invocation of equivalent endpoints), and composite (combinations of the aforementioned). However, client-side caching and other disconnected operations techniques are not considered in this work.

Many scientific works are focused on adding resilience to distributed network applications, but only few of them consider the client as a point of network and service fault handling. Among the introduced works, FT-REST can be considered as highly related, as it provides fault handling support for the client and is aimed at consuming RESTful services. However, no previous approaches have been found which provide developers with an out-of-the-box solution that helps to implement RESTful mobile application with necessary fault tolerance.

3   Service Consumption Concept

In this section, the design choices and concepts behind a framework for reliable, adaptive and fault-tolerant RESTful service consumption (RAFT-REST) will be presented. This includes a detailed description of the logical and the derived structural architecture, a service consumption workflow and a consideration of component interactions.

3.1   Logical Architecture

RAFT-REST is a conceptual framework which ensures a high level of reliability, resilience, adaptivity and fault tolerance for service consumption subject to network and service failures. It is intended to achieve service-oriented architectures of higher quality, in particular for mobile clients and embedded cyber-physical systems connected to often brittle service interfaces in the cloud.

The high-level logical architecture of RAFT-REST is shown in Fig. 1. It consists of an API Mapping Component, a Request Executor, a Network Manager as well as a Cache and a Request Queue. The purpose of the *API Mapping Component* is to transform requests and messages into a format understood by the service interface. The *Network Manager* monitors the network connections maintained by the client device and notifies the other componentens of the RAFT-REST framework about changes of connectivity. The heart of the RAFT-REST logical architecture is the *Request Executor*. As an active component it manages the Cache and Request Queue and handles incoming request from clients as well as response messages from services. Access to the network is managed based on the connectivity information provided by the Network Manager. The *Request Queue* fulfills the requirement of asynchrony by enqueuing all outgoing request received from a client. The *Cache* is responsible for temporarily storage of requested resources in the persistent memory of the client device. Thus, it is a key component to handle short-time network failures and longer disconnection phases.

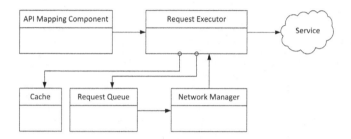

Fig. 1. RAFT-REST Logical Architecture

As a particular design choice, the framework should be as generic as possible, while allowing for almost-REST service-specific workarounds. Therefore, messages can be adapted by the API mapper when instructed to do so by the application. A typical use case is to substitute an error code for a success indication in cases of occurred problems.

3.2 Structural Architecture

The structural architecture of RAFT-REST, which is derived from the logical one, is shown in Fig. 2. It describes the framework from the perspective of a developer.

Client and Service. The Service component represents a RESTful service, which provides a RESTful service API. The Client component represents the Application client which intents to consume the RESTful service.

The Core Structure of the framework is build around the *RequestQueue* for request messages and the *Cache* for resource representations. The **Request Execution Manager** acts as mediator with fault tolerance and adaptation functions. The fault tolerant part checks network and message errors, including response error codes, makes decisions about whether such errors can be mitigated, and applies fault handling techniques. The adaptive part is mostly specific to certain services. It adapts resources to the device context apart from general adaptations, e.g. to work around wrongly modelled response codes. The Request Execution Manager provides an interface, via which clients can pass requests and receive responses. During the instantiation a client can configure some of the network and performance related parameters using the **Configuration** component.

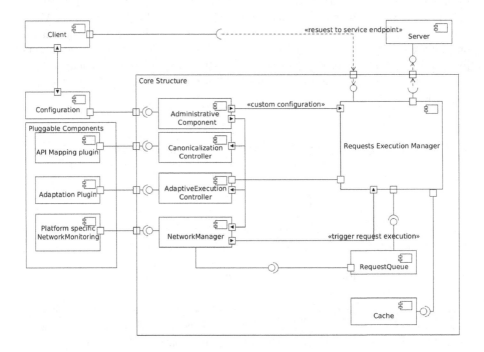

Fig. 2. RAFT-REST Structural Architecture

The **Network Manager** is aware of network conditions, and supply this information to other components, which rely on it (i.e. Requests Queue and RequestExecution Controller). As it is possible to have more than one type of network connection on mobile devices, and retrieving information about connection state is associated with inquires to hardware, Network Manager must rely on **Network Monitoring** components, which are platform specific. Thus, the framework can be extended with custom Network Monitoring components at this point.

The **Canonicalization component** is present in the architecture to supply the framework with canonical entities of the requests and responses. The most widespread service descriptions now exist as plain text, which can be understood by human. In such situation RESTful service endpoints, corresponding HTTP methods and responses should be transformed manually by the developer. Pluggable components can be added to achieve automatic transformation.

Finally, the **Administrative component** collects statistics and manages the level of information that is printed into log messages.

3.3   Service Consumption Workflow

The intended workflow for RAFT-RESTful service consumption is represented in Fig. 3 to illustrate the behavior of the RAFT-REST framework. The complete workflow is organized into three phases.

In *Phase 1* the client initiates the interaction with a service by handing a service request over to the framework. As a first step this request is transformed into a canonical representation which allows the framework to process different types of service interfaces in a common way. As a second step, the cache is checked. If the reply to this request is found in the cache, e.g. the result of an idempotent request which is always cacheable, it is returned immediately to the client.

Otherwise, *Phase 2* is entered and the request is placed into a request queue where it stays until an active network link to the service is available. For mitigating the absence of a connection, a random delay time is added before messages can be forwarded using a re-established network connection to avoid request overhead after service ior network failures.

In *Phase 3* the resource is requested from the service and eventually error responses could be received. In this phase the framework is responsible for evaluating the cause of an error and deciding about appropriate error handling. For instance a retry of a message can be triggered. Parameters for error handling such as the maximum number of retries and the back off time between retries are configurable. Finally the response is handled (e.g. response data is cached) and forwarded to the initiating client.

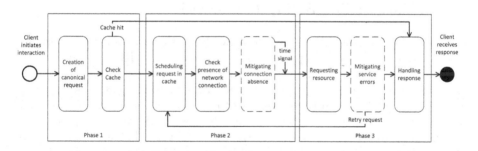

Fig. 3. Workflow of RESTful service consumption according to the RAFT-REST concept

Table 2 offers a comparative summary of the characteristics of RAFT-REST and FT-REST. While RAFT-REST lacks a structured description of faults, for which a domain-specific language is yet to be defined, it offers additional functionality especially through caching and error mitigation. Equivalent endpoint invocation is a feature already found in general adaptive service proxies and therefore can be combined with RAFT-REST while keeping the framework lean.

Table 2. Comparison of characteristics: FT-REST vs RAFT-REST

Characteristics	FT-REST	RAFT-REST
Separation of concerns - separating of fault-tolerant layer from application logic	yes	yes
Fault condition description	for each endpoint, in XML document	for each endpoint (optionally hierarchical), in generated classes
Handling strategies configuration	for each endpoint	for all application
Timeout handling	yes	yes
HTTP response error codes handling	yes	yes
Mitigation of errors, embedded in the message	no	yes
Service binding code	no	yes
Fault handling techniques		
Retrying of request	yes	yes
Equivalent endpoints invocation	yes	no
Cache	no	yes
Asynchronous request invocation (due to network conditions)	no	yes

4   Validation: The ReSup Framework

ReSup (RESTful Support), a Java framework for the development of service-bound mobile and desktop applications, turns the RAFT-REST concepts into practice for service clients implemented with the Java language and corresponding networking libraries. ReSup consists of a proxy library located between the application and the network stack, similar to existing HTTP client libraries, and an Eclipse wizard to generate service-specific message classes by mapping API specifications to code. A screenshot of the wizard in Fig. 4 highlights the possibility to import WADL (Web Application Description Language) service descriptions to reduce the manual class modelling effort [8]. Both the wizard and the library need to be present as JAR files (`org.tud.resup.apimapper_1.0.0.2013MMDD.jar`, `Resup_1.0.0.2013MMDD.jar`) in the plugins folder of Eclipse. The library is subsequently copied into the resulting project archive and used at runtime.

The ReSup library delivers and caches message objects which may be created manually in the application code or as instantiations of the generated classes. Each message object represents a service resource or a request targeting one. The way ReSup is used depends mainly on the application requirements. Fig. 5 demonstrates the possible configuration directive combinations.

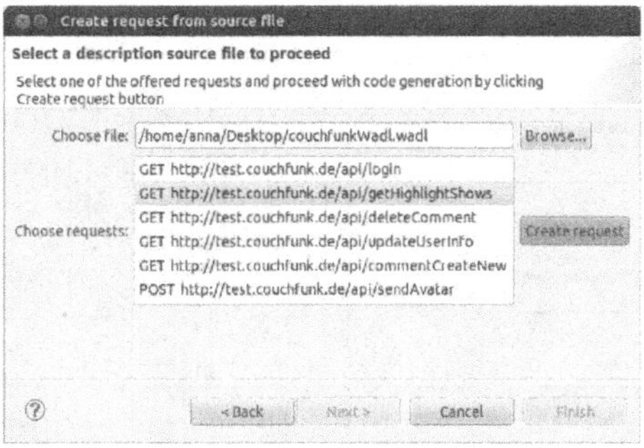

Fig. 4. Eclipse wizard to generate API mapping classes for use with the ReSup library

Step 1		
Caching		
Yes		No
`factory` = `EManagerFactory(ClientConfiguration, CachingStyle, AbstractCacheStorageFactory, int) or factory` = `EManagerFactory(CachingStyle, AbstractCacheStorageFactory, int)`		`factory` = `EmanagerFactory() or EmanagerFactory (ClientConfiguration)`
Step 2		
Asynchrony		
Yes		No
`manager` = `factory.createNetworkAwareExecutionManager(IQueueStorage, IReSupNetworkMonitoring) or manager` = `factory.createNetworkAwareExecutionManager(IReSupNetworkMonitoring)`		`manager` = `factory.createExecutionManager()`

Fig. 5. Flexible configuration of the ReSup objects depending on the desired application behaviour

The integration of ReSup is particularly easy by its HttpClient interface which mimicks the API of the widely used Apache `HttpClient` library. Hence, developers can switch to ReSup by just substituting a Java import statement and afterwards gradually turning on and testing its RAFT features. ReSup can also run as a transparent stand-alone proxy so that applications do not have to be modified except for a system-wide forced HTTP proxy configuration. Proxies, gateways and networked intermediaries are common architectural elements for RESTful service consumption [5]. However, on mobile systems such as Android, this requires system modification access and is therefore often not a viable solution.

In order to demonstrate the capabilities of ReSup, and therefore acknowledge the RAFT-REST concepts, we have performed a number of measurements and experiments in an evaluation study which includes existing services with RESTful interfaces in both simulated and real imperfect networks. Fig. 6 shows the setup of the experiment. Off-the-shelf networking tools such as Burp, an intercepting proxy, Trickle, a bandwidth variator, and Netem, a packet loss generator, are used to simulate reproducible low-quality connections. Trickle allows scaling the bandwidth within the constraints imposed by the hardware from a zero-throughput connection to the typical speeds of mobile networks, WLANs and LANs. Netem varies typical WAN parameters such as delay, loss, duplication and re-ordering (shuffling).

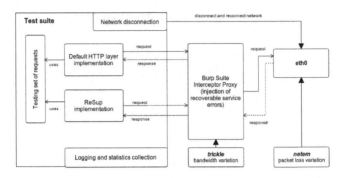

Fig. 6. Test suite for the experiments involving RESTful services and clients using the ReSup library

The test environment consisted of the test suite running on an Intel Core i5 machine with 4 times 2.4 GHz CPUs, 3 GB DDR2 RAM, the Ubuntu 12.04 operating system and Java 1.6.

The results are shown in Fig. 7 and 8, respectively. The first diagram shows the distribution of error responses still successfully received from one of the test runs, in this case a mobile connection with 50 kbps. On the whole range of possible network losses, ReSup retrieves a higher number of error reponses compared to a pure HttpClient connection. The increase is between 35% and 92%, but still recovers less than half of the lost packets when the loss rate exceeds 80%. The second diagram measures the overall response times over a bivariate range from a perfect connection (100 Mbps with 0% loss) to a nearly unusable one (50 kbps with 80% loss). Due to the caching, ReSup is much faster for all good-enough connections and considerably slower than HttpClient for all worse ones due to the retries. Yet, the retries contribute to the higher success rate as shown in 7, therefore even the highest run-time overhead of 55,4% for a 500 kbps connection with 60% loss will eventually improve the user experience in practice.

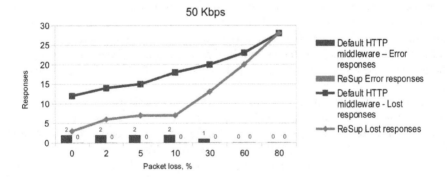

Fig. 7. Error response numbers evaluation

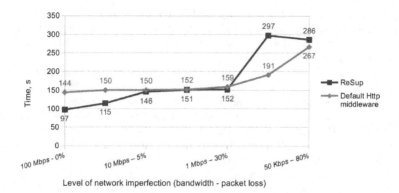

Fig. 8. Response times evaluation

5   Conclusion

We have motivated and discussed RAFT-REST, a client-side RESTful service integration concept which addresses reliability, safety and quality concerns. Compared to previous integration concepts, the combination of conventional fault-tolerance schemes, graceful error handling and caching achieves a great user experience for distributed applications connected by imperfect networks. The ReSup framework targets mobile application developers through an API-compatible HTTP client library and an Eclipse code engineering plugin with the aim to increase real-world application robustness through RAFT-REST. It is made available as open source toolkit for use and further improvements[1].

Subsequent research questions focus on the global view, i.e. the server-side and total load behaviour when using any of the offered RAFT-REST mechanisms, as well as on extended validation with real-time statistics collection and visualisation for immediate feedback about the waiting state of applications to the user.

Acknowledgements. This work has received funding under project number 080949277 by means of the European Regional Development Fund (ERDF), the European Social Fund (ESF) and the German Free State of Saxony.

References

1. Aihkisalo, T., Paaso, T.: Latencies of Service Invocation and Processing of the REST and SOAP Web Service Interfaces. In: Eighth IEEE World Congress on Services (SERVICES), Hawaii, USA, pp. 100–107 (June 2012)
2. Belqasmi, F., Glitho, R.H., Fu, C.: RESTful Web Services for Service Provisioning in Next-Generation Networks: A Survey. IEEE Communications Magazine 49(12), 66–73 (2011)

---

[1] ReSup website and source code: `http://serviceplatform.org/wiki/ReSup`

3. Edstrom, J., Tilevich, E.: Reusable and Extensible Fault Tolerance for REST-ful Applications. In: 11th International Conference on Trust, Security and Privacy in Computing and Communications (TrustCom), pp. 737–744 (June 2012), doi:10.1109/TrustCom.2012.244

4. Fielding, R.T.: Architectural Styles and the Design of Network-based Software Architectures. Ph.D. thesis, University of California, Irvine (2000)

5. Kelly, M., Hausenblas, M.: Using HTTP Link: Header for Gateway Cache Invalidation. In: Proceedings of the First International Workshop on RESTful Design (WS-REST), Raleigh, North Carolina, USA, pp. 23–26 (April 2010)

6. Kwon, Y.-W., Tilevich, E., Apiwattanapong, T.: DR-OSGi: Hardening Distributed Components with Network Volatility Resiliency. In: Bacon, J.M., Cooper, B.F. (eds.) Middleware 2009. LNCS, vol. 5896, pp. 373–392. Springer, Heidelberg (2009)

7. Leitner, P., Rosenberg, F., Dustdar, S.: Daios – Efficient Dynamic Web Service Invocation. Internet Computing 13(3), 72–80 (2009)

8. Maleshkova, M., Pedrinaci, C., Domingue, J.: Supporting the creation of semantic RESTful service descriptions. In: 8th International Semantic Web Conference (ISWC), Washington D.C., USA (October 2009)

9. Masse, M.: REST API Design Rulebook. O'Reilly (2011)

10. Mulligan, G., Gracanin, D.: A comparison of SOAP and REST implementations of a service based interaction independence middleware framework. In: Proceedings of the Winter Simulation Conference (WSC), Austin, Texas, USA, pp. 1423–1432 (December 2009)

11. Mulloy, B.: Web API Design: Crafting Interfaces that Developers Love. e-Book (March 2012)

12. Salatge, N., Fabre, J.C.: Fault Tolerance Connectors for Unreliable Web Services. In: 37th Annual IEEE/IFIP International Conference on Dependable Systems and Networks (DSN), Edinburgh, UK, pp. 51–60 (June 2007)

13. Santos, G.T., Lung, L.C., Montez, C.: FTWeb: A Fault Tolerant Infrastructure for Web Services. In: Proceedings of the Ninth IEEE International EDOC Enterprise Computing Conference, Enschede, The Netherlands, pp. 95–105 (September 2005)

14. Tilkov, S.: REST Anti-Patterns. InfoQ Article (July 2008)

15. VanderMeer, D., Datta, A., Dutta, K., Ramamritham, K., Navathe, S.B.: Mobile User Recovery in the Context of Internet Transactions. IEEE Transactions on Mobile Computing 2(2), 132–146 (2003)

Contract Compliance Monitoring
of Web Services

Gregorio Díaz[1] and Luis Llana[2]

[1] Computer Science Dept. University of Castilla-La Mancha
[2] Computer Science Dept. Complutensis University of Madrid
gregorio.diaz@uclm.es, llana@dfi.uclm.es

Abstract. Design and implementation via contractual specifications helps designers and programmers understand and analyze when the requirements have been elicited according to the client' desires. In general, software is released when some tests have been successfully passed. However, these tests only cover a finite set of possible executions. But in systems such as web services, which involve a set of heterogeneous parties, it is difficult to identify an appropriate set of tests because their execution tends to be nondeterministic since most rely on underlying software systems where most of the information is hidden due to copyright or security concerns. In this work, we propose that the use of contract specifications, such us C-O Diagrams, allow one to specify and codify a system, where once the software has been released it is still possible to check if the execution conforms to a given contract. To achieve this goal, we purpose a monitoring technique, where all actions specified in a contract are recorded in a log that will be used by the monitor software to check if the contract is being fulfilled and alerting all parties when it is not so that the system can force reparations.

1   Introduction

A *contract* from a software perspective refers to a set of statements agreed between the involved parties. These statements have different detail level depending on the case. One of the first approaches to use contracts in software designs dates to the mid-eights, with the Eiffel language, where the contract refers to a set of pre and post conditions and invariants following the ideas defined by Hoare. These ideas have proven effective for the development of Object Oriented designs. However in more recent paradigms such as component-based and interaction-based developments, the abstraction level has changed and therefore new definition of contracts need to be introduced.

In the context of SOA, there are different service contract specification languages, such as ebXML, WSLA, and WS-Agreement. These standards and specification languages suffer from one or more of the following problems: They are restricted to bilateral contracts, lack formal semantics (so it is difficult to reason about them), their treatment of functional behaviour is rather limited and the sub-languages used to specify security constraints, for instance, are usually

K.-K. Lau, W. Lamersdorf, and E. Pimentel (Eds.): ESOCC 2013, LNCS 8135, pp. 119–133, 2013.
© Springer-Verlag Berlin Heidelberg 2013

limited to small application-specific domains. The lack of suitable languages for contracts in the context of SOA is a clear conclusion of the survey [15] where a taxonomy is presented.

In [12] *C-O Diagrams* were introduced, a graphical representation not only for electronic contracts but also for the specification of any kind of normative text (Web service composition behaviour, software product lines engineering, requirements engineering, ...). *C-O Diagrams* allow the representation of complex clauses describing the obligations, permissions, and prohibitions of different signatories (as defined in deontic logic [14]), as well as *reparations* describing contractual clauses in the case of non-fulfillment of obligations and prohibitions. Also, *C-O Diagrams* permit defining real-time constraints. In [11] some of the satisfaction rules needed to check if a timed automaton satisfies a *C-O Diagram* specification were defined. In [13], *C-O Diagrams* were equipped with a formal semantics, based on a transformation of these diagrams into a network of timed automata (NTA). Finally, some conformance relationships are given in [4], where contract and implementation, are compared. The contribution of this work pursues the further development of our previous work. Here, we focus on the development of a software system implementing the conformance relationships between contracts and implementations to check if implementation executions corresponds to its contracts. The software developed in this case is a monitoring system and is based in a subscription and notification system where the different involved services subscribe to a specific contract under a specific role and are notified in case a service violates the contract.

2   Related Work

The use of deontic logic for reasoning about contracts is wide spread in the literature and was proposed in [5] for modelling communication processes. In [10] Marjanovic and Milosevic present their initial ideas for formal modelling of e-contracts based on deontic constraints and verification of deontic consistency, including temporal constraints. In [6] Governatori et al. go a step further, providing a mechanism to check whether business processes are compliant with business contracts. They introduce the logic FCL to reason about the contracts, based again on deontic logic. In [9] Lomuscio et al. provides another methodology to check whether service compositions are compliant with e-contracts, using WS-BPEL to specify both, all possible behaviours of each service and the contractually correct behaviours, and translating these specifications into automata supported by the MCMAS model checker to verify the behaviours automatically.

None of the previous works provide a visual model for the definition of contracts. However, there are several works that define a meta-model for the specification of e-contracts, with the purpose of their enactment or enforcement. In [3] Chiu et al. present a meta-model for e-contract templates written in UML, where a template consists of a set of contract clauses of three different types: obligations, permissions and prohibitions. These clauses are later mapped into ECA rules for contract enforcement purposes, but the templates do not include any kind of reparation or recovery associated to the clauses. In [7] Krishna et al. purpose another meta-model, based on entity-relationship diagrams to generate workflows supporting e-contract enactment. This meta-model includes clauses, activities, parties and the possibility of specifying exceptional behaviour, but this approach is not based on deontic logic and says nothing about including real-time aspects natively.

3   C-O Diagrams Syntax and Semantics

We first introduce a motivation example to understand the diagrams in a more intuitive manner. Figure 1 depicts our running example. This example consists of the auction of an item. The online auction starts when a *seller* wants to auction an item. Therefore, the *seller* has **one day** to upload valid information about the item he wants to sell, taking into account that the sale of inadequate items such as counterfeit items or wild animals is forbidden. Once an item is cleared for auction, the *auction service* has **one day** to publish the auction of the item. After that, the *buyer* can place bids during **seven days**. When this period of time is over, if the bid placed by the *buyer* is the highest, the activities concerning the payment and the shipment of the item start.

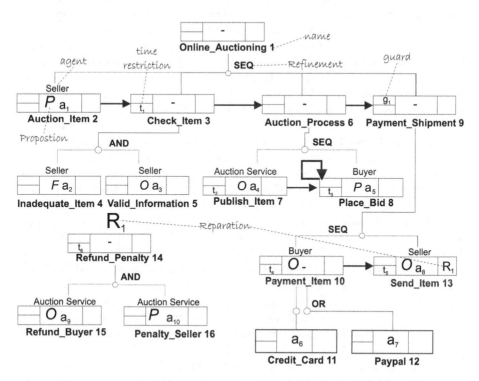

Fig. 1. *C-O Diagrams* examples

At first sight, *C-O Diagrams* are top down hierarchical structures with several boxes and branches. In Figure 1, we observe two examples, a contract and a reparation of a clause of this contract corresponding to our running example. The basic construction element of these diagrams is called **box**, also referred to as proposition or clause, and is divided into four fields. The *guard*, top left hand side field, **g** specifies·the conditions under which the contract clause must be taken into account (boolean expression). The *time restriction* **tr**, bottom left hand side field, specifies the time frame during which the contract clause must be satisfied (deadlines, timeouts, etc.). The *propositional content* **P**, in the centre, is the main field of the box, and it is used to specify normative aspects such as obligations (**O**), permissions (**P**) and prohibitions (**F**), that are applied over actions, and/or the specification of the actions themselves. The last field, on the right-hand side, is the *reparation* **R**. This reparation, if specified by the contract clause, is a reference to another contract that must be satisfied in case the main norm is not satisfied (a *prohibition* is violated or an *obligation* is not fulfilled, there is no reparation for *permission*), considering the clause eventually satisfied if this reparation is satisfied. Each box has also a *name* at the bottom and an *agent* at the top.

These are the basic boxes, which can be composed by using a few refinements. Refinements are classified into three types: joining *AND-refinements*, disjunctive *OR-refinements* and sequential *SEQ-refinement*. Joining refinements require that all the hanging propositions should be accomplished to declare the upper proposition accomplished; on the contrary, disjunctive propositions only require one to be accomplished; whereas, sequential propositions require a left-to-right ordered sequential satisfaction of every proposition to obtain the same result. In Fig. 1 we show a *C-O Diagram* that we specify for the process, called *Online_Auctioning*, to start from the permission specified in clause **1**, that has been called *Auction_Item*. We have grouped the rest of the clauses into four more general clauses with a sequence relationship between them: 1) *Check_Item* decomposed via a conjunction of clauses **2** and **3**, 2) *Auction_Process* refined as a sequence of Clause (**4** and **5**), 3) *Payment_Shipment* other sequence of clauses.

The clause *Check_Item* is decomposed into two subclauses, where an *AND-refinement* is used in the decomposition and the real-time constraint t_2, one day, equivalent to t_3 is affecting the whole composition[1]. We have, on the left-hand side of the specification the prohibition specified in clause **2**, that has been called *Inadequate_Item*, and on the right-hand side the obligation specified in clause **3**, that has been called *Valid_Information*. The decomposition of clause *Auction_Process* into two subclauses is performed via a *SEQ-refinement*. We have on the left-hand side the specification of the obligation specified in clause **4**, that has been called *Publish_Item*, including the real-time constraint t_4, one day, and on the right-hand side the permission specified in clause **5**, that has been called *Place_Bid*, including the real-time constraint t_5, seven days. We can see in this clause that the repetition structure of *C-O Diagrams* is used to model

---

[1] Since they are equivalent we have assumed that the conjunction can be affected by the same restriction. Similar approach is taken when the all the subclauses of the parent clause are affected by the same temporal restriction.

that the *buyer* is allowed to place multiple bids. The clause *Payment_Shipment*, which only shows the name and guard g_1 (this guard checks if the buyer is the auction winner) is decomposed into two sub-clauses via sequential composition, that is, *Payment_Item*, on the left hand side, and, afterwards, *Send_Item*, on the right hand side. The first is the **obligation** (O) of payment with the temporal restriction t_4, three days in this case, then this obligation is decomposed via an *OR-refinement* into clause **11** and clause **12** composing the actions of paying by credit card or PayPal by means of an *OR-refinement*. On the right-hand side we have the **obligation** (O) specified in clause **13**, which has been called *Send_Item*, including the real-time constraint t_5 14 days and a reference to reparation R_1. Since reparations are references to new contracts, in Figure 1 we can see the diagram corresponding to reparation R_1. It has been called *Refund_Penalty*, including the real-time constraint t_6, and it is decomposed into two subclauses by means of an *AND-refinement*. The subclause on the left corresponds to the **obligation** (O) specified in clause **15**, which has been called *Refund_Buyer*, and the subclause on the right corresponds to the **permission** (P) specified in clause **16**, which has been called *Penalty_Seller* regarding the possibility of performing some kind of penalization over the seller by the *Auction Service*.

The **syntax** of *C-O Diagrams* was first presented in [12]. Next, we just present a brief description of the EBNF grammar followed in the diagrams:

$$C := (agent, name, g, tr, O(C_2), R) \mid \qquad C_1 := C\,(And\,C)^+ \mid C\,(Or\,C)^+ \mid C\,(Seq\,C)^+$$
$$(agent, name, g, tr, P(C_2), \epsilon) \mid \qquad C_2 := a \mid C_3\,(And\,C_3)^+ \mid$$
$$(agent, name, g, tr, F(C_2), R) \mid \qquad C_3\,(Or\,C_3)^+ \mid C_3\,(Seq\,C_3)^+$$
$$(\epsilon, name, g, tr, C_1, \epsilon) \qquad\qquad C_3 := (\epsilon, name, \epsilon, \epsilon, C_2, \epsilon)$$
$$R := C \mid \epsilon$$

The C-O diagram **semantics** is defined by using NTAs (*Network of Timed Automata*) [1] as semantic objects. Here we omit this formal translation and the technical definitions can be found in [13,4]. Instead, we present an informal intuitive interpretation of the NTA behaviors. When transforming a C-O diagram into a network of timed automata, the states of the generated automata are decorated with the set of contractual obligations, prohibitions and permissions that are either violated or satisfied.

Definition 1. *(Normative timed automaton) Let us consider the set of contractual obligations and prohibitions CN ranged over cn, cn',... standing for identifiers of obligations and prohibitions and the set of contractual permissions CP ranged over cp, cp', ...*

A normative timed automaton is a timed automaton (N, n_0, E, I) (see [1]) where the state $s \in S$ is defined as the tuple (n, v, Cla) where $n \in N$, v corresponds to the clock and variable valuation and a new tuple to extend the automata with normative propositions $Cla = (Vio, Sat, Per)$ with Vio, $Sat \subseteq CN$ and $Per \subseteq CP$. The subset Vio stands for the obligations and prohibitions violated, whereas Sat stands for the satisfied. Although, the subset Per stands for the permission that have been granted, already. The initial state is $s_0 = (\bar{n}_0, u, v, Cla_0)$, where Cla_0 is the set of clauses that are violated, satisfied or permitted at this initial state.

Let us recall that the intuitive meaning of an NTA is the parallel composition of several timed automata. We consider a set of actions ACT, in which we have the following actions:

- An internal action $\tau \in ACT$.

- An input action $m? \in ACT$.

- An output action $m! \in ACT$.

- A synchronization action $m \in ACT$ that comes from a synchronization of an input action $m?$ and an output action $m!$.

The semantics of timed automata is well known [1]. It is based on a timed labeled system, where states are pairs $s = (n, v)$ where n is a node of the automaton and v is a valuation of the clocks and variables. However, as stated in the previous definition, the state has been extended with the information regarding the clauses that have been either violated, satisfied or permitted. There are two types of transition:

- timed transitions[2] $s \xrightarrow{d} s'(d \in \mathbb{R}^+)$

- and action transitions $s \xrightarrow{a} s'(a \in ACT)$.

A *Network of Timed Automata* (NTA) is then defined as a set of timed automata that run simultaneously, using the same set of clocks and variables, and synchronizing on the common actions, where the state corresponds to the union of all the independent states. Internal actions can be executed by the corresponding automata independently, and they are ranged over the letters $a, b, \ldots$ whereas synchronization actions must be executed simultaneously by two automata. Synchronization actions are ranged over letters $m, m', \ldots$ and come from the synchronization of two actions $m!$ and $m?$, executed from two different automata[3].

The operational semantics of a network of timed automata has the following transitions:

- A delay transition of d time units requires that all involved automata are able to perform this delay individually.
- Autonomous action transitions that correspond to the evolution of a single timed automaton.
- Synchronization transitions that require two automata to perform two complementary actions, $m!$ and $m?$, respectively.

Definition 2. *(Semantics of an NTA)*
Let $N = (A_1, , \ldots, A_k)$ be an NTA. A state of N is a tuple $\bar{s} = (s_1, \ldots, s_k)$, where s_i is a state of the automaton A_i (for $i = 1, \ldots, k$). We have the following transitions:

---

[2] Timed transitions only change the valuation of clocks.
[3] In the original definition, the only internal action is τ, and synchronizations always yield internal actions.

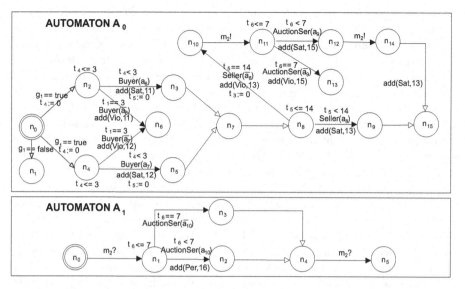

Fig. 2. Automata for the Payment_Shipment clause, A_0 and A_1

- *Timed transitions. If* $\forall 1 \leq j \leq k :$ $s_j \xrightarrow{d} s'_j$, *then:* $(s_1, \ldots, s_k) \xrightarrow{d} (s'_1, \ldots, s'_k)$ *with* $d \in \mathbb{R}^+$.

- *Autonomous transitions. If* $\exists 1 \leq j \leq k : s_j \xrightarrow{a} s'_j$ *for* $a \in ACT$, $a \neq m!$ *and* $a \neq m?$, *then:*
$$(s_1, \ldots, s_j, \ldots s_k) \xrightarrow{a} (s_1, \ldots, s'_j, \ldots s_k).$$

- *Synchronization transitions.* $\exists 1 \leq i, j \leq k :$ $s_j \xrightarrow{m?} s'_j$, $s_i \xrightarrow{m!} s'_i$ *for* $m?, m! \in ACT$, *then:*
$(\ldots, s_j, \ldots, s_i, \ldots,) \xrightarrow{m} (\ldots, s'_j, \ldots, s'_i, \ldots)$, *assuming that* $j \leq i$, *the other case is similar.*

The complete semantics for *C-O Diagrams* in terms of NTAs translation can be found in [13]. Figure 2 shows the resulting NTA once these transformations are applied over the *Payment_Shipment* clause of Fig. 1. This NTA consists of two automata running in parallel, that is, $NTA_{P\&S} = \{A_0, A_1\}$. Automaton A_0 is where the main part is translated and the starting point of this example. The main translated structures observed here are the three kind of refinements and the reparation of a violated clause. Besides these main structures, we can see how guards and time restrictions are translated. The nodes are labeled with invariants defining the maximum amount of time the state of the system will stay in this node and transitions are labeled in this order 1st) guards to enable the transitions, 2nd) actions to be performed, 3rd) updates of the violation, satisfaction and permission subsets, and 4th) modifications and resets of clocks and variables, but only if they are specified.

In A_0, this clause starts with a SEQ-refinement of two clauses 10 and 13, which assemble in sequence via the transition between nodes n_7 and n_8, that is, the end of clause 10 and the beginning of clause 13, respectively. From node n_0, where clause 10 starts, we may reach either n_2 or n_4, which correspond to an OR-refinement representing the payment made either by credit card or Paypal. Node n_6 only captures termination in the event that that the time for the payment expires without performing any of these actions. Notice that once the payment has been made (nodes n_3 or n_5) we move into node n_7, from which the "sending item action" clause 13 starts, which corresponds to action a_8. In this case we have 14 time units. If this time expires and the client has not received the item, the reparation clause is activated (node n_{10}). In this case we have an AND-refinement, so a second timed automaton (A_1) is created, which corresponds to the right-hand side part of the AND-refinement (the left-hand side is performed by A_0). Both automata synchronize at their beginning and at their termination in order to be executed simultaneously using channel m_2. The obligation to refund the money is captured by action a_9 in A_0, whereas the permission to penalize the seller is captured by action a_{10} in A_1. Over-line actions label those transitions enabled when the main action is not performed.

guards are here translated as guards in the transitions and time restrictions are used to denote the invariants of certain states and some guards in transitions, which determine whether a clause is satisfied in time. In reference to the different violation, satisfaction and permission sets, they are modified as follows. Whenever obligations of actions are performed in time, the clauses defining them are added to the satisfaction set, otherwise they are added to the violation set. An example of this situation can be observed in our example of the transitions connecting node 2 to node 3 and node 2 to node 6 from automata A_0, respectively. If the actions specified in prohibitions are performed during the forbidden period of time[4] specified in the **tr** field, then they are added to the violation set otherwise to the satisfaction set. Finally, permissions are optional and when their actions are performed the clauses are added to the permission set, but if they are not performed then no modification to any set is done. In the transitions from nodes 1 to 2 and 1 to 3 of the automata A_0 this situation is shown, respectively.

4 Conformance Relations

In this section we define a set of conformance relations to establish whether an implementation of a contract conforms to the contract we want to satisfy. We will consider a semantic relation inspired in the *conformance testing* relation given in [16]. We take as starting point a normative document written in terms of a C-O Diagram, which is then translated into a network of timed automata. We also consider an implementation I of this contract, with at least the same actions we had in the contract. We intend to define a black box conformance relation, which means that we do not know how the implementation has been done, so we can only use the information about the actions it performs.

Definition 3. *A timed trace is a sequence* $[a_1 d_1 a_2 d_2 \cdots a_n d_n] \in (ACT \times \mathbb{R}^+)^*$. *We will use the symbols* t, t_1, t_2, t_n,... *to denote traces. The empty trace is denoted by* $[]$. *The concatenation of* t_1 *and* t_2 *will be denoted by* $t_1 \cdot t_2$. *We will*

---

[4] Note that this time can be an unbounded period of time, i.e., infinite, and therefore forbidden during all the time the contract is valid.

say that t_1 is a subtrace of t_2, written $t_1 \leq t_2$, if there is a trace t such that $t_2 = t_1 \cdot t$.

Let N be an NTA, where we define the timed computations *of N as follows:*

- $\overline{s} \xoverset{[]}{\Longrightarrow} \overline{s}$.
- $\overline{s} \xoverset{t \cdot [ad]}{\Longrightarrow} \overline{s'}$ *for $a \in ACT$ and $d \in \mathbb{R}^+$ if there exist states $\overline{s_1}, \overline{s'_1}, \ldots, \overline{s_l}, \overline{s'_l}$ of N with $l \geq 1$ such that*

$$\overline{s} \xoverset{t}{\Longrightarrow} \overline{s_1} \xoverset{d_1}{\longrightarrow} \overline{s'_1} \xoverset{\tau}{\longrightarrow} \overline{s_2} \xoverset{d_2}{\longrightarrow} \overline{s'_2} \cdots \overline{s_{l-1}} \xoverset{d_{l-1}}{\longrightarrow} \overline{s'_{l-1}} \xoverset{\tau}{\longrightarrow} \overline{s_l} \xoverset{d_l}{\longrightarrow} \overline{s'_l} \xoverset{a}{\longrightarrow} \overline{s'} \text{ and}$$
$$d = \sum_{1 \leq i \leq l} d_i$$

We define the set of timed traces *of N as $\mathrm{tr}(N) = \{t \mid \exists \overline{s} : \overline{s_0} \xoverset{t}{\Longrightarrow} \overline{s}\}$, being $\overline{s_0}$ the initial state of N.*

The following definition introduces the sets V, S and P to traces, as the values of Vio, Sat and Per of the last state of a trace since they may be modified by any transition in the trace.

Definition 4. *Let $N = (A_1, \ldots A_k)$ be an NTA and $t \in \mathrm{tr}(N)$, we define the sets of* violation *(denoted $V(N,t)$),* satisfaction *(denoted $S(N,t)$), and* permission *(denoted $P(N,t)$) as follows:*

- $V(N,t) = \{\bigcup_{1 \leq i \leq k} Vio_i \mid \overline{s_0} \xoverset{t}{\Longrightarrow} (s'_1, \ldots, s'_k), \ s'_i = (n_i, v_i, (Vio_i, Sat_i, Per_i))\}$
- $S(N,t) = \{\bigcup_{1 \leq i \leq k} Sat_i \mid \overline{s_0} \xoverset{t}{\Longrightarrow} (s'_1, \ldots, s'_k), \ s'_i = (n_i, v_i, (Vio_i, Sat_i, Per_i))\}$
- $P(N,t) = \{\bigcup_{1 \leq i \leq k} Per_i \mid \overline{s_0} \xoverset{t}{\Longrightarrow} (s'_1, \ldots, s'_k), \ s'_i = (n_i, v_i, (Vio_i, Sat_i, Per_i))\}$

Where $\overline{s_0}$ is the initial state of N. We say that t is a good *trace, denoted by $t \in \mathrm{good}(N)$ if it is maximal[5], $S(N,t) \neq \varnothing$, and $V(N,t) \subseteq S(N,t)$.*

We say that t is a clean *trace, denoted by $t \in \mathrm{clean}(N)$, if $V(N,t) = \{\varnothing\}$.*

Table 1. Trace examples for $NTA_{P\&S}$

Trace	Description	V	S	P
$t_0 = [\overline{a_6}4]$	4 days without paying.	10	$\varnothing$	$\varnothing$
$t_1 = [a_6 3 a_8 8]$	Credit card payment in 3 days and then item shipped in 8 days.	$\varnothing$	11, 13	$\varnothing$
$t_2 = [a_6 3 \overline{a_8} 15 \overline{a_9} 8]$	Similar to t_1 but the item is not shipped.	13, 15	11	$\varnothing$
$t_3 = [a_6 3 \overline{a_8} 15 a_1 02 \overline{a_9} 6]$	Similar to t_2 but with a penalization.	13	11	16
$t_4 = [a_7 2 \overline{a_8} 15 a_9 4]$	Paypal payment in 2 days, item not received but refunded in 19 days.	13	12, 15, 13	$\varnothing$
$t_5 = [a_7 2 \overline{a_8} 15 a_9 4 a_1 01]$	Similar to t_4 but a penalization is made.	13	12, 15, 13	16

---

[5] A maximal trace is a trace that cannot be extended anymore: if $t \in \mathrm{tr}(N)$ but $t \cdot [ad] \notin \mathrm{tr}(N)$ for all $a \in ACT$ and $d \in \mathbb{R}^+$.

Comming back to our running example $NTA_{P\&S}$ in Fig. 2, let us analyze the following maximal traces of Table 1. The *good* traces will be t_1, t_4 and t_5 because a) the satisfaction set is not empty and b) the violation set are either empty or repaired since the violation set is a subset of the satisfaction. From these traces only t_1 corresponds to a *clean* trace since t_4 and t_5 have violated the shipment clause 13, however they have been recovered via R_1.

Definition 5. *Let C be an NTA corresponding to a C-O diagram. We say that C is consistent if the following conditions hold:*

- $\mathsf{clean}(C) \cap \mathsf{good}(C) \neq \varnothing$. *This means that there is a way to meet contracts without making any violations.*
- $\forall cn \in CN\ \exists t \in \mathsf{clean}(C) \cap \mathsf{good}(C)\ :\ \exists S \in \mathsf{S}(C,t)\ :\ cn \in S$. *That is there is a way to meet all obligations and prohibitions without making any violation.*

Our $NTA_{P\&S}$ example satisfies both conditions since trace t_1 is a *good* and *clean* trace that meets both obligations, the payment and the shipment.

Next, we assume that implementations are given as networks of timed automata, however they can be given in any other way since the conformance relationship we define works as a black box relationship and only reasons about the actions specified in the contract, as we will see in the next section. Implementations usually need to implement a single action by making several simple actions. For instance let us suppose that a contract specifies that a payment can be done by credit card. When implementing the payment procedure, several invisible steps such us contacting the bank or checking the credit card should be performed. All these actions are not considered in the specification of the contract and they should not be taken into account. All we need in this case is the amount of time required to perform these actions. Thus, these implementation traces may contain actions that are not considered in the contract, so we need to *hide* these actions and therefore a function called *hide* is used in the next definition.

Definition 6. *Let us consider $ACT \subseteq ACT'$ and $t \in (ACT' \times \mathbb{R}^+)^*$. We consider the operator hide_{ACT} defined as follows:*

- $\mathsf{hide}_{ACT}([\,]) = [\,]$
- $\mathsf{hide}_{ACT}([ad] \cdot t) = [ad] \cdot \mathsf{hide}_{ACT}(t)$ *for $a \in ACT$, $a \neq \tau$*
- $\mathsf{hide}_{ACT}([ad] \cdot t) = d + \mathsf{hide}_{ACT}(t)$ *for $a \notin ACT$ or $a = \tau$, where the operator $+$ adds d units of time to the last action of t. Formally it is defined as follows:*
  - $d + [\,] = [\,]$
  - $d + ([ad_1] \cdot t) = [a(d_1 + d)] \cdot t$

Let us consider the following trace $t_6 = [a_1 3 a'_3 2 a''_3 2 a_3 4]$ belonging to a possible implementation of our contract. The actions a'_3 and a''_3 are internal actions of the implementation (for instance the seller obtains the delivery company list related to the shipment address a'_3 and sends the shipment info to the deliverer a''_3). Therefore, the result of $\mathsf{hide}_{ACT}(t_6) = [a_1 3 a_3 8]$, where the internal actions have been omitted and the intermediate time delays are $2 + 2 + 4 = 8$.

Now, we have all the machinery needed to define our conformance relation. We will consider that an implementation satisfies a contract if a) there is at least one trace that executes all the actions expressed in the obligations in due time, and no actions from the prohibitions; that is, satisfying all the obligations and prohibitions expressed in the contract, and b) if at any time a violation occurs, then it will be repaired in the future. In our example, the ideal implementation should be able to "allow the user to at least pay with either credit card or Paypal in 3 days, and then, the seller send the item in time". This ideal behavior is represented by condition a), since it gathers all contract obligations and prohibitions. However we should be most realistic and think that all systems are prone to errors, then implementations can as well fail in some occasions. But if they do, then they should been able to recover somehow. That is the idea behind the second condition, that is, if a seller does not send the item, he should at least refund the buyer.

Definition 7. *Let us consider a consistent contract specification C and an implementation I, we say that I conforms C, written I conf C, iff*

- *For any $cn \in CN$ there exists $t \in \text{tr}(I)$ such that $\text{hide}_{ACT}(t) \in \text{clean}(C) \cup \text{good}(C)$ and $cn \in \text{S}(I, \text{hide}_{ACT}(t))$.*
- *If there exists $t \in \text{tr}(I)$ and $cn \in CN$ with $cn \in \text{V}(C, \text{hide}_{ACT}(t))$, there exists t' such that $t \cdot t' \in \text{tr}(I)$ such that $\text{hide}_{ACT}(t \cdot t') \in \text{tr}(C)$ and $cn \in \text{S}(C, \text{hide}_{ACT}(t \cdot t'))$.*

Let us consider the following implementations I_1, I_2 and I_3 where $\text{tr}(I_1) = \{t_1, t_2\}$, $\text{tr}(I_2) = \{t_4\}$ and $\text{tr}(I_3) = \{t_1, t_4\}$ of our running example $NTA_{P\&S}$. The implementation I_1 satisfies the first condition since t_1 is good and clean and satisfies all the $cn \in CN$, although it does not satisfy the second because t_2 violates clause 5, which is never repaired. Thus implementation I_1 does not conform to the given contract. Regarding I_2, we have the opposite situation, here trace t_4 violates clause 5, but reparation R_1 is now applied to refund the buyer. Therefore this trace satisfies the second condition but not the first because it does not include all $cn \in CN$. Finally, implementation I_3 is the only one that conforms the contract written as I_3 conf $NTA_{P\&S}$, since it includes t_1 and t_2, which fulfil both conditions.

5   Design of the Monitoring Software

To follow the conformance relationship given before, it is necessary to generate all possible traces from a given contract and implementation, which in some cases is impossible since recursion can result in an infinite set of traces. To avoid this problem we use a different approach that we call "on-the-fly" monitoring. Instead of producing a set of all traces, we check step-by-step if the trace produced by the implementation can be produced by the given contract in terms of its equivalent automata. In this case the implementation is not given via an NTA automata, as it has been stated above that the conformance relationship is a black box relation, where only the information present in the traces is taken into account, that is, the actions specified in the contract and the time of its executions. On the contrary, our goal is to monitor implementations of given contracts.

The algorithm implemented in the monitor is based on the forward reachability algorithm implemented in the model checking UPPAAL tool [8]. This algorithm is presented in Algorithm 5.1, which accepts as the input parameter the trace[6] to be checked. The initialization declares the *Waiting* list of states. The main structure is a repeat-until that ends when the waiting list is empty. The statements in this structure start by getting the first state in the waiting list and the first part of the trace, i.e., the first action-delay tuple. Afterwards, the algorithm checks for all the transitions starting from this state using the action and delay obtained from the trace. If this action and delay corresponds with the last action and delay in the trace two situations are studied. The first codifies that in case a violation have occurred but not repaired then the contract is breached and therefore notified to the involved parties. However if there have been no violations or they are properly repaired then the trace conforms the contract. Once these two cases have been studied every new reached state is added to the waiting list. Finally, the state already visited and the action and delay studied are discarded. Note that, the state is not removed until all their descendants have been added to the waiting list; but if there is no descendant it is removed as well. This last chance can result in an empty waiting list and therefore a negative response, that is, the trace would not conform the contract.

Algorithm 5.1: MONITORING($Trace$)

$Trace := \{(a_0, d_0), (a_1, d_1) \ldots (a_n, d_n)\}$;
$Waiting := (n_0, v_0, Cla_0)$;
repeat
    $\Big\{$ get$(n, v, Cla) : Cla := (Vio, Sat, Per)$ from Waiting;
    get(a, d) from Trace;
    for each transition $(\overline{n}, v, Cla) \xrightarrow{(a,d)} (\overline{n}', v', Cla')$
    do $\Big\{$ **then** $\Big\{$ **if** (a, d) equal to (a_n, d_n)
            if $Vio \neq \{\} \wedge Vio \not\subseteq Sat$
            then return Not;
            else return Yes;
    add$(\overline{n}', v', cl')$ to Waiting;
    remove$(\overline{n}, v, cla)$ from Waiting;
    remove(a, d) from Traces;
until $Waiting = \{\}$;
return Not;

The conformance notion defined above varies from the algorithm given in this case since it does not have access to all of the traces belonging either to the contract or its implementation.

---

[6] The trace is shortened according to the delays before treated due to latencies in the communicating media and all actions not belonging to the contract are *hide*.

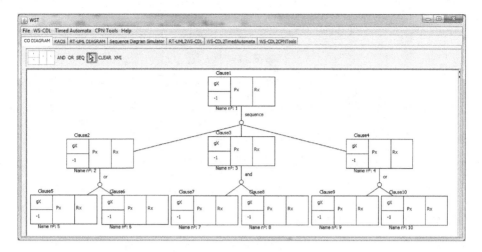

Fig. 3. WST plugin to model *C-O Diagrams*

Our current work is focused on the development of a plugin for WST[7] [2] implementing the transformations and monitoring system. A prototype of this plugin can be seen in Fig. 3. This plugin will be available in the next release of the tool and it is aimed at helping users to model the system and perform the automatic translation to be used by the monitor. In addition, WST is a general framework to develop Web Service Transformations using XSLT technologies applied to the area of web services and any others related to this main area of application. The objective of this tool is the inclusion of formal validation and verification techniques in the life cycle of software development. This tool already performs several translations from languages such as WS-CDL and WS-BPEL or visual models including UML sequence diagrams and KAOS goal models into the formalism supported by UPPAAL and CPN-tools[8].

As a proof of concept the Online Auctioning Process has been implemented. This implementation consists of the diagram classes shown in Fig. 4. Here, however some details have been hidden for the sake of readability, we can still see the design patterns observer (white) and bidder (green), which have been used to implement the example. The design pattern observer is divided into two parts; the observer and the subject. In our system, we have identified the subject to observe as the Auctioning Service and the state to be observed as the monitor (yellow). The Auctioning Service notifies whether the trace of the system is correct or not. Whereas the observers are the sellers and buyers that will be notified in case the contract is breached. This design pattern is known in the web service context as a subscribe/publisher notification protocol, indeed the WS-Notify language defines all the needed machinery. On the other hand, the bidder is a pattern to manage the auction itself and the bidder class is merged with the observers, i.e., the sellers and buyers.

---

[7] Available at http://dsi.uclm.es/retics/wst/
[8] Available at http://www.cpntools.org/.

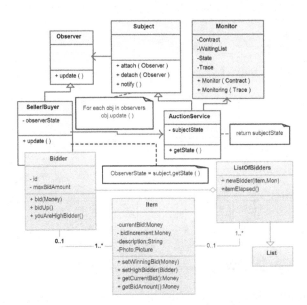

Fig. 4. UML Class Diagram to implement the Online Auction Process

6 Conclusions

In this paper we have used the conformance relationship based on the formal semantics given by NTAs (Network of Timed Automata) for normative contracts written in terms of C-O diagrams in order to implement a monitoring mechanism for web services. For that purpose, we have introduced an on-the-fly algorithm to check if implementation traces either satisfy all obligations and prohibitions stated in contracts, or in the event of a violation, the corresponding reparation is executed. These implementations are said to conform to the contract. We have also implemented our running example as a proof of concept. Furthermore a new plugin for the tool WST has been presented. This plugin allows the design of normative contracts in terms of C-O Diagrams.

As a future work, we plan to improve the implementation of the conformance relationship detecting, those traces that include the performance of all the obligations and the absence of all prohibitions. The idea is to keep a record of how adequate the implementation is with respect to the contract. However, even if, these traces are still present, the presence of traces non consisting with the contract is sufficient to determine that the contract is violated.

References

1. Alur, R., Dill, D.L.: A Theory of Timed Automata. Theoretical Computer Science 126(2), 183–235 (1994)
2. Cambronero, M.E., Díaz, G., Martínez, E., Valero, V., Tobarra, M.L.: WST: a tool supporting timed composite Web Services Model transformation. Simulation 88(3), 349–364 (2012)

3. Chiu, D., Cheung, S., Till, S.: A Three-Layer Architecture for E-Contract Enforcement in an E-Service Environment. In: Proceedings of the 36th Hawaii International Conference on System Sciences (HICSS-36), pp. 74–83 (2003)

4. Díaz, G., Llana, L., Valero, V., Mateo, J.A.: Conformance Verification of Normative Specifications using C-O Diagrams. In: Proceedings Sixth Workshop on Formal Languages and Analysis of Contract-Oriented Software, FLACOS, pp. 1–10 (2012)

5. Dignum, F., Weigand, H.: Modelling Communication between Cooperative Systems. In: Iivari, J., Rossi, M., Lyytinen, K. (eds.) CAiSE 1995. LNCS, vol. 932, pp. 140–153. Springer, Heidelberg (1995)

6. Governatori, G., Milosevic, Z., Sadiq, S.: Compliance checking between business processes and business contracts. In: Proceedings of the 10th IEEE Conference on Enterprise Distributed Object Computing, pp. 221–232 (2006)

7. Krishna, P.R., Karlapalem, K., Dani, A.R.: From Contract to E-Contracts: Modeling and Enactment. Information Technology and Management 6(4), 363–387 (2005)

8. Larsen, K.G., Pettersson, Z., Wang, Y.: UPPAAL in a Nutshell. STTT: International Journal on Software Tools for Technlogy Transfer 1(1-2), 134–152 (1997)

9. Lomuscio, A., Qu, H., Solanki, M.: Towards verifying contract regulated service composition. In: Proceedings of IEEE International Conference on Web Services (ICWS 2008), pp. 254–261 (2008)

10. Marjanovic, O., Milosevic, Z.: Towards formal modeling of e-Contracts. In: Proceedings of 5th IEEE International Enterprise Distributed Object Computing Conference, pp. 59–68 (2001)

11. Martínez, E., Díaz, G., Emilia Cambronero, M.: Contractually Compliant Service Compositions. In: Kappel, G., Maamar, Z., Motahari-Nezhad, H.R. (eds.) ICSOC 2011. LNCS, vol. 7084, pp. 636–644. Springer, Heidelberg (2011)

12. Martínez, E., Díaz, G., Cambronero, M.E., Schneider, G.: A Model for Visual Specification of e-Contracts. In: The 7th IEEE International Conference on Services Computing (IEEE SCC 2010), pp. 1–8 (2010)

13. Martínez, E., Díaz, G., Cambronero, M.E., Schneider, G.: Specification and Verification of Normative Specifications using C-O Diagrams (2012), http://dsi.uclm.es/descargas/thecnicalreports/DIAB-12-05-1/TSE11.pdf

14. McNamara, P.: Deontic Logic. In: Gabbay, D.M., Woods, J. (eds.) Handbook of the History of Logic, vol. 7, pp. 197–289. North-Holland Publishing (2006)

15. Okika, J.C., Ravn, A.P.: Classification of SOA Contract Specification Languages. In: 2008 IEEE International Conference on Web Services (ICWS 2008), pp. 433–440. IEEE Computer Society (2008)

16. Tretmans, J.: Testing Concurrent Systems: A Formal Approach. In: Baeten, J.C.M., Mauw, S. (eds.) CONCUR 1999. LNCS, vol. 1664, pp. 46–65. Springer, Heidelberg (1999)

Service-Oriented Distributed Applications in the Future Internet: The Case for Interaction Paradigm Interoperability

Nikolaos Georgantas[1], Georgios Bouloukakis[1],
Sandrine Beauche[2], and Valérie Issarny[1]

[1] Inria Paris-Rocquencourt, France
`firstname.lastname@inria.fr`
[2] Ambientic, France
`sandrine.beauche@ambientic.com`

Abstract. The essential issue of interoperability in distributed systems is becoming even more pressing in the Future Internet, where complex applications will be composed from extremely heterogeneous systems. Open system integration paradigms, such as service oriented architecture (SOA) and enterprise service bus (ESB), have provided answers to the interoperability requirement. However, when it comes to integrating systems featuring heterogeneous interaction paradigms, such as client-service, publish-subscribe and tuple space, existing solutions are typically ad hoc and partial, applying to specific interaction protocol technologies. In this paper, we introduce an interoperability solution based on abstraction and merging of the common high-level semantics of interaction paradigms, which is sufficiently general and extensible to accommodate many different protocol technologies. We apply this solution to revisit the SOA- and ESB-based integration of heterogeneous distributed systems.

Keywords: Interoperability, interaction paradigms, interaction abstractions, service oriented architecture, enterprise service bus.

1 Introduction

The Future Internet (FI) is emerging as, among others, a global application space where People, Services and Things will be always-connected and interact in numerous ways. Accordingly, complex distributed applications in the FI will be based, to a large extent, on the open integration of extremely heterogeneous systems, such as lightweight embedded systems (e.g., sensors, actuators and networks of them), mobile systems (e.g., smartphone applications), and resource-rich IT systems (e.g., systems hosted on enterprise servers and Cloud infrastructures). These heterogeneous system domains differ significantly in terms of interaction paradigms, communication protocols, and data representation models, which are most often provided by supporting middleware platforms. In particular with regard to middleware-supported interaction, the client-service (CS), publish-subscribe (PS), and tuple space (TS) paradigms are among the most

K.-K. Lau, W. Lamersdorf, and E. Pimentel (Eds.): ESOCC 2013, LNCS 8135, pp. 134–148, 2013.
© Springer-Verlag Berlin Heidelberg 2013

widely employed ones, with numerous related middleware platforms, such as: Web Services, Java RMI for CS; JMS, SIENA for PS [1, 2]; and JavaSpaces, Lime for TS [3, 4]. In the following, we outline a representative application scenario, where a complex distributed application needs to be devised by integrating heterogeneous networked systems that interact with differing interaction paradigms.

Search and Rescue (S&R) operations after a disaster, such as a flood or earthquake, are carried out in hazardous environments and require personnel from multiple agencies (e.g., fire-fighters, police) to coordinate. To detect survivors, sensors are installed at various places of the hazardous area. Such sensors communicate their location. S&R personnel also notify at short intervals of their current positions via their PDAs. Upon sensing some life sign, sensor nodes send out notifications. At the same time, nearby light-emitting actuators start lighting the place to facilitate the rescuing effort. Sensors, PDAs, and actuators interact among them and with external actors via a TS. TS location and life sign data are sent via CS invocations to a planning service that recommends at real time the optimal deployment of rescue forces. This output is notified via a PS system to the coordinator of the operation on her smartphone and also to a number of control/monitoring centers. The coordinator may approve and command S&R personnel via the PS system and the TS system to rush into the spot.

To enable such a scenario, the heterogeneity between the involved system domains needs to be tackled. Existing cross-domain interoperability efforts are based on, e.g., bridging communication protocols [5], wrapping systems behind standard technology interfaces [6], and providing common API abstractions [7–10]. In particular, such techniques have been applied by the two currently dominant system integration paradigms, that is, service oriented architecture (SOA) and enterprise service bus (ESB) [11]. Both SOA and ESB employ the CS paradigm. Certainly, there are extensions, such as event-driven SOA [11] or industrial-strength ESBs supporting the PS paradigm. Additionally, research efforts have proposed the TS paradigm as interaction substrate for Web services or for ESBs [9, 12]. Nevertheless, most of these cross-paradigm interoperability efforts are ad hoc and partial, applying to specific cases. On the other hand, interaction paradigms have been widely studied, with theoretical approaches providing them with formal semantics by relying on concurrency theory, process algebras and architectural connectors (e.g., see [13]). These approaches typically identify semantics for individual paradigms but not cross-paradigm semantics.

In this paper[1], we introduce a model-based system integration solution that can deal with diverse existing systems, focusing in particular on integrating their heterogeneous interaction paradigms. Our systematic approach is carried out in two stages. First, a middleware platform is abstracted under a corresponding interaction paradigm among the three base ones, i.e., CS, PS and TS. To this aim, we elicit a *connector model* for each paradigm, which comprehensively cov-

---

[1] This work has been partially supported by the European Union's Seventh Framework Programme FP7/2007-2013 under grant agreement number 257178 (project CHOReOS).

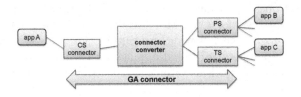

Fig. 1. GA-based connector interoperability

ers its essential semantics. Then, these three models are abstracted further into a single *generic application (GA) connector* model, which encompasses their common interaction semantics. Based on GA, we build abstract *connector converters* that enable interconnecting the base interaction paradigms. A high-level representation of our approach is depicted in Figure 1. We realize our interoperability solution as an *extensible service bus (XSB)*, which is an abstract service bus that employs GA as its common bus protocol. Furthermore, we provide an implementation of the XSB, building upon existing SOA and ESB realizations. Based on our XSB platform, we propose a comprehensive solution to the peer-to-peer integration of services relying on heterogeneous interaction paradigms into complex applications. Our overall approach generalizes the way to design and implement service-oriented distributed applications, where the employed interaction paradigms are explicitly represented and systematically integrated. We demonstrate the applicability of our solution by implementing the scenario introduced above, and evaluate it in terms of extensibility and performance.

The rest of this paper is structured as follows. In Section 2, we introduce our connector models for abstracting and interconnecting interaction paradigms. In Section 3, we present the application of our models to the XSB solution, as well as its implementation. Then, in Section 4, we discuss the results of our evaluation. We finally complement this paper with a comparison of our approach with related work in Section 5, and conclude, also discussing future work, in Section 6.

2   Abstractions for Interaction Paradigm Interoperability

In this section, we identify the semantics of the three principal interaction paradigms, i.e., CS, PS and TS, and elicit a connector model for each paradigm (Section 2.1). Our modeling proposition is the outcome of an extensive survey of these paradigms as well as related middleware platforms in the literature. In a second step, we introduce our GA connector model, which enables cross-paradigm interoperability (Section 2.2). Before getting into the specifics of each connector, we briefly introduce in the following our global approach to connector modeling and point out the specific focus of this paper.

Our models represent the essential semantics of interaction paradigms, concerning *space coupling, time coupling* [14] and *concurrency*. Space coupling determines how peer applications interconnected via the connector identify each other and, consequently, how *interaction elements* (e.g., messages for a CS connector) are routed from one peer to the other. Time coupling determines if peers need to be present and available at the same time for an interaction or if the interaction can take place in phases occurring at different times. Concurrency characterizes the exclusive or shared access semantics of the virtual channel established between interacting peers. These three categories of semantics are of primary importance, because these are end-to-end semantics: when interconnecting different connectors, we seek to map and preserve these semantics.

We represent interaction paradigm semantics in the connector's abstract *API (Application Programming Interface)*. This API presents the programming model supported by the connector and offered to the peer applications that use the connector for their interaction. The API is a set of *primitives* expressed as operations or functions supported by the middleware. This abstract API can be refined to a specific middleware platform by mapping to the primitives and incorporating the data structures and types of the middleware platform. Besides a connector's API, we introduce an abstract *interface description language (IDL)* for specifying the open interfaces of systems that rely on middleware represented by the specific connector. Our IDLs are largely inspired from WSDL. We specify the IDLs conceptually, while we have also implemented each one of them as an XML schema document. Based on the flexibility of XML schema, an IDL can be easily refined in order to enable the description of a concrete system that is based on the connector, e.g., we can refine the abstract XML elements into the precise data structures and types of the specific middleware and system.

Based on the informal identification of semantics as discussed in the previous, we further specify the connector's *formal behavioral semantics* in terms of LTS (Labeled Transition Systems). This formal behavior specification focuses on time coupling and concurrency semantics, while space coupling semantics is mainly represented by the connector's API and IDL. Additionally, we *formally verify* the correctness of these behavioral specifications with respect to time coupling and concurrency properties expressed in LTL temporal logic. This allows stating the correctness of our base connector models with respect to the semantics that they must have. This further enables identifying the semantics of the GA connector derived from the interconnection of base connectors.

The focus of this paper is the application of our connector modeling and analysis approach to the practical integration of heterogeneous services. Hence, and due to space limitations, we introduce in the following sections our connectors only informally – concentrating on their space coupling, time coupling and concurrency semantics – and mainly in terms of their respective IDLs, which are used to describe open interfaces of services.

2.1   Connector Models for Base Interaction Paradigms

This section introduces connector models for the CS, PS and TS paradigms.

Client-Service Connector. The CS connector model integrates a wide range of semantics, covering both the *non queue-based messaging* and *remote procedure call* paradigms. In terms of *space coupling* between two interacting peers, CS requires that the sender must hold a reference of the receiver. With respect to *time coupling*, both entities must be connected at the time of the interaction.

CS-based service interface			
element	sub-element	attributes	S&R scenario - planning service
message	data fields	semantics, <u>name</u>, type	{sensorId, sensorType, locationData, lifeSign}
main scope of message	service system identity	<u>name</u>, address type, address value	planningService
sub-scope of message	operation	semantics, <u>name</u>, type, value	planOperation
interaction semantics of message		{one-way, notification, request-response, solicit-response}	request

Fig. 2. CS IDL

Regarding *concurrency*, a dedicated virtual channel is used between a sender and a receiver: as long as servers do not have an excessive load of messages to process, all messages sent by different clients will be received by the designated servers. CS semantics is reflected on the CS-IDL presented in Figure 2, where the last column presents the example of the planning service of the S&R scenario (note that we provide an example for the underlined attributes of the third column). *Message* is the essential interaction element in CS-IDL; its interaction semantics is borrowed from WSDL. The main new concept here is that a message is assigned two qualifiers, *main scope* and *sub-scope*, which are, in inverse order, the operation served by the message and the URL of the service providing the operation. These qualifiers delimit the set of peer entities that will receive the message – actually only one service and, more finely, its specific operation.

Publish-Subscribe Connector. The PS connector model abstracts comprehensively different types of publish-subscribe systems, such as *queue-*, *topic-* and *content-based systems* [14]. In PS, multiple peers interact via an intermediate *broker*. Publishers produce events, which are received by peers that have previously subscribed for receiving the specific events. In terms of *space coupling*, interacting PS peers do not need to know each other; e.g., in topic-based systems, events are diffused to subscribers only based on the topic. With respect to *time coupling*, peers do not need to be present at the same time: subscribers may be disconnected at the time that events are published; they can receive the pending events when reconnected and before the events expire. Regarding *concurrency*, the broker maintains a dedicated buffer for each subscriber. Hence, all published non expired events will be eventually received by interested subscribers. We note that standardization of open PS interfaces (in the way SOA has done for CS systems) is far less developed. Hence, to introduce our PS-IDL (Fig. 3), we rely on our PS connector semantics, which has been extracted from a wide range of PS systems. The figure includes the example of the coordinator of the S&R scenario. The essential interaction element in PS-IDL is *event*; its interaction semantics denotes whether this event is published or received by the system in question and its lifetime, determined by *lease*. An event's *main scope* and *sub-scope* are the PS system URL and the *filter*, respectively, used for qualifying the event. *Filter* may represent a queue, topic or content. Similarly to CS, these qualifiers delimit the set of peers that will receive the event.

PS-based service interface			
element	sub-element	attributes	S&R scenario - coordinator
event	data fields	semantics, name, type	{personnelId, personnelType, locationData}
main scope of event	pub-sub system identity	name, address type, address value	SRcoordinationBroker
sub-scope of event	filter	semantics incl. {queue, topic, content}, name, type, value	topic, planningServiceInput
interaction semantics of event	produce/consume	{publish, subscribe}	subscribe
	lease	type, value	forever

Fig. 3. PS IDL

TS-based service interface			
element	sub-element	attributes	S&R scenario - sensor
tuple	data fields	semantics, name, type	{sensorId, sensorType, locationData, lifeSign}
main scope of tuple	tuple space system identity	name, address type, address value	SRdataSpace
sub-scope of tuple	extent	semantics, name, type, value	-
	template	semantics, name, type, value	sensorTemplate
interaction semantics of tuple	produce/consume	{write, take, read}	write
	consume policy	{one, all}	-
	lease	type, value	forever

Fig. 4. TS IDL

Tuple Space Connector. The *TS connector model* is based on the classic tuple space semantics [15]. In TS, multiple peers interact via an intermediate *shared data space*. Peers can post data into the space and retrieve data from it, either by taking a copy or removing the data. Data take the form of tuples; a tuple is an ordered list of typed elements. Data are retrieved by matching based on a tuple *template*, which may define values or expressions for some of the elements. Regarding *space coupling*, TS peers may write and read/take data from the space with no knowledge of each other. As for *time coupling* semantics, peers can act without any synchronization. With respect to *concurrency*, peers have access to a single, commonly shared copy of the data. Then, concurrent access semantics of the data space is non-deterministic: the order among accessing peers is determined arbitrarily. Hence, if a peer that intends to take specific data is given access to the space before other peers that are interested in the same data, the latter will never access these data. The TS-IDL is depicted in Figure 4, including the example of a sensor of the S&R scenario. Same as for PS systems, there are no standard open interfaces for TS systems, hence we rely on the generality of our TS connector. The essential interaction element in TS-IDL is *tuple*. Its interaction semantics denotes whether this tuple is produced or consumed by the system in question and its lifetime, determined by *lease*. In the case of tuple consumption, only *one* or *all* tuples matching a template may be retrieved. A tuple's *main scope* and *sub-scope* are the TS system URL and the pair {*extent, template*}, respectively, used for qualifying the tuple. *Extent* may be used to access only an identified part of the shared space. These qualifiers delimit the set of peer entities that will potentially receive the tuple.

2.2   Generic Application Connector Model

Given the three base connector models, we now introduce the *Generic Applica-tion (GA)* connector model. Our objective is to devise a single generic connector that comprehensively represents the end-to-end cross-paradigm interaction se-mantics of application peers that employ different base connectors.

We identify two main high-level API primitives for the GA connector: (i) *post* employed by a peer for sending data to one or more other peers, and (ii) *get* employed by a peer for receiving data. For example, a PS *publish* primitive can be abstracted by a *post*. We identify *space coupling* semantics for the GA connec-tor by appropriately mapping among the space coupling semantics of the base connectors. Hence, we define the essential interaction element for GA to be *data*. *Data* can represent any one of CS *message*, PS *event* or TS *tuple*. Same as for the base connectors, GA uses the qualifiers *main scope* and *sub-scope* to characterize a data element. These qualifiers can represent the corresponding qualifiers of any of the CS, PS or TS. Hence, GA's {*main scope, sub-scope*} maps, for CS, to {*CS system identity, operation*}, for PS, it maps to {*PS system identity, filter*}, and for TS, to {*TS system identity, {extent, template}*}. In this way, GA generalizes and unifies addressing for the different interaction paradigms.

In order to identify the *time coupling* and *concurrency* semantics of GA and construct a converter among the base connectors (see Fig. 1), we have built upon the formal method of *protocol conversion via projections* [16]. According to this method, conversion between two different protocols is possible if both protocols can be projected (where projection is an abstraction defined as a set of transformations on the protocol LTS) to a *functionally sufficient* common *image protocol*. Then, the end-to-end protocol of the interconnection of the two protocols is this image protocol. However, this work is out of the scope of this paper. In the following, we present informally some of the outcomes of this work.

In the case of CS-PS-TS interconnection, GA is the common image protocol and represents the common time coupling and concurrency semantics. However, as shown in Section 2.1, time coupling and concurrency semantics of CS, PS, TS are not directly compatible. In particular, we saw that for successful interaction, for CS, the CS server must be online, for PS, a subscription is necessary, and for TS, all interested peers must be allowed to read the shared data before one of the peers takes them. This means that, in Fig. 1, *app A, B* and *C* may assume and perceive different semantics, which can be problematic for the composed application. The solution is to constrain the semantics of the heterogeneous con-nectors to a compatible subset *by application-side enforcement*. This means that if each one of *app A, B* and *C* enforces with its behavior the identified condition for successful interaction proper to its connector, common time coupling and concurrency semantics will apply to the end-to-end GA connector. In another example, a CS two-way interaction does not have an equivalent in the PS and TS connectors. In this case, the PS and TS applications should take care of enforc-ing the additional semantics. In general, CS is the more restrictive of the three paradigms, while PS and TS allow more flexibility to the applications; hence, the PS and TS applications should apply the missing semantics, if required by

GA-based service interface			
element	sub-element	attribute	S&R scenario - coordinator
data	data fields	semantics, _name_, type	{personnelId, personnelType, locationData}
main scope of data	system identity	_name_, address type, address value	SRcoordinationBroker
sub-scope of data	data qualifier(s)	semantics, _name_, type, value	topic, planningServiceInput
interaction semantics of data		{post, get, post-get, get-post}	get

Fig. 5. GA IDL

the CS application. While each case should be treated individually, we can state in general that in a CS-PS-TS interconnection, the resulting end-to-end GA semantics is the one of CS.

Based on the above and by mapping among the IDLs of the base connectors, we elicit the IDL for the GA connector as shown in Fig. 5. We can see that interaction semantics of _data_ corresponds to the one of CS. The figure includes the example of the coordinator of the S&R scenario as mapped from PS-IDL (see Fig. 3) to GA-IDL. Concluding, we point out three important features of GA that result from the previous. First, although GA semantically intersects the CS, PS and TS paradigms, it represents _rich_ interaction functionality, which means that interconnecting CS, PS and TS systems – under certain identified conditions – results in satisfactorily functional systems. Second, GA-IDL, which unifies the description of heterogeneous systems, is not heavier or more complex than the native CS/PS/TS-IDL descriptions. Third, GA applies at the middleware layer, and hence it allows _full expressivity_ – only subject to the intersected end-to-end interaction semantics – of application-layer languages that specify the internal or external behavior of application components, such as WS-BPEL.

3   eXtensible Service Bus

We apply our connector models and resulting middleware interoperability method to an enhanced service bus paradigm, the _eXtensible Service Bus (XSB)_. XSB features richer interaction semantics than common ESBs to deal effectively with the increased Future Internet heterogeneity. Moreover, from its very conception, XSB incorporates special consideration for the cross-integration of heterogeneous interaction paradigms. In particular, XSB is an abstract bus that prescribes only the high-level semantics of the common bus protocol, which is the GA semantics. Services relying on different interaction paradigms can be plugged into XSB by employing _binding components (BCs)_ that adapt between their native middleware and the common bus protocol. This adaptation is based on the abstractions discussed in Section 2, and in particular on the conversion between the native middleware, the corresponding CS/PS/TS abstraction, and the GA abstraction, as depicted in Figure 6. Hence, XSB BCs are half-converters in relation to Fig. 1.

XSB, being an abstract bus, can have different implementations. This means that it needs to be complemented with a _substrate bus_ which supports deployment of services and a communication protocol that implements GA semantics.

This substrate bus may be designed and built from scratch or, alternatively, an existing one can be used, as long as GA primitives can be conveyed on top of the available protocol. The latter solution can be attractive, as it enables XSB realizations in different domains. We provide a generic *architectural framework* for XSB. This enables implementing XSB on top of a substrate bus of choice, and offers systematic support for building XSB BCs for different middleware platforms that apply one of the CS, PS, TS interaction paradigms. Furthermore, the framework can be extended with support for a new interaction paradigm. In the following, we present our architectural framework and the implementations we carried out by using this framework.

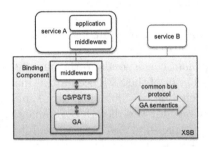

Fig. 6. eXtensible Service Bus

Architectural Framework. The architecture of an XSB BC as provided by our architectural framework is depicted in Fig. 7, where the main components are the *xDL Processor*, *Core Engine*, and *Envelope for Substrate Bus*. On its lower side, the BC communicates with the substrate bus, while on its upper side, it communicates with the middleware of the corresponding service by employing an instance of the same middleware, e.g., as an external library. In order to support extensibility, each component of an XSB BC is designed with three *architectural levels*: the first one is the most generic and can be refined stepwise into the two other levels, where refinement refers to class inheritance and XML schema transformation. The *generic level* provides APIs and functionalities that are shared among all supported interaction paradigms. The *interaction paradigm level* specializes the APIs and functionalities of the previous level for each one of the CS, PS and TS interaction paradigms. The *middleware platform level* specializes the APIs and functionalities of the previous level for a concrete middleware. In the following, we briefly sketch the main components of an XSB BC, and how a developer can make use of them.

The *xDL Processor* processes the descriptions of services deployed on the XSB. It performs both parsing of CS/PS/TS-IDL descriptions and mapping of them to GA-IDL descriptions, where the latter relies on XSLT-based transformations [17]. We use the XML schema extensibility mechanisms to specialize these functions from one architectural level to another. The *Core Engine* provides mechanisms to: (i) transform and map between service data and CS/PS/TS/GA XML data; (ii) execute service primitives, and map between them and CS/PS/TS

/GA primitives; and (iii) manage connections to the service middleware. The above mechanisms cooperate with each other, as well as with the xDL Processor for retrieving service information. The *Envelope for Substrate Bus* makes the BCs deployable on top of different substrate buses. It provides the mechanisms to: (i) communicate GA primitives over substrate bus connections, while exchanging them with the Core Engine; and (ii) manage the lifecycle of the service on the substrate bus, after retrieving service information from the xDL Processor. These mechanisms can be refined to support a new substrate bus.

Use by the Developer. Targeting facilitated extensibility of our solution, we provide a highly-optimized design, where the common reusable part of the BC functionalities is already implemented by the different architectural levels, leaving to the developer the required specialization for introducing a new service, middleware platform, or interaction paradigm. More specifically, a developer wishing to deploy a new service on the XSB should write an xDL description of the service, and then invoke the tools provided by our solution to generate a corresponding BC deployable on the bus. A developer wishing to develop an XSB BC supporting a new middleware platform should refine the interaction paradigm levels of the xDL Processor and Core Engine. A developer wishing to support a new interaction paradigm should refine the generic levels of the xDL Processor and Core Engine.

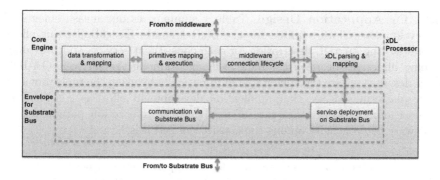

Fig. 7. Binding Component architecture

Implementation. We have implemented XSB on top of the EasyESB[2] enterprise service bus, which is an open source lightweight service bus. In particular, we have refined our architectural framework to support building XSB BCs on top of EasyESB, and have provided interaction paradigm level BCs for CS, PS and TS. We demonstrate the applicability of our approach by implementing the S&R scenario. Our scenario implementation integrates: (1) sensors, actuators and personnel equipment communicating over a Jini JavaSpaces TS[3]; (2) the

---

[2] https://research.linagora.com/display/easyesb
[3] http://www.jini.org/wiki/JavaSpaces_Specification

planning service implemented as a JMEDS DPWS Web Service[4]; and (3) a JMS
PS system based on Apache ActiveMQ[5] that the coordinator of the operation
uses to receive recommendations and to send commands. We provide support
for the three mentioned middleware platforms by producing appropriate middleware platform level BCs. Our XSB prototype implementation is available as
open source software at `http://xsb.inria.fr`.

4   Evaluation

Based on the implementation of our solution discussed in Section 3, we evaluate our approach with respect to three criteria. First, we evaluate the effort
for the application developer and accordingly the provided support by our solution for developing complex applications from the integration of services that
employ heterogeneous interaction paradigms. Second, we have designed our architectural framework with particular consideration for its extensibility. Thus,
we evaluate the easiness in integrating new middleware platforms, in particular with regard to building related binding components (BCs). Third, we have
introduced a number of extensions to the typical SOA & ESB infrastructure,
such as transfer of GA primitives as payload of ESB communication primitives,
and, more importantly, runtime model transformations inside the BC. Hence,
we evaluate the performance of our solution and the time overhead introduced.
We discuss our evaluation results in the following.

Effort for Application Design. Table 1 summarizes our measurements of
the development effort required for the S&R scenario. Essentially, this effort
includes writing an xDL description for each constituent service, and providing
mapping directives between the data exchanged among the services. GA-IDL
service descriptions are then generated automatically by using the tools provided
by our platform. We see that application development effort is considerably
low, since our platform takes care of resolving the interaction paradigm and
middleware heterogeneity among the constituent services.

Table 1. Development effort for the application developer

	xDL description (XML lines)	Generated desc. (XML lines)	Mapping directives (XML lines)
Java Spaces system	148	98	72
DPWS system	50	61	76
JMS system	209	90	78
Total	407	249	226

Extensibility. Referring to the architectural framework of Fig. 7, we measure
the effort for building a BC for the JMS Apache ActiveMQ middleware platform.

---

[4] `http://ws4d.e-technik.uni-rostock.de/jmeds/`

[5] `http://activemq.apache.org/`

Table 2. Development effort for the JMS binding component

	Lines of code	XML schema (lines)	Configuration (XML lines)
xDL Processor	7520	2617	111
Core Engine	9993	219	137
Envelope for Substrate Bus	508	0	0
Total	18021	2836	248
Written by the developer	1162	191	12
Effort	6%	6%	4%

Table 3. Interaction latency on the bus for each interconnection

Interconnection	Latency (ms)
one-way CS - CS via EasyESB	258
one-way CS - CS via XSB	261,5
CS - PS via XSB	283
CS - TS via XSB	276
PS - TS via XSB	298

Table 2 summarizes this effort, in terms of implemented numbers of: (1) Lines of code, (2) XML schema lines regarding the xDL descriptions, and (3) XML lines of configuration files for the architectural framework. We have performed our measurements with the Metrics 1.3.6 Eclipse plugin[6]. We provide measurements for each one of the three components of the framework, as well as the ratio of the effort specific to the JMS platform (refinement of subcomponents) over the total effort (i.e., including the generic code written once and reusable each time). We see that considerably small effort, no more than 6% of the total effort, is required for the integration of a new middleware platform. This points out the significant support offered, resulting in considerable easiness for integrating new middleware platforms and related high extensibility of our approach.

Performance. We measure execution times for a number of layouts: (i) one-way and two-way interaction inside our implemented CS system; (ii) end-to-end interaction between a publisher and a subscriber inside our implemented PS system; (iii) end-to-end interaction between a writer and a reader inside our implemented TS system; (iv) one-way and two-way interaction between two CS peers via EasyESB; and (v) interaction between all pair combinations of CS, PS and TS peers via XSB. We repeat each measurement a 100 times and calculate mean values. Based on these experiments, we evaluate the latency overhead introduced by the EasyESB for an one-way CS-CS communication, and the latency overhead introduced by the XSB for an one-way CS-CS as well as all other pair combinations of communication. Our results are summarized in Table 3. We see that the latency overhead introduced by the XSB for a CS-CS interconnection is only 1% greater than the latency overhead introduced by the

---

[6] http://metrics.sourceforge.net

EasyESB itself. When conversion between heterogeneous interaction paradigms is involved, the XSB latency overhead ranges from 7% to 15,5%, where we note that we always compare with the EasyESB CS-CS homogeneous interconnection, since EasyESB support for other interaction paradigms is not available. We see that the performance cost introduced by the XSB remains at reasonable levels.

5   Related Work

Distributed system interoperability approaches at the middleware level are classically based on bridging communication protocols, wrapping systems behind standard technology interfaces, and providing common API abstractions. Most efforts focus on a single interaction paradigm, which is already a hard problem. Nevertheless, there are some solutions combining diverse interaction paradigms.

Common API abstractions enable developing applications that are agnostic to the underlying interaction paradigm. Then, some local mapping is performed between the API operations and the diverse interaction paradigms/related interaction protocols supported. In our previous work [18], we made a first attempt towards modeling the CS, PS and TS interaction paradigms. We also proposed a TS-based model as higher-level API abstraction for representing all three paradigms. Even if under certain conditions any of the three paradigms can be used as common abstraction, our introduction of GA in this paper makes things clearer and facilitates extension with new interaction paradigms. Additionally, that work was about heterogeneous service orchestrations, while our current work is more general and enables service choreographies. In the same category, ReMMoC [7] is an adaptive middleware for mobile systems, enabling clients that can interact with both RPC servers and PS systems via a common programming interface. Such systems are described with extended WSDL descriptions. Our solution is much more general: it covers as well TS systems and introduces the higher-level GA abstraction that can accommodate new interaction paradigms. Following a similar approach, an API conforming to one interaction paradigm can be locally mapped to an interaction protocol conforming to another paradigm. Thus in [8], the authors implement the LIME TS middleware on top of a PS substrate. Similarly, work in [9] enables Web services SOAP-based interactions over a TS binding. Contrary to these specific solutions, our approach aims to cover a much wider range of interaction paradigm interoperability.

Wrapping systems behind standard technology interfaces enables accessing these systems by using interaction paradigms that are different from their native ones. In [6], a gateway allows high-level access to the data and operations of a wireless sensor network via Web service interfaces. Again, our solution is much more general, relying on technology-independent abstractions.

Bridging is about interworking between heterogeneous interaction protocol stacks. The ESB paradigm is currently the dominant bridging solution for the integration of heterogeneous systems, with realizations that are established industrial (open- and closed-source) products, such as Apache ServiceMix[7] and

---

[7] http://servicemix.apache.org

IBM Websphere ESB[8]. Certain efforts have provided binding components (BCs) for ESBs that map between different interaction paradigms. For instance in [5], an external TS is connected through a BC to a distributed ESB topology and is accessible via the bus messaging-based interface. However, such solutions are typically ad hoc and concern each time a specific case, while we propose a generic and systematic approach that can be applied to many different middleware technologies. Other efforts propose extensions to SOA and ESB infrastructures, such as event-driven SOA [11], while now most industrial-strength ESBs support the PS paradigm. Still, these remain partial, they do not support the TS paradigm. Acknowledging the flexibility of the TS model, a number of system integration efforts have adopted TS as the common interaction facility. Some of these approaches enrich TS with PS semantics, or offer a REST-based API in addition to the TS-based API [19]. Similar efforts introduce extended TS as an alternative solution to the realization of the ESB paradigm [12]. Some of these ESBs offer various interaction semantics (by emulating different interaction paradigms) and related APIs, such as CS- and PS- in addition to TS-based. With respect to these efforts, the comparative advantage of our approach is its generality and extensibility thanks to the introduction of the higher-level GA abstraction.

6   Conclusion

Integrating services that employ heterogeneous interaction paradigms is challenging. We have introduced a modeling approach abstracting heterogeneous middleware platforms into their corresponding interaction paradigms, and the latter to a single higher-level interaction paradigm that enables cross-paradigm interconnection. We apply our modeling abstractions to extend an SOA & ESB infrastructure for supporting development of complex applications by seamless peer integration of heterogeneous services. A development platform is provided to application designers. Using this platform, they can easily develop composite applications: they only need to build descriptions for the constituent services and directives for data mapping among them. Our platform then deals with reconciling among the heterogeneous interaction paradigms and protocols of the services. Additionally, support for new middleware platforms, new ESB infrastructures, or even new interaction paradigms can be incorporated in a facilitated way thanks to our architectural framework. Our evaluation demonstrates the application design support, high extensibility, and low performance cost of our solution.

In our current and future work, besides publishing on the formal foundation of our interoperability approach, we aim to enrich our modeling abstractions with support for continuous interactions in addition to discrete ones. Continuous interactions are commonly found in data streaming protocols, which are increasingly important in the Future Internet, due to the vast spread of media content and sensor-generated data streams.

---

[8] http://www.ibm.com/developerworks/websphere/zones/businessintegration/wesb.html

References

1. Monson-Haefel, R., Chappell, D.: Java Message Service. O'Reilly & Associates, Inc., Sebastopol (2000)
2. Carzaniga, A., Wolf, A.L.: Content-based Networking: A New Communication Infrastructure. In: König-Ries, B., Makki, K., Makki, S.A.M., Pissinou, N., Scheuermann, P. (eds.) IMWS 2001. LNCS, vol. 2538, pp. 59–68. Springer, Heidelberg (2002)
3. Freeman, E., Arnold, K., Hupfer, S.: JavaSpaces Principles, Patterns, and Practice. Addison-Wesley Longman Ltd., Essex (1999)
4. Murphy, A.L., Picco, G.P., Roman, G.C.: LIME: A Coordination Model and Middleware Supporting Mobility of Hosts and Agents. ACM Transactions on Software Engineering and Methodology (TOSEM) 15(3), 328 (2006)
5. Baude, F., Filali, I., Huet, F., Legrand, V., Mathias, E., Merle, P., Ruz, C., Krummenacher, R., Simperl, E., Hammerling, C., Lorre, J.P.: ESB Federation for Large-scale SOA. In: Proceedings of the 2010 ACM Symposium on Applied Computing, SAC 2010, pp. 2459–2466. ACM, New York (2010)
6. Avilés-López, E., García-Macías, J.: TinySOA: A Service-oriented Architecture for Wireless Sensor Networks. Service Oriented Computing and Applications 3(2), 99–108 (2009)
7. Grace, P., Blair, G.S., Samuel, S.: A Reflective Framework for Discovery and Interaction in Heterogeneous Mobile Environments. SIGMOBILE Mob. Comput. Commun. Rev. 9(1), 2–14 (2005)
8. Ceriotti, M., Murphy, A.L., Picco, G.P.: Data Sharing vs. Message Passing: Synergy or Incompatibility?: An Implementation-driven Case Study. In: Proceedings of the 2008 ACM Symposium on Applied Computing, New York, USA, pp. 100–107 (2008)
9. Wutke, D., Martin, D., Leymann, F.: Facilitating Complex Web Service Interactions through a Tuplespace Binding. In: Meier, R., Terzis, S. (eds.) DAIS 2008. LNCS, vol. 5053, pp. 275–280. Springer, Heidelberg (2008)
10. Pietzuch, P., Eyers, D., Kounev, S., Shand, B.: Towards a Common API for Publish/Subscribe. In: Proceedings of the 2007 Inaugural International Conference on Distributed Event-based Systems, pp. 152–157. ACM, New York (2007)
11. Papazoglou, M.P., Heuvel, W.J.: Service Oriented Architectures: Approaches, Technologies and Research Issues. The VLDB Journal 16, 389–415 (2007)
12. Mordinyi, R., Kühn, E., Schatten, A.: Space-Based Architectures as Abstraction Layer for Distributed Business Applications. In: Proceedings of the 2010 International Conference on Complex, Intelligent and Software Intensive Systems, CISIS 2010, pp. 47–53. IEEE Computer Society, Washington, DC (2010)
13. Busi, N., Zavattaro, G.: A Process Algebraic View of Shared Dataspace Coordination. The Journal of Logic and Algebraic Programming 75(1), 52–85 (2008)
14. Eugster, P.T., Felber, P.A., Guerraoui, R., Kermarrec, A.M.: The Many Faces of Publish/Subscribe. ACM Comput. Surv. 35(2), 114–131 (2003)
15. Gelernter, D.: Generative Communication in Linda. ACM Transactions on Programming Languages and Systems (TOPLAS) 7(1), 80–112 (1985)
16. Lam, S.S.: Protocol Conversion. IEEE Trans. Softw. Eng. 14(3), 353–362 (1988)
17. Kay, M.: XSLT 2.0 Programmer's Reference. Wiley Pub. (2004)
18. Georgantas, N., Rahaman, M.A., Ameziani, H., Pathak, A., Issarny, V.: A Coordination Middleware for Orchestrating Heterogeneous Distributed Systems. In: Riekki, J., Ylianttila, M., Guo, M. (eds.) GPC 2011. LNCS, vol. 6646, pp. 221–232. Springer, Heidelberg (2011)
19. Nixon, L.J.B., Simperl, E., Krummenacher, R., Martin-Recuerda, F.: Tuplespace-based Computing for the Semantic Web: A Survey of the State-of-the-Art. Knowl. Eng. Rev. 23(2), 181–212 (2008)

An App Approach Towards User Empowerment in Personalized Service Environments

Mario Hoffmann

Fraunhofer AISEC, Parkring 4, 85748 Garching near Munich, Germany
mario.hoffmann@aisec.fraunhofer.de

Abstract. The laws of identity and privacy protection goals are major requirements of user-centric personalized service environments. The goal is that users can send master data, preferences, attributes and claims together with policies to relying parties such as Cloud Services Providers in order to control purpose, usage, and availability of personally identifiable information. In order to meet the requirements and to establish a trusted end point this paper introduces a virtual representation of a user called $Life_{App}$ that can be downloaded and installed by relying partners. On the one hand this approach aims at empowering the user to control access, enforce policies, minimize misusage and enjoy – nonetheless – personalized contextual services. On the other hand relying parties benefit from synchronizing data whenever it changes at the user's or the requester's side. The advantages are up-to-date and authentic user data, simplified customer relationship management, and if needed compliance to local data protection. The paper introduces the app approach to personalized service environments based on the Kantara-UMA protocol.

Keywords: Internet Identity Management, Life Management Platforms, Personal Clouds, Personally Identifiable Information, Privacy by Design, User Empowerment, Kantara UMA Protocol.

1 Introduction

Although privacy is an inherent necessity people when asked have their difficulties to value possible consequences and implications of disregard. Moreover, people are used to disclose their personal preferences, relationships, and behaviors to online services; typical examples of services managing huge amounts of personally identifiable information (PII) are online stores, social and business networks as well as dating agencies. Latest prominent examples of – from the users' point of view – misuse of PII are mobile apps: In the case of the smartphone-based social network *Path* for example a developer in Feb'12 discovered that the app was uploading users' address books to its server without their explicit consent. Other examples, where users not in all cases have been asked for their approval when uploading personal data, are apps from *Facebook, Instagram, Foursquare, Foodspotting,* and *Yelp.*[1] Implications range from

---

[1] For testing purposes and detailed reports Android apps can be uploaded for example to AppRay (www.app-ray.de).

K.-K. Lau, W. Lamersdorf, and E. Pimentel (Eds.): ESOCC 2013, LNCS 8135, pp. 149–163, 2013.
© Springer-Verlag Berlin Heidelberg 2013

targeted marketing and predicting behavior to analyzing social and business relationships or even identity theft.

However, "Privacy compliant cloud computing is feasible"[2] states a press release from the data protection office Schleswig-Holstein in July 2012. In order to fulfill the privacy protection goals transparency, unlinkability and intervenability (see Marit Hansen's definitions in [1]) mechanisms for protecting and minimizing personal data, monitoring it's usage as well as binding it to specific purposes have to be in place during the complete life cycles of identities, information, and services. In addition Article 29 Data Protection Working Party published their "Opinion 05/2012 on Cloud Computing" in July 2012 [6]; the document "outlines how the wide scale deployment of cloud computing services can trigger a number of data protection risks, mainly a lack of control over personal data as well as insufficient information with regard to how, where and by whom the data is being processed/sub-processed."

This paper will introduce a "privacy by design" approach to support privacy protection goals. The core mechanism is based on the well known download of apps. Users, nowadays, are used to download apps, trust the issuers, and install and configure them on their mobile phones. The app approach introduced in this paper supposes the same from the service provider's perspective. The service provider downloads an app representing a virtual identity from a user and installs it in an encapsulated virtual machine running in his Cloud infrastructure. This so called Life$_{App}$ is supposed to establish a secure channel to the users' Life Management Platform and to grant, monitor, and control access to data that is requested by the service provider. (Note: The paper will use the terms "service provider", "requester" and "relying party" synonymously. Here, they do all refer to the same sense of collaboration partner.)

The paper is organized as follows: The next chapter will first give an overview of the state of the art of relevant areas. Then the Life$_{App}$ approach is described followed by promising application scenarios and the architectural concept. An evaluation of the concept based on the seven laws of identity (see Kim Cameron's definition in [3]), finally, supports the conclusion that the app approach proposed in this paper can be a large step towards more privacy protection and user empowerment in personalized service environments.

2   State of the Art

2.1   The Laws of Identity

The laws of identity are based on an open blog of the identity community initiated by Kim Cameron (Microsoft) in 2005 and have become an important reference for all identity systems introduced afterwards. They are described in detail in [3] and comprise (1) User Control and Consent, (2) Minimal Disclosure for a Constraint Use, (3) Justifiable Parties, (4) Directed Identity, (5) Pluralism of Operators and Technologies,

---

[2] Press release: ULD: "Privacy compliant cloud computing is feasible", 13.07.2012, https://www.datenschutzzentrum.de/presse/20120713-datenschutzkonformes-cloud-computing_en.htm

(6) Human Integration, and (7) Consistent Experience across Contexts. The Life$_{App}$ approach will be evaluated against the laws of identity in chapter 6 "Compliance to the Laws of Identity".

2.2   Relevant Approaches and Concepts

On a conceptual level laws of identity and privacy protection goals are best supported by Vendor Relationship Management (VRM[3]), Personal Clouds, and Life Management Platforms[4]. According to its definition VRM provides customers with both independence from vendors and better means for engaging with vendors, which is a cornerstone of the approach presented in this paper. Personal Clouds provide the necessary functionality of personal data storage; examples are personal.com, mydex.com, and qiy.com. Only the combination of both, however, enhanced by the user's full control over his personally identifiable information fulfils the characteristic of so called Life Management Platforms[5] - see below.

The big picture is also addressed by a number of EU funded projects such as PrimeLife, ABC4Trust, GINI-SA, and TClouds. PrimeLife[6] for example has developed a user-side transparency enhancing tool "which gives the user an overview of what data have been sent to different data controllers and also makes it possible for a data subject to access her personal data and see information on how her data have been processed and whether this was in line with privacy laws and/or negotiated policies." ABC4Trust[7] is a successor of PrimeLife and focuses on attribute based credentials for trust. GINI-SA[8] is a support action and "works towards the vision of a Personal Identity Management environment." TClouds[9] finally "develops an advanced cloud infrastructure that can deliver computing and storage that achieves a new level of security, privacy, and resilience." However, to the author's knowledge none of them has introduced a user represented as an app that can be downloaded yet.

2.3   Authentication, Authorization, and Identity Management

On protocol level the most relevant developments for the Life$_{App}$ approach during the last two years are Kantara UMA and OAuth 2.0 (both described in the next paragraph) as well as OpenID Connect[10] "a suite of lightweight specifications that provide a framework for identity interactions via REST like APIs." Additionally, SAML[11] provides an underlying XML-based format for exchanging authentication and

---

[3] http://blogs.law.harvard.edu/vrm/
[4] http://www.economist.com/blogs/babbage/2011/11/personal-data
[5] http://www.discoveringidentity.com/2012/07/11/life-management-platforms/
[6] http://primelife.ercim.eu/
[7] https://abc4trust.eu/
[8] http://www.gini-project.eu
[9] http://www.tclouds-project.eu/
[10] http://openid.net/connect/
[11] https://www.oasis-open.org/committees/download.php/27819/

authorization data between parties; Life$_{App}$ benefits from its single-sign-on feature. Higgins[12] is relevant because it provides a Personal Data Service (PDS) that lets you control how your personal data is shared with friends and organizations you trust but the framework is still under development. In the future personal clouds might be based on Higgins. Last but not least SCIM[13] is a new system for cross-domain identity management and "is designed to make managing user identities in cloud-based applications and services easier." SCIM will be evaluated in more detail in the next months.

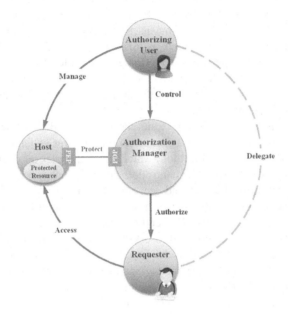

Fig. 1. Kantara UMA Protocol

The integration of Life$_{App}$ in a Life Management Platform is based on Kantara UMA. The protocol U(ser) M(anaged) A(ccess) is a powerful authorization protocol specified by Kantara Work Group UMA[14] and accepted by IETF (see Fig. 1 and [3]). It is a profile of OAuth 2.0 and implements two OAuth 2.0 cycles; the first cycle specifies and manages the authorization between the *authorizing user*, the *host(s)* containing *protected resources*, and the so-called *authorization manager*; the second cycle defines the sequence of sharing information and enforcing access rights between the host(s), the authorization manager as well as the *requester*.

The UMA protocol is mainly characterized by the introduction of an independent authorization manager (AM) which will play an important role in the Life$_{App}$ approach described in chapter 5. The AM provides a central point of managing access policies to the authorizing user. The user can manage policies of all protected resources in a

---

[12] http://www.eclipse.org/higgins/
[13] http://www.simplecloud.info/
[14] http://kantarainitiative.org/confluence/display/uma/Home

standardized and centralized way, which are actually distributed to and stored at hosts such as business networks, location services or document sharing providers. The advantage for hosts is that they can outsource the complete management of granting access rights to protected user resources to the AM.

3   The Life$_{App}$ Approach

Now, imagine you are an app – an app for Android, iOS, any kind of mobile or desktop operating system and let's call it your Life$_{App}$. Assume your Life$_{App}$ consists of personal information and policies how to deal with that information. This personal information could be your name, your address, contacts, and preferences – or in general any kind of personally identifiable information that belongs to you, characterizes you, and personalizes your interactions with other people, services, or things. Moreover, your Life$_{App}$ can contain references to your existing personal data stores in the Cloud or remote data stores you would like to integrate such as your social and business networking platforms, your eGovernment services or your business accounts. Life$_{Apps}$ might even be part of the larger vision of Life Management Platforms in the future Internet. Fig. 2 shows this vision of a complete life management infrastructure including the Life$_{App}$.

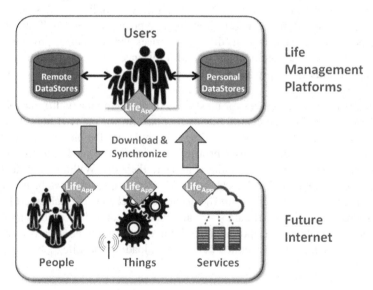

Fig. 2. Using Life Management Platforms in Future Internet Infrastructures

The new paradigm of being an app has several advantages for both the users themselves as well as for relying parties. The main benefit for users is an enhanced user-controlled access rights management. Since the Life$_{App}$ needs to be downloaded, installed, configured, and – may be – bought by an interested relying party, this party needs to agree on the users' terms and conditions. This might include particular user defined policies as well as regulations from third party and local data protection regulations. Inside the Life Management Platform every download of the user's Life$_{App}$ triggers the set up of corresponding profiles, preferences, and policies that reflect a specific part of the user's virtual identity and the intended usage of the services offered by other people, things, or services.

The goal is that the user is empowered to minimize the individual information flow and control the purpose of the usage of PII (both are also requirements identified in the draft report of the European Parliament with regard to the General Data Protection Regulation, see [5]). At any time the user is supposed to monitor, modify, deny or cancel access rights. The update mechanism of the Life$_{App}$ ensures that latest revisions are available for all subscribers.

Relying parties subscribe to the user's life management service. Besides of having the latest revision of the Life$_{App}$ itself requesters benefit from having up-to-date and authentic information supported by a synchronization mechanism between the Life Management Platform and the Life$_{Apps}$. In case of for example address data, phone numbers, email addresses, and credit card information there is no longer inconsistencies between relying parties and latest user information; once the user changes an information in his or her personal data store all communication partners that have corresponding access rights will get the latest information as soon as they interact with the Life$_{App}$ again.

Furthermore, the Life$_{App}$ can take care of fulfilling compliance rules such as national data protection rights if a corresponding component is built in. That is a huge benefit especially for small and medium enterprises that cannot afford appropriate customer relationship management software, for instance. Such service providers now have the opportunity to simply agree on the terms and conditions the Life$_{App}$ provides in order to be compliant.

Eventually, the model changes for most users of managing many different accounts independently to having one central managing platform for many if not all accounts and relationships. And for the corresponding relying parties the model changes from a centralized model of managing user profiles to a distributed model where the users control access rights, policies and authorizations to their PII. With the introduction of the Life$_{App}$ the existing relationships between users and requesters have been reversed.

Both parties, finally, benefit from the secure channel that is established between the data source, e.g. a personal data store, and the Life$_{App}$ residing at the service provider through any kind of transportation medium, e.g. the Internet. This is enabled by crypto keys that have been generated *before* downloading the Life$_{App}$ by the service provider.

4   Application Scenarios

The application scenarios for Life$_{Apps}$ are manifold and comprise at least social and business networks, cloud services, and intelligent environments. The following paragraphs describe how Life$_{Apps}$ can be integrated in each of those:

4.1   Personal Networks

In the future new social and business networks can be based on the direct exchange of Life$_{Apps}$. Assume for example that you attend a special session at a conference on Life Management Platforms. The conference is taking place in Malaga, a city you have never been to before. During the conference week – and only during that week – you would like to exchange local recommendations for sightseeing or restaurants with the other participants and only with them (and *not* with your 500+ followers at Facebook). (Anabel González-Tablas et al. describe such contextual information sharing in detail in [6].)

So, whenever people will meet – in their jobs, doing some sports, in their leisure time, at public places or private environments – they will have the opportunity to share personal information by exchanging their Life$_{Apps}$ directly from device to device (e.g. based on NFC). The Life$_{Apps}$ contain references and access policies. So, for example, whenever one user would like to send a new recommendation he or she requests the receiver's Life$_{App}$ first in order to check authorization and to get the most appropriate communication channel.

The users' privacy benefits from exchanging access rights to references instead of the information itself. The most important advantage, however, is that no third party Internet service is needed which maintains a social or business network platform. Building up people's networks is simply based on their contextual peer-to-peer relationships.

4.2   Cloud Services

Valid and authentic contact information is a very important commodity for service providers in Cloud and service environments. At the same time managing user accounts and identifying out-of-date information is complex and costly – usually handled in customer relationship management systems (CRMs). Once a critical mass of Life$_{App}$ users has been reached service providers will start supporting Life$_{App}$-enabled services by downloading Life$_{Apps}$ themselves. Such relying parties will benefit from decentralizing and simplifying CRM and – at the same time – having access to up-to-date and authentic customer information the synchronization mechanism is taking care of. In addition Life$_{App}$ software updates ensure state-of-the-art security mechanisms and provide the integration of latest data protection rules in order to fulfill compliance to national and international regulations.

Note: The app approach assumes that business models of relying parties that take advantage of users' Life$_{Apps}$ do not rely on analyzing, aggregating and archiving PII.

4.3   Intelligent Environments

The vision is that even intelligent environments will benefit from downloading Life$_{Apps}$. In the envisioned future Internet of people, things, and services intelligent environments are supposed to deliver contextual services to users in a trustworthy and secure way respecting their privacy. EU-projects such as SWAMI and HYDRA addressed these challenges during the last decade.

A user's Life$_{App}$ could be downloaded, for instance, by a hotel room. According to the user's profile "hotel room" the Life$_{App}$ grants access to his favorite films and music, preferred dishes or allergies, room temperature etc. Also the different Life$_{App}$-enabled models in a car sharing scenarios could take advantage of a corresponding profile "car". As soon as entering a shared car seat, mirrors, favorite radio stations and recent destinations are set up. The user can immediately start her journey.

5   UMA Based Life$_{App}$ Architecture

Life Management Platforms take advantage of the UMA protocol (see section 2.3) by adapting the protocol schema integrating the authorizing user, the requesters, the authorization manager, and the host(s) where protected information is stored. The only new component that is added to the protocol is the Life$_{App}$ (see Fig. 3).

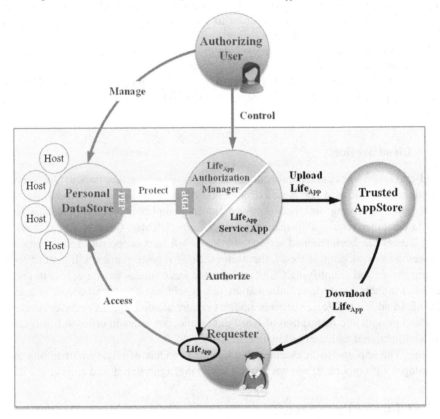

Fig. 3. LifeApp integration into the UMA protocol

Principally, two scenarios can be distinguished: Online: The Life$_{App}$ contains a reference to the user's authorization manager and a default set of access policies and a default user profile; Offline: For autonomous usage the Life$_{App}$ hosts a minimal set of attributes, values, and claims as well as appropriate policies. In both cases the relying party is supposed to download and install the Life$_{App}$ from the corresponding trusted App Store before.

The *Personal Data Storage* (PDS) on the left side of Fig. 3 is a specific implementation of the host of UMA's architecture. It serves, firstly, as an adapter to the existing hosts, where users have stored protected data already; here, the Life Management Platform integrates existing relationships. Secondly, the PDS provides encrypted storage saving and archiving PII directly. The PDS in this concept could be securely hosted by standard Cloud storage providers because the PII is encrypted on the client side as well as on transportation.

5.1   Example: eGov Citizen Portal

The last twelve months the public sector has recognized the potential of cloud computing. Some pilot cities in Germany, such as Münster and Ingolstadt, are featuring especially the consistent integration of the new German ID card into citizen-centric service portals. The most interesting and complex case with respect to Life Management Platforms is the support of service chains where processes have to be operated across several administrative positions – sometimes even with the involvement of the private sector; examples include motor vehicle registration, moving to another city or applying for social benefits.

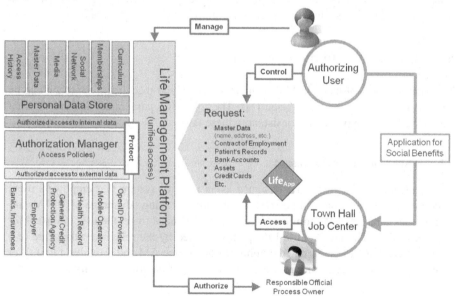

Fig. 4. Example: A Life Management Platform in an eGov Scenario

The application for social benefits is illustrated as an example in Fig. 4:

1. Let's assume a user applies for social benefits at the town hall's website.

2. At the website of the public authority the user has to provide a lot of different personalized information such as master data, patient's record, bank accounts, etc.
3. He has three opportunities: (a) Some data can be sent and/or filled in a form by hand, (b) some fields are automatically completed by the Life$_{App}$ and a corresponding auto-complete service, (c) the Life$_{App}$ redirects the request and authorizes access to the Life Management Platform. Here access to internal and external sources is specifically protected and bound to specific purposes.
4. The goal is to support two kinds of processes: (a) In a synchronized interaction the user controls every single step; (b) in the asynchronous alternative the user authorizes the complete service chain accessing information when needed.

In general users who would like to apply for example for social benefits or any other kind of digital services for citizens are authorizing users in UMA terminology. They manage their personal data in internal and external repositories and care about identity theft and data protection. UMA's so called authorization manager is implemented as a Life Management Platform. The platform empowers the authorizing user to control and authorize access to protected resources. Requesters, e.g. a town hall/job center, need personalized information from the authorizing user in order to feed a service chain and operate a process. The requester receives particular access rights by the Life Management Platform. Internal and external repositories are hosts in UMA terminology. Internal repositories contain any kind of user controlled content and can be organized as a personal data store. External sources are typically based on references to 3rd parties and other Identity Providers – note: some are not controlled by the authorizing user.

6   Compliance to the Laws of Identity

The main features of the Life Management Platform and the Life$_{App}$ approach can be mapped to the laws of identity (see [3]). The following paragraphs analyze to what extent the Life$_{App}$ approach is consistent to these laws.

6.1   User Control and Consent

Life Management Platforms are designed as an identity system that empowers users to control access to protected personal information. Taking advantage of UMA's authorization manager (AM) component relying parties need to get the user's consent for any transaction. The user-centric Life$_{App}$ downloaded by the requester takes care of a secure channel and a standardized communication to the AM and provides a first filter enforcing policies already on the requester's side. The first law of identity is fulfilled.

6.2   Limited Disclosure for Limited Use

Limited disclosure for limited use relies on two aspects of policy management. The first aspect "definition" is realized in most identity systems: The user can define rules and policies who are supposed to get access to what, why, and when. The second aspect "enforcement" is not that easy to fulfill since any user data is traditionally considered lost as soon as it is sent to the requester. The Life$_{App}$ residing on the requester's side is a first step towards user-centric policy enforcement. It integrates compliance rules such as data protection laws and, when interacting with the requester, monitors and binds the usage of protected data to the purpose(s) intended. The second law is partially fulfilled.

6.3   Justifiable Parties

Relationships of the parties involved in the Life Management infrastructures are well-defined and limited. The introduction of an AM to an identity system decreases complexity significantly and frees the hosts of managing users' policies in detail. Disclosure of personally identifying information is restricted to relying parties "having a necessary and justifiable place in a given identity relationship." The PDS, moreover, decreases the number of communication partners significantly since it hides the access to other hosts and identity providers behind a standardized interface. The third law of identity is fulfilled.

6.4   Directed Identity

On the one hand UMA's authorization manager basically can be securely addressed by a well-known URL and public key certificate. According to the definition of the forth law of identity, thus, the AM supports omni-directional identifiers. On the other hand a (short-lived) unidirectional identity relation could be established between the Life$_{App}$ and the relying party. Providing both omni-directional as well as unidirectional identifiers fulfills the forth law of identity.

6.5   Pluralism of Operators and Technologies

The integrated approach of Life Management Platforms addresses the fifth law that states that a universal identity system might channel and enable the inter-working of multiple identity technologies run by multiple identity providers. Both Life$_{Apps}$ as well as the Life Management Platform are designed to be identity agnostic. That means that the user can choose with what means he would like to authenticate himself to his user management interface and what kind of authentication he expects from the relying party. Different identity providers are integrated as hosts through the personal data store.

6.6   Human Integration

The user is the most important architectural component of UMA's protocol extension illustrated in Fig. 3. The user-centric approach enables the user to store his personal information sustainably and securely at the PDS. Information stored at other identity providers can be referenced and integrated by corresponding adapters. Policies for granting access rights are managed under user's control at the AM. And, finally, the Life$_{App}$ is the user's trust and compliance anchor at the relying party. The sixth law is fulfilled.

6.7   Consistent Experience Across Contexts

The strength of Life Management Platforms is the management of contextual identities. The platform is designed for supporting the user's experience in intelligent environments where contexts might switch dynamically and quickly. Switching contexts transparently providing a consistent user experience is a very important aim for Life Management Platforms. How these context switches are supposed to be supported by the user management interface is described in the next chapter.

7   User Experience

User interfaces in identity management aim at a transparent, comprehensible and context-independent way of dealing with personally identifiable information. The user needs to be able to relate to how his or her virtual identities are used, whether the usage is compliant to their policies and bound to a specific purpose, as well as whether the complete life-cycle is user-controlled. In short: It needs to support the privacy protection goals: transparency, unlinkability and intervenability.

Usable security and privacy is the key to acceptance of any identity system balancing user requirements and requirements of providers of context-aware personalized services. The following paragraphs introduce a user interface design for managing the information and identity life cycle at a smartphone.

The creation of new virtual identities and corresponding profiles is one of the key features of the Personal Information Assistant (PIA); see Fig. 5 (a). Some services rely on one's real name and address, sometimes on birth date and credit card information, some services, however, just ask for an email address to verify one's real interest in a white paper or article. So, for different purposes users can define specific contextual profiles containing subsets of PII.

Editing such profiles and preferences is illustrated in Fig. 5 (b). Basically, it is an open list of attributes, claims, and credentials that can be reused in different virtual identities and profiles. The goal is that PIA – in addition to predefined ones – can learn new attributes from relying parties. For a first realization it is planned, however, that the user himself establishes links between attributes with the same semantics explicitly. The result will be user defined ontologies; standardized ontologies will be part of future research.

An example of PIA during run-time shows Fig. 6. Part (a) lists the registered people, environments, and services Bob shares personal information with and which are authorized to access certain corresponding profiles. As a prerequisite each of them has downloaded Bob's Life$_{App}$. Part (b) illustrates the other way around. Details of communication partners Bob has downloaded are presented. Here, the list contains Alice, Bob's wife, his best friend Thomas, his boss, as well as his lovely dog Brutus. How Bob benefits from PIA managing his relationships explain the paragraphs below:

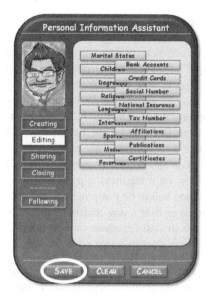

a) Create new
    virtual identities

b) Edit your profiles
    and preferences

Fig. 5. LifeApp User Interface Mockup – Part 1

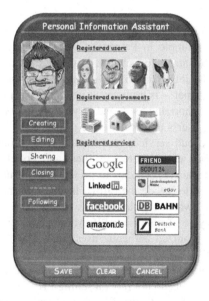
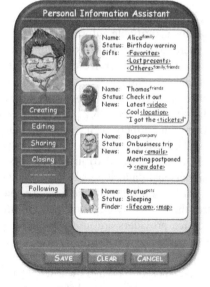

a) Manage access rights
    and policies

b) Follow your
    interests and data

Fig. 6. LifeApp User Interface Mockup – Part 2

1. Alice is Bob's wife and as such part of the group *family*. Bob and Alice share almost everything from each other's Life$_{Apps}$. Bob certainly knows Alice's birthday – however, not to forget it the calendar throws a birthday warning. Bob checks Alice's favorites in her profile, compares it with his history from last celebrations and agrees with others from *family* and *friends* in order to avoid doublings.
2. Bob and Thomas are *friends*. As friends Bob and Thomas share specific Life$_{App}$ configurations. Thomas recommends a good restaurant from his latest trip and he informs Bob that he got the tickets for the forthcoming football game on Saturday.
3. Bob's boss is part of the group *company*. The Life$_{App}$ profile that Bob shares with his boss and other colleagues is pretty restricted. According to his calendar Bob's boss in on a business trip. In Bob's inbox are five new emails from his boss. A meeting had to be postponed. A new appointment has to be agreed.
4. Brutus is Bob's dog and belongs to the group *pets*. Via Brutus' Life$_{App}$ Bob has access to vital functions such as breath, pulse, and blood sugar. So, Bob knows that Brutus is sleeping right now. The lifecam offers a stream from the dog's place.

User interface design is manifold. The mock-up presented above is just one example based on a smartphone layout. Since the logic of the personal information assistant is separated from the presentation layer alternatives such as laptops, desktops, tablets and even smart TVs can be supported efficiently.

8   Conclusion

Life Management Platforms are designed for users to centralize their management of personally identifiable information (PII) for example in Personal Clouds. Management, here, basically refers to the life cycles of attributes, claims, profiles, and policies in personalized service environments. The introduction of the Life$_{App}$ approach into such environments – as proposed in this paper – is a powerful new paradigm to establish new forms of relationships between authorizing users and service providers.

The novelty of the Life$_{App}$ approach is the user's app that can be downloaded by collaboration partners such as other people, Cloud services, and intelligent environments. The Life$_{App}$ might contain content such as attributes, profiles, and policies already or (recommended) just references plus access policies to protected information at personal data stores. At the service provider's side the Life$_{App}$ is able to establish a trusted contact point and a secure channel which enables the user to monitor and control the access to, usage of, and the life cycle of his or her PII. Main advantages for service providers are up-to-date and synchronized authentic user data, avoiding inconsistencies and non-active users, as well as being compliant to data protection regulation when needed (and if integrated into the Life$_{App}$). Note: The concept assumes collaboration partners whose business models do not rely on selling PII.

The paper evaluated the Life$_{App}$ concept according to the 7 Laws of Identity and could show that the new privacy protection goals transparency, unlinkability and intervenability are supported. Therefore, the integration of the Life$_{App}$ concept in a Life Management Platform enables developers of personalized service environments to implement privacy by design.

Roadmap for a proof of concept: The mock-up has been partly underpinned by specific implementations already. The UMA protocol has been implemented last year. Currently, as part of a nationally funded project[15], first components of the proposed Life Management Platform such as the personal data store are under development and authentication technologies such as OpenID Connect and the new German ID card are supposed to be integrated soon. The implementation of the $Life_{App}$ component, finally, is planned for the end of 2013.

References

1. Hansen, M.: Top 10 Mistakes in System Design from a Privacy Perspective and Privacy Protection Goals. In: Camenisch, J., Crispo, B., Fischer-Hübner, S., Leenes, R., Russello, G. (eds.) Privacy and Identity 2011. IFIP AICT, vol. 375, pp. 14–31. Springer, Heidelberg (2012) http://www.csc.kth.se/~buc/PPC/Slides/marit.pdf
2. Rost, M., Bock, K.: Privacy by Design and the New Protection Goals. Datenschutz und Datensicherheit 35, 30–35 (2011), https://www.european-privacy-seal.eu/results/articles/BockRost-PbD-DPG-en.pdf
3. Hardjono, T. (ed.): User Managed Access (UMA) Profile of OAuth 2.0. IETF Internet-Draft (2013), http://docs.kantarainitiative.org/uma/draft-uma-core.html
4. Cameron, K.: The Laws of Identity (2005), http://www.identityblog.com/stories/2005/05/13/TheLawsOfIdentity.pdf
5. Albrecht (Rapp.), J.P.: Draft Report on the proposal for a regulation with regard to the processing of personal data and on the free movement of such data (General Data Protection Regulation) (December 2011), http://www.europarl.europa.eu/meetdocs/2009_2014/documents/libe/pr/922/922387/922387en.pdf
6. Article 29 Data Protection Working Party, Opinion 05/2012 on Cloud Computing (July 2012), http://ec.europa.eu/justice/data-protection/article-29/documentation/opinion-recommendation/files/2012/wp196_en.pdf
7. González-Tablas, A.I., Alam, M., Hoffmann, M.: An architecture for user-managed location sharing in the Future Internet of Services. In: The 4th International Workshop on Trustworthy Internet of People, Things & Services, co-located with the Internet of Things 2010 Conference, Tokyo, Japan, November 29-December 1 (2010), http://www.seg.inf.uc3m.es/papers/2010tiopts.pdf
8. Fischer-Hübner, S., Hoofnagle, C., Krontiris, I., Rannenberg, K., Waidner, M. (eds.): Online Privacy: Towards Informational Self-Determination on the Internet, http://drops.dagstuhl.de/opus/volltexte/2011/3205/

---

[15] http://www.aisec.fraunhofer.de/de/kompetenzen/projekte/sealed-cloud.html

A Life-Cycle Model
for Software Service Engineering

Erik Wittern[1] and Robin Fischer[2]

[1] eOrganization Research Group
FZI Research Center for Information Technology
wittern@fzi.de
[2] eOrganization Research Group
Karlsruhe Institute of Technology (KIT)
robin.fischer@kit.edu

Abstract. Applying existing life-cycle models to software service engineering, we identify shortcomings: they do not focus on engineering activities, lack a clear underlying definition of software services, do not address both service roles of consumer and provider, and assume longevity and sequence of activities. We present a life-cycle model for software service engineering to tackle these shortcomings. We illustrate the model's prescriptive use by applying it to assess *software service variability* and *software service standardization*.

Keywords: Software service engineering, service variability, cloud standards.

1 Introduction

The Internet has fundamentally changed the nature and delivery of services. Providers of software services can effortlessly serve a tremendous amount of globally distributed consumers. Methods and tools, best practices, and structure-providing methodologies are required for providers to efficiently develop and provision services. Service consumers require support to master consumption-related tasks like service selection, service integration, or system scaling.

Software service engineering is the systematic application of methods and tools for the creation and provision of a software service. *Life-cycle models* structure service engineering. Their nature is *descriptive* in that they capture common service engineering approaches. In addition, life-cycle models are *prescriptive* in that they guide providers in service development and provision and consumers in service consumption. They denote relevant activities at different stages of the life-cycle and recommend their order.

Despite the important role that life-cycle models play, we find that current models have flaws with regard to service engineering. Many models have broad focus (e.g., include organization aspects), hampering their applicability to software service engineering. Also, the service concept underlying most service life-cycle

K.-K. Lau, W. Lamersdorf, and E. Pimentel (Eds.): ESOCC 2013, LNCS 8135, pp. 164–171, 2013.
© Springer-Verlag Berlin Heidelberg 2013

models is not made explicit or is too generic. Many models focus on provider activities, leaving the consumer side open. Finally, many models imply a longevity and sequence of activities that does not necessarily reflect reality.

To overcome these problems, we discuss software service in section 2. We relate to existing work in section 3. In section 4, we present our software service life-cycle model. We illustrate its prescriptive use by discussing a) activities to support service variability and b) software service standardization in section 5. Section 6 concludes our findings and gives an outlook to future work.

2 Tems and Definitions

Generic Services. A service, generically, is "[...] an abstract resource that represents a capability of performing tasks that form a coherent functionality from the point of view of providers entities and requesters entities. To be used, a service must be realized by a concrete provider agent." [14].

The involvement of two *roles*, namely *provider* and *consumer*, is a universal characteristic of services. Generically, the provider performs activities for the sake of the consumer. In return, the consumer compensates the provider, e.g., in form of payments. Some authors identify additional roles (cf. [7]), like *service creator* or the *service broker* in Web services. Because these roles are only sensible in particular contexts, we concentrate on the two fundamental roles (and assume the provider to have also created the service). Considering services as *activities* reveals their procedural nature. Services take an input, often provided by the consumer in form of information or physical goods, and transform it. Services enable consumption on demand. Service consumers can invoke a service (only) when they actually need them.

Software Services. Given these fundamental characteristics of services generically, we now focus on *software services*. We define a software service as a deployed capability that is realized by software and provided and consumed on-demand over networks.

This conceptual view of software services is illustrated in Figure 1. On the left side, *software* depicts the implementation of a capability to be provided as a service. The capability that the software realizes can be an application, a platform, or even an infrastructure. The implementation contains the specification of interfaces. The interfaces are, however, not accessible before the software is deployed. Through deployment, the capability is made accessible to consumers, transforming software into a software service. Technically, through deployment the software is packed (e.g., within a jar or virtual machine) and loaded into an execution environment (e.g., a Web server or virtual infrastructure). The interfaces defined as part of the software are made accessible to consumers by the execution environment as service interfaces. The necessity of software services to be deployed is important to differentiate them from classical software products.

The concept of software services comprises sub-ordinate service classes, two of which we introduce in the following. *Web services* denote software that provides

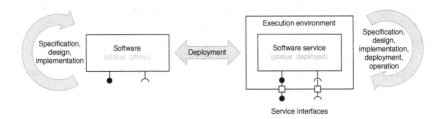

Fig. 1. Software service engineering

interoperable machine-to-machine interaction over a network [14]. Atomic Web services provide a single functionality while composite services *compose* multiple Web services. Composite Web services can, again, be offered as service, making composition a recursive operation [5]. Another class of software services are *cloud services*. Cloud computing is about on-demand provisioning of scalable, network-centric, abstracted IT infrastructures (IaaS), platforms (PaaS) and applications (SaaS) with a pay-per-use model, utilizing virtual processing and storage resources [2]. While cloud services build on Web service standards, cloud standard challenges remain, e.g. managing virtual compute or data resources.

3   Related Work

Life-cycle models define phases that a software or service goes through from its conceptualization to its discontinuation. The goal of such models is to provide an overview and order of tasks that are relevant for provision and consumption.

Software life-cycle models have long been guiding the practice in the software engineering domain. They define a set of related activities whose execution leads to the creation of a software product. These activities typically are *specification, design and implementation, validation*, and *evolution* [13]. Sequential, non-iterative descriptions, often referred to as *waterfall models*, were first formally described in the 1970s [12]. Recommending approaches foresee that activities are repeatedly executed to refine software or to continuously approve and adapt it. For example, the correspondingly named *spiral model* [4] or the development models used in *agile development* [1] are cyclic by nature. An example of a flexible and iterative software life-cycle model is *Rational Unified Process (RUP)*. It includes four phases, namely *inception, elaboration, construction*, and *transition*, and activities performed in them, referred to as *workflows* [9].

Software life-cycle models focus on engineering tasks. *Service life-cycle models* are diverse, addressing different service types and different scopes. *IT governance*, applies service life-cycle models to prescribe the introduction and enforcement of company-wide policies for adopting and operating service-oriented architectures [7]. The *Information Technology Infrastructure Library (ITIL)* encompasses the phases service design, transition, and operation as well as a variety of related processes. The *Web service development life cycle* denotes a methodology to software service engineering, fostering analysis, change, and evolution of Web services [11]. Engineering cloud service comprises requirements, discovery, negotiation, orchestration, and consumption and monitoring phases [8]. Recently, DevOps proposes the integration of development and operation activities independent of a service's status [6].

Assessing how the presented *service* life-cycle models reflect software service characteristics, we notice the following shortcomings:

Missing focus on consumption: IT governance and management models provide holistic views, encompassing organizational aspects. Agile and DevOp methods focus on parallel provider activities. However, integration of engineering-related aspects of consuming software services is missing.

Coupling activities with service status: In service engineering, activities can be performed independent of the service's status. For example, while a service's status is running, providers and consumers may perform design activities to evolve the service or, respectively, plan its consumption. Current models assume coupling of service status and activities.

Implied longevity of activities: Frequently used phases imply that a service remains in a corresponding engineering activity for long time. However, activities may in reality only be short-lived, e.g. deployment to cloud infrastructure can be a matter of seconds.

4   Our Software Service Life-Cycle Model

Our software services life-cycle model is inspired from existing approaches in software engineering (especially the RUP) and (Web) service engineering. It considers three dimensions: (1) two *service status*, (2) five types of *activities*, and (3) two *roles*, namely *providers* and *consumers*.

Service Status are *offline* or *deployed*. While a service is offline, it is not available for consumers. The two status are mutually exclusive, i.e. a service may only be in one status of the two status at a given time. A service's status impacts how activities are performed in software service engineering. For example, changing a deployed service requires deployment activities to be performed so that continuous service availability is ensured. A service's status is global in that it affects both provider and consumer activities.

Activity Types include *specification, design, implementation, deployment*, and *operation*. An overview of the set of provider and consumer activities and their typical sequence is provided in Figure 2.

Similar to software engineering [13], *specification activities* define requirements and constraints on service provision or consumption. Both, provider and consumer check the technical feasibility and perform, e.g., requirements analysis, specification, or validation. Providers will focus more on the realizability of a service, while the consumer will, e.g., analyze whether to consume a service. Consumers perform a service candidate identification in cohesion with the feasibility and requirements activities.

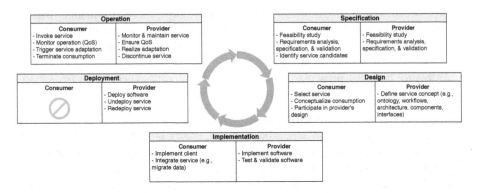

Fig. 2. Common provider and consumer activities

In *design activities*, service providers conceptualize the service and its provision. Results are the service's architecture, components, data models, or algorithms. In contrast to software design, software service design activities include service interfaces, deployment, and runtime methods and tools. The consumers' design activities plan and conceptualize service consumption. Based on requirements, preferences, and service candidates, service selection is performed. New interfaces or systems to integrate the service with are conceptualized.

Service providers apply *implementation activities* to realize the service based on designs. Implementation includes the development of the software artifact, its testing, and validation. Service consumers realize the envisioned service consumption. Contracting must be performed with the provider, specifying e.g., the service's price or service level agreements (SLAs). The consumer's implementation activities also include the creation of client components. Integration efforts may be required to utilize a new service with existing services or systems. When utilizing services to host systems or data, e.g., cloud infrastructure services, migration of these systems and / or data is required [10].

Deployment activities transfer the software implementation to a deployed status. We differentiate deployment from implementation activities as they do not necessarily co-occur. For example, recurring deployment of once implemented cloud services is a common approach to realize horizontal scalability [2]. *undeployment* transfers a service's status back to being offline.

Provider-side *operation activities* ensure ongoing service provision matching quality of service (QoS) properties. The provider maintains the service, reacting e.g., to errors, changing amounts of requests and resulting performance impacts, or adaptation needs. When the provider decides to discontinue the service provision, corresponding activities, e.g., data retrieval or consumer notification, may be required. The consumer's operation activities include, foremost, the actual invocation of the service. Furthermore, consumers may trigger service adaptation, e.g., in reaction to changed context. When terminating consumption, consumers may have to retrieve their data or actively dissolute running contracts.

Figure 1 summarizes the relationship of status, activities and software services. Gray arrows indicate activities on the service. While the service is offline, specification, design, implementation activities can be performed. Deployment activities lead to a transition of the status. While the service is in deployed status, any activity can be performed. This characteristic of our life-cycle model allows, e.g., consumers to perform design activities while a service is deployed. Such flexibility is not supported by existing service life-cycle models.

5   Applying the Software Service Life-Cycle Model

We illustrate the usage of our model in a *prescriptive* way for software service engineering in this section.

Software Service Variability Service variability denotes the capability of a service to be provisioned in variants. Variant selection depends on context, e.g., on consumer or provider requirements and preferences or external factors. We use our life-cycle model to structure these activities (see Figure 3).

For providers, offering service variability begins with feasibility assessment as a specification activity. In design activities, providers conceptualize, assess, and select variants, using, e.g., methods from software product line engineering [15]. Providers implement selected variants to be offered to all consumers or customized variants offered only to a subset of consumers. Implemented variants are deployed, either in parallel or as a single service where variability is often realized through multi-tenancy [2]. Re-deployment furthermore realize variability. Operation activities concern the adaption of a service.

Consumers specification activities concern the impact of variability for consumption. For example, the flexibility and configuration options that variability brings might strengthen the case for service consumption. Consumers' design activities include selection of service variants. Configuration can be used to select a service variant through provision of predetermined information. Implementation activities concern client variants. Operation activities include assessing the consumption of the service variant and eventually triggering adaptation. Adaptation may be performed solely as an operation activity, if changing the service variant does not require re-deployment or selecting another service all together.

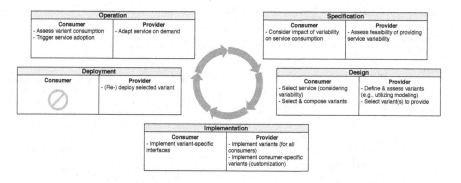

Fig. 3. Service variability activities throughout our life-cycle model

Software Service Standardization. Standards define rules, guidelines or features for generic and repeated use. Using standards in service engineering reduces complexity of decisions, e.g., while specifying or designing interfaces. Existing standards classifications assess standards according to main contributions. Selecting standards according to status, activity or role of the service engineering life-cycle, however, is not supported. Table 1 shows three standards for engineering cloud service that a recent study classified most mature [3]. While not being representative for the current state of standardization, we use these examples to illustrate the use how our life-cycle model in classifying standards for service engineering.

The *Cloud Data Management Interface (CDMI)* defines an interface for storing and managing data in the cloud. CDMI affects specification and design activities of both provider and consumer in offline status. Providers benefit from adopting CDMI because it guides the specification and design of functional and managerial data interfaces. Likewise, consumers receive guidance for identifying their requirements or for evaluating general capabilities of potential cloud services. CDMI further provides guidance to consumers in designing a specific service consumption. The standard supports selection of services based on functional requirements through querying capabilities. Moreover, CDMI offers service consumers guidance for operating their cloud storage. For example, it addresses data management abstractions or access rights management capabilities.

The *Open cloud Computing Interface Core (OCCI)* defines a set of interfaces and protocols to manage cloud compute resources. It supports the specification and design of software artifacts for providers and consumers. Similar to CDMI, OCCI defines functions for the discovery of a service's capabilities. In doing so, OCCI supports consumers with design activities for deployed services, e.g., feature-based selection among a set of cloud compute services.

The *Open Virtualization Format (OVF)* describes a file and exchange format for virtual appliances. It provides guidance for service providers and consumers for specifying and designing software features while the service is offline. Moreover, OVF supports consumers with operating the services as it provides the format that is used to import and export virtual machines.

Table 1. Example: Classification of cloud standards

Standard	Scope	Roles	Status	Activities
CDMI	Cloud Data Management Interface	Provider, Consumer	Offline	Specify, Design
		Provider	Deployed	Design, Operate
OCCI	Interface and protocol for managing cloud infrastructures	Provider, Consumer	Deployed	Design
		Provider	Offline	Specify, Design
OVF	File and exchange format for virtual appliances	Provider, Consumer	Offline	Specify, Design
		Consumer	Deployed	Operate

6 Conclusion

We presented a software service life-cycle model for the engineering of service provisioning and consumption. It considers the dimensions service status, activities, and roles. Our model is capable to foster the discussion about activities related to service variability. It states and structures the activities of providers and consumer when engineering or consuming variable services. The presented classifications of cloud service standards allow to better understand these approaches in the context service engineering. Having influence on the evolution of software service engineering approaches or their uptake, our life-cycle model acts in a *prescriptive* way. We will use this model in future work as a framework to structure discussions about software service engineering approaches.

References

1. Abrahamsson, P., Salo, O., Ronkainen, J., Warsta, J.: Agile Software Development Methods. Review and Analysis. VTT Publications (2002)
2. Baun, C., Kunze, M., Nimis, J., Tai, S.: Cloud Computing. Web-Basierte Dynamische IT-Services, Springer-Verlag New York Incorporated (March 2011)
3. BMWi: The standardisation environment for cloud computing. Tech. rep. (2012)
4. Boehm, B.W.: A Spiral Model of Software Development and Enhancement. Computer 21(5), 61–72 (1988)
5. Curbera, F., Khalaf, R., Mukhi, N., Tai, S., Weerawarana, S.: The next step in Web services. Communications of the ACM 46(10), 29–34 (2003)
6. Humble, J., Farley, D.G.: Continuous delivery: reliable software releases through build, test, and deployment automation. Addison-Wesley, Upper Saddle River (2010)
7. Janiesch, C., Niemann, M., Steinmetz, R.: The TEXO governance framework. Tech. rep., SAP Research (2011)
8. Joshi, K.P., Finin, T., Yesha, Y.: Integrated Lifecycle of IT Services in a Cloud Environment. In: Proceedings of the Third International Conference on the Virtual Computing Initiative (ICVCI 2009), Research Triangle Park, NC (2009)
9. Kruchten, P.: The Rational Unified Process: An Introduction, 3rd edn. Addison-Wesley (2004)
10. Menzel, M., Ranjan, R.: CloudGenius: Decision Support for Web Server Cloud Migration. In: Proceedings of the 21st International Conference on World Wide Web (WWW 2012), Lyon, France, pp. 979–988 (March 2012)
11. Papazoglou, M.P., Van Den Heuvel, W.J.: Service-oriented design and development methodology. International Journal of Web Engineering and Technology 2(4), 412–442 (2006)
12. Royce, W.W.: Managing the Development of Large Software Systems. In: Proceedings of IEEE WESCON, pp. 1–9 (August 1970)
13. Sommerville, I.: Software Engineering, 9th edn. Addison-Wesley (2011)
14. W3C Working Group: Web Services Glossary (2004),
    http://www.w3.org/TR/ws-gloss/ (accessed February 21, 2013)
15. Wittern, E., Schuster, N., Kuhlenkamp, J., Tai, S.: Participatory Service Design through Composed and Coordinated Service Feature Models. In: Liu, C., Ludwig, H., Toumani, F., Yu, Q. (eds.) ICSOC 2012. LNCS, vol. 7636, pp. 158–172. Springer, Heidelberg (2012)

A Tale of Millis and Nanos: Time Measurements in Virtual and Physical Machines

Ulrich Lampe[1], Markus Kieselmann[1], André Miede[2],
Sebastian Zöller[1], and Ralf Steinmetz[1]

[1] Multimedia Communications Lab (KOM), TU Darmstadt, Germany
{firstName.lastName}@KOM.tu-darmstadt.de
http://www.kom.tu-darmstadt.de/
[2] Fakultät für Ingenieurwissenschaften, HTW des Saarlandes, Saarbrücken, Germany
andre.miede@htw-saarland.de
http://www.htw-saarland.de/

Abstract. Cloud computing makes large infrastructure capacities available to users in a flexible and affordable fashion, which is of specific interest to scientists for conducting experiments. Unfortunately, our past research has provided first indications that virtual machines – the most popular type of cloud-based infrastructure – have substantial deficits with respect to time measurements, which are an important tool for researchers. In this paper, we provide a detailed analysis on the accuracy of time measurements based on various machine configurations. They cover influence factors such as machine type, virtualization solution, and programming language. The results indicate that not the use of virtualization as such, but the potentially uncontrollable utilization of the physical host is a decisive factor for the accuracy of time measurements. Different virtualization solutions and programming languages play an inferior role. Our findings, along with the publicly released tool *TiMeAcE.KOM*, can provide a valuable decision support for researchers in the selection and configuration of cloud-based experimental infrastructures.

Keywords: cloud computing, infrastructure, virtual machine, experiment, time measurement, accuracy, timeace.

1 Introduction

A key feature of cloud computing is elasticity, i. e., the ability to access Information Technology (IT) resources in a flexible and affordable fashion [1]. Apart from small and medium enterprises, this characteristic is specifically relevant for researchers, who frequently require large capacities on short term in order to conduct scientific experiments. In this context, Infrastructure as a Service (IaaS) offers are of specific interest. They provide flexible environments, i. e., Virtual Machine (VM) instances, which permit the execution of practically any existing software without major adaptation [2].

Unfortunately, our past work has provided initial indications that VMs suffer from deficits with respect to the accuracy of time measurements [3]. This is

K.-K. Lau, W. Lamersdorf, and E. Pimentel (Eds.): ESOCC 2013, LNCS 8135, pp. 172–179, 2013.
© Springer-Verlag Berlin Heidelberg 2013

problematic in so far as time measurements are an important tool in scientific research, e. g., in the comparative evaluation of exact and heuristic optimization approaches [4]. In this paper, we substantially extend our past research through the consideration of additional influence factors, e. g., different virtualization solutions and programming languages. This work also extends a recently published work-in-progress paper [5], which is based on similar results, through the inclusion of statistical test results and an overview of related work.

The remainder of this paper is structured as follows: Section 2 describes our experimental design and setup. The results and practical conclusions are described in Section 3. Subsequently, Section 4 provides an overview of related work. Section 5 concludes the paper with a summary and outlook.

2   Experimental Setup

2.1   Measurement Tool

In this work, we pursue the same principal experimental approach as in our past research [3]: We repeatedly measure the computation time of a deterministic function in order to quantify potential inaccuracies in time measurement. Deterministic, in this context, means that the function exhibits the same *computational* complexity for a given input parameter. Thus, the observed computation time for each execution should also be identical under ideal conditions. Accordingly, variations in the computation times can directly be related to measurement inaccuracies.

For our experiments, we have implemented a measurement tool, which features a simple counter function as its core component. The function accepts a single integer a as argument and returns the required computation time as result. The tool can be configured to conduct a series of $b \in \mathbb{N}$ batches. Each batch comprises $c \in \mathbb{N}$ calls of the aforementioned counter function, using the arguments $a \in A = \{2^0, 2^1, \ldots, 2^m\}$, where $m \in \mathbb{N}$. The tool automatically adapts the given argument through multiplication by a so-called *machine speed index*. This index is initially determined by the program and ensures that for a given argument a, the computation time is approximately $a \times 10$ ms, regardless of the underlying processor. This guarantees that the observed runtimes feature roughly the same *absolute* values for identical arguments.

2.2   Experimental Configurations

The aim of our work is to quantify the impact of different potential influence factors on the accuracy of time measurements, which constitutes the *dependent variable* in our experiments. Thus, we employ a multitude of different *machine configurations* in our experiments, where the influence factors are modeled through five *independent variables*.

The first independent variable of interest is the *machine type*, with respect to which we distinguish two options. As previously outlined, *VMs* are the most common form of IaaS, and are commercially offered based on flexible pay-as-you-go pricing models today. In contrast, Physical Machines (*PMs*) represent traditional,

dedicated experimental infrastructure. The *deployment model* is the second independent variable in our experiments. Specifically, we consider VMs from a *public
cloud* (Amazon EC2) and a *private cloud* that is operated on the basis of multiple
IBM Blade servers at our research lab (KOM). In addition, we made VMs available
using a *local host* computer. As third independent variable, we regard the *virtualization software*. Concerning this factor, we distinguish between *ESXi*, a solution
that is commercially marketed by VMware, and *Xen*, an open-source software that
forms the basis for Amazon's Elastic Compute Cloud (EC2). As fourth independent variable, we consider the *host utilization*, i. e., computational load that the
PM or host system for the VMs is subjected to. Concerning this factor, we distinguish between three options. In the case of *low load*, the PM exclusively hosts one
instance of the measurement tool or VM. In the case of *high load*, the system runs
multiple tool instances or VMs in parallel. Lastly, in the case of *random load*, the
host utilization is out of our control sphere, and potentially fluctuates during the
experiments. As fifth and final independent variable, we regard the *programming
language*. For that purpose, we have implemented the measurement tool in similar form in *C* and *Java*. This choice was made because Java as such uses a form of
virtualization, the so-called Java VM, which may potentially influence the measurement accuracy independent of the underlying infrastructure. In contrast, C
does not feature such a concept.

2.3 Measurement Procedure

In principal, we follow a *full-factorial approach* in our experiments. That is, we
examine each possible combination of values for the five independent variables,
i. e., influence factors, that were introduced in the previous section. However, as
can easily be reasoned, some combinations are mutually exclusive: For example,
Amazon does not provide a choice between different virtualization systems, but
uses Xen as standard solution. Nevertheless, our experiments encompass a total
of 16 different machine configurations, which should provide a comprehensive
overview of different influence factors.

As PM and local host for the VMs, we used a desktop computer, equipped
with an Intel Core 2 Duo processor at 2.0 GHz and 2 GB of memory. Given
that our previous research showed no major differences between Linux and Windows concerning the accuracy of time measurements [3], we exclusively employed
the former as guest operating system in our experiments. Specifically, we chose
Ubuntu Server 12.04.1 LTS, which was booted into the default text-based shell to
minimize the influence of background services. In order to generate high load for
the corresponding configurations, we either launched three parallel VM instances
or measurement tool instances on the physical host.

For every configuration, we conducted 20 experimental batches with 100
method calls each (i.e., $b = 20$, $c = 100$). The set of applicable arguments
was specified as $A = \{2^0 = 1, ..., 2^9 = 512\}$, i. e., $m = 9$. Thus, we obtained a
total *sample* of 20,000 runtime observations per configuration, with *subsamples*
of 2,000 observations per argument and machine configuration. In total, across
all 16 configurations, 320,000 individual observations were collected.

3 Experimental Results and Practical Recommendations

In accordance with our previous work [3], we use the normalized standard deviation, i. e., the *Coefficient of Variation* (CV), as measure of accuracy. It is given by the ratio between the standard deviation (commonly denoted as σ) and the mean value of the observations (μ) in a sample [6]. The CV numerically represents the dependent variable in our experiments. Due to the definition of the CV, *higher* values indicate *lower* accuracy and vice versa; hence, in the case of ideal accuracy, the observed CV would correspond to zero.

A comprehensive overview of all machine configurations, along with the CVs that were observed of each argument of the counter function, is given in Table 1 in the appendix. The table also provides the relative rank for each configuration with respect to the observed accuracy per argument.

Given the findings of our previous work [3], which indicated general deficits of VMs with respect to time measurements, our new experiments provide some surprises. Specifically, the VMs from the *private* cloud at our institute provide the best accuracy for small arguments, i. e., $a \leq 2$, among all tested configurations (cf. #13 and 14 in Table 1). For increasing arguments, the VMs lose some ground to the PMs, specifically when the Java-based implementation of the measurement tool is used (cf. #2 in Table 1). Nevertheless, a *Friedman test* at the common confidence level of 95% shows no significant difference between the PM-based configurations and the configurations that used VMs from our cloud ($p = 0.5034$).

Yet, the results confirm the deficits of *public* clouds with respect to time measurements. Notably, the VM instances from Amazon EC2 exhibit the highest CVs, i. e., lowest accuracy, for most arguments, specifically those in the subsecond range (cf. #15 and 16 in Table 1). Correspondingly, the Friedman tests show that VMs from the public cloud perform significantly worse compared to PMs with low utilization ($p = 0.0000$). However, in comparison to a PM under high load, the Friedman test shows no significant difference ($p = 0.2632$).

Concerning the two virtualization solutions, ESXi and Xen, we obtained mixed results. On the basis of the locally hosted VMs and low utilization, the observed CVs indicate some advantages for ESXi with respect to small arguments (i. e., $a \leq 2$), while the relative performance of Xen improves with growing arguments (cf. #5, 6, 9, and 10 in Table 1). In addition, Xen achieves more favorable accuracy once high host utilization comes into play; in this case, ESXi generally appears to perform very poorly (cf. #7 and 8 in Table 1). Correspondingly, a Friedman test indicates a significant difference between both solutions and confirms a superior measurement accuracy for Xen across the considered programming languages and host utilization ($p = 0.0038$).

From the above discussion, one may conclude that the host utilization plays a key role in the accuracy of measurements, and this is strikingly confirmed in our experiments. Regardless of the machine type and virtualization software, imposing additional load on the physical host results in sharp increases in the observed CVs (cf. #7, 8, 11, and 12 in Table 1). The same applies for the PM (cf. #3 and 4 in Table 1). Accordingly, the Friedman tests confirm the role of

Table 1. Observed time measurement accuracies, i.e., *coefficients of variation*, by machine configuration. Values in parentheses denote the rank among all configurations for the given argument, ordered from most accurate (1) to least accurate (16). Absolute runtimes for the counter function approximately correspond to $a \times 10$ ms. Abbreviations: M/T (Machine Type), D/M (Deployment Model), V/S (Virtualization Software), H/U (Host Utilization), P/L (Programming Language).

| # | Machine Configuration | | | | | Function Argument | | | | | | | | | |
	M/T	D/M	V/S	H/U	P/L	$a = 1$	$a = 2$	$a = 4$	$a = 8$	$a = 16$	$a = 32$	$a = 64$	$a = 128$	$a = 256$	$a = 512$
1	PM	n/a	n/a	Low	C	0.0123 (3)	0.0090 (3)	0.0065 (5)	0.0048 (5)	0.0034 (5)	0.0025 (5)	0.0018 (5)	0.0014 (5)	0.0011 (3)	0.0008 (5)
2	PM	n/a	n/a	Low	Java	0.0328 (6)	0.0403 (6)	0.0005 (1)	0.0003 (1)	0.0002 (1)	0.0003 (2)	0.0001 (1)	0.0001 (2)	0.0000 (1)	0.0000 (1)
3	PM	n/a	n/a	High	C	0.3990 (9)	0.2213 (9)	0.1304 (9)	0.1205 (9)	0.1352 (12)	0.1306 (13)	0.1205 (13)	0.1061 (15)	0.0965 (15)	0.0823 (15)
4	PM	n/a	n/a	High	Java	0.5527 (10)	0.3876 (10)	0.3152 (10)	0.2814 (12)	0.2501 (14)	0.2290 (14)	0.2078 (16)	0.1795 (16)	0.1667 (16)	0.1496 (16)
5	VM	Local	ESXi	Low	C	0.0172 (4)	0.0096 (4)	0.0078 (6)	0.0065 (6)	0.0105 (7)	0.0067 (7)	0.0063 (6)	0.0127 (8)	0.0040 (6)	0.0044 (7)
6	VM	Local	ESXi	Low	Java	0.0290 (5)	0.0203 (5)	0.0226 (7)	0.0085 (7)	0.0057 (6)	0.0045 (6)	0.0195 (8)	0.0086 (6)	0.0048 (7)	0.0033 (6)
7	VM	Local	ESXi	High	C	1.5958 (14)	1.1553 (15)	0.8151 (15)	0.6014 (16)	0.4440 (15)	0.3063 (15)	0.1725 (14)	0.0789 (13)	0.0406 (13)	0.0211 (13)
8	VM	Local	ESXi	High	Java	1.6590 (15)	1.2490 (16)	0.8356 (16)	0.5877 (15)	0.4783 (16)	0.3420 (16)	0.1934 (15)	0.0822 (14)	0.0424 (14)	0.0234 (14)
9	VM	Local	Xen	Low	C	0.0892 (7)	0.0677 (7)	0.0494 (8)	0.0346 (8)	0.0259 (8)	0.0181 (8)	0.0132 (7)	0.0104 (7)	0.0081 (8)	0.0066 (10)
10	VM	Local	Xen	Low	Java	0.2463 (8)	0.0733 (8)	0.0029 (3)	0.0005 (2)	0.0002 (2)	0.0001 (1)	0.0001 (2)	0.0001 (1)	0.0002 (2)	0.0002 (2)
11	VM	Local	Xen	High	C	1.1925 (13)	0.7790 (13)	0.5021 (13)	0.2873 (13)	0.1266 (11)	0.0681 (11)	0.0361 (11)	0.0198 (12)	0.0115 (11)	0.0077 (12)
12	VM	Local	Xen	High	Java	1.0830 (11)	0.7112 (12)	0.4449 (12)	0.2489 (11)	0.1135 (10)	0.0597 (10)	0.0296 (10)	0.0157 (9)	0.0090 (9)	0.0055 (8)
13	VM	Private	ESXi	Low	C	0.0028 (1)	0.0023 (1)	0.0027 (2)	0.0021 (3)	0.0018 (3)	0.0014 (3)	0.0011 (3)	0.0008 (3)	0.0013 (5)	0.0005 (3)
14	VM	Private	ESXi	Low	Java	0.0118 (2)	0.0074 (2)	0.0029 (4)	0.0022 (4)	0.0022 (4)	0.0017 (4)	0.0017 (4)	0.0010 (4)	0.0013 (4)	0.0006 (4)
15	VM	Public	Xen	Random	C	1.7477 (16)	1.0945 (14)	0.6565 (14)	0.3150 (14)	0.1503 (13)	0.0886 (12)	0.0405 (12)	0.0196 (11)	0.0118 (12)	0.0061 (9)
16	VM	Public	Xen	Random	Java	1.1398 (12)	0.6293 (11)	0.3576 (11)	0.1783 (10)	0.0974 (9)	0.0499 (9)	0.0271 (9)	0.0159 (10)	0.0108 (10)	0.0075 (11)

the host utilization as decisive factor in measurement accuracy, both for PMs and VMs ($p = 0.0000$ in both cases).

Concerning the impact of the programming language, we observe very mixed results. Neither C nor Java consistently achieves higher accuracy across all considered machine configurations (cf., for example, #1, 2, 15, and 16 in Table 1). In accordance, a Friedman test indicates no significant differences between both programming languages at a 95% confidence level ($p = 0.8701$).

In conclusion, the experimental results in this paper – to some extent – relativize the preliminary findings of our previous work: Most notably, we have found that contemporary virtualization technology as such does *not* necessarily imply deficits with respect to the accuracy of time measurements. In fact, the lowest CVs, i. e., best accuracies, among all machine configurations in our experiments were observed on VM instances from a private cloud. Likewise, those VMs that were hosted on a single physical host performed very similarly to a "raw" PM.

Our experiments have shown that a different influence factor, namely host utilization, is the key determinant for time measurement inaccuracies. Unfortunately, this is the very factor that commonly lies out of the control sphere of the end user when leasing resources from a public cloud; in fact, from the viewpoint of the cloud provider, the consolidation of multiple VMs on a single physical host is highly desirable in order to reduce operational cost. The same also applies to a private cloud in principal, even though the level of control may be higher for the end user in such deployment model. To state it more explicitly, virtualization does not hurt the accuracy time measurement, but high host utilization – which is a key benefit of virtualization – does.

Hence, our results confirm the most important recommendation of our previous work: If accurate time measurements, specifically in the sub-second range, are required in scientific experiments, dedicated PMs should be preferred over VMs. Yet, if host utilization as the key influence factor can be effectively controlled by the end user, VMs may also provide acceptable accuracy. In this context, dedicated VM instances with performance guarantees – which have recently appeared in the public cloud market – could be of interest as well.

In order to help scientists in the assessment of experimental infrastructures, we have created a lightweight tool called *Time Measurement Accuracy Estimation* (TiMeAcE.KOM). This tool, which is available through our Web site[1], automatically conducts a small set of measurements using a simple counter function, and provides a textual assessment of measurement accuracies.

4   Related Work

To the best of our knowledge, our previous work [3] and the present paper is the only research that specifically examines the accuracy of time measurements in physical and virtual environments. However, with the renewed interest in virtualization technology and the hype around cloud computing, various research efforts have been undertaken in related fields recently.

---

[1] http://www.kom.tu-darmstadt.de/timeace/

In this context, timekeeping on VMs is the first major area of interest. A comprehensive overview of this topic has been provided in a whitepaper by VMware [7]. The authors provide an extensive background on timekeeping mechanisms on PMs. Based on this, they outline different options for timekeeping in virtualized environments and also provide hints for improving timekeeping accuracy. A specific proposal for improving the timekeeping VMs in Xen has been made by Chen et al. [8]. Their approach, called XenHVMAcct, aims to provide the same accuracy in hardware-assisted VMs, which use an unmodified guest operating system, as in para-virtualized VMs that rely on modified systems. Broomhead et al. [9] also introduce an improved timekeeping mechanism in the context of Xen. Their work specifically targets clock inaccuracies that are introduced by live migration operations.

The second notable area of related research concerns performance evaluations in cloud computing environments. El-Khamra et al. [10], for example, have examined the runtime fluctuations of a scientific workflow in FutureGrid, a scientific Grid testbed, and the commercial Amazon EC2 cloud. The authors also find relatively large variations in runtime, but attribute them to performance fluctuations, rather than timekeeping deficits. Schad et al. [11] have conducted a longitudinal study of performance variations in Amazon EC2 using a suite of benchmarks. They find substantial fluctuations in the performance of different system components, such as processor and network, and conclude that the conduction of performance experiments on leased VMs can be problematic. However, Schad et al. do not take the potential systematic weaknesses of time measurements in virtualized environments into account either.

5   Summary and Outlook

Commercial cloud providers make large pools of compute capacity available to end users based on a pay-as-you-go scheme. This is of specific interest to researchers, who can exploit VM instances to conduct scientific experiments. However, past research has indicated that VMs suffer from inaccuracy when it comes to time measurements, which are a common instrument in science, e. g., in the assessment of heuristic optimization approaches. Based on this notion, this work provided an extensive analysis concerning the accuracy of time measurements depending on different influence factors, namely machine type, deployment model, virtualization software, host utilization, and programming language.

We found that the machine type, i. e., the use of virtualization as such, is *not* a key determinant of time measurement inaccuracies; instead, the utilization of the physical host plays a decisive role. According to our observations, a high degree of load on the physical host – as it can likely be expected in cloud data centers due to the use of consolidation techniques – results in dramatic loss of accuracy. Furthermore, we concluded that the virtualization software Xen has small advantages over ESXi. For the two considered programming languages, C and Java, we observed no statistically significant results with respect to time measurement accuracy. Based on our findings, we recommend scientists to either use PMs or VMs from a controlled environment if accurate time measurements, specifically in the sub-second range, are required.

For the future, we plan to extend our existing work through a longitudinal (i. e., long-term) study with different commercial cloud providers. With such design, we expect to identify the impact of potential performance fluctuations on the accuracy of time measurements. Furthermore, these additional experiments may permit fellow scientists to make a more educated decision among competing cloud offers.

Acknowledgments. This work has been sponsored in part by the E-Finance Lab e. V., Frankfurt a. M., Germany (www.efinancelab.de).

References

1. Owens, D.: Securing Elasticity in the Cloud. Comm. of the ACM 53(6), 46–51 (2010)
2. Briscoe, G., Marinos, A.: Digital Ecosystems in the Clouds: Towards Community Cloud Computing. In: Proc. of DEST 2009 (2009)
3. Lampe, U., Miede, A., Richerzhagen, N., Schuller, D., Steinmetz, R.: The Virtual Margin of Error – On the Limits of Virtual Machines in Scientific Research. In: Proc. of CLOSER 2012 (2012)
4. Silver, E.: An Overview of Heuristic Solution Methods. J. of the Operational Research Society 55, 936–956 (2004)
5. Lampe, U., Kieselmann, M., Miede, A., Zöller, S., Steinmetz, R.: On the Accuracy of Time Measurements in Virtual Machines. In: Proc. of CLOUD 2013 (2013)
6. Jain, R.K.: The Art of Computer Systems Performance Analysis: Techniques for Experimental Design, Measurement, Simulation, and Modeling. Wiley (1991)
7. VMware, Inc.: Timekeeping in VMware Virtual Machines (2011), http://www.vmware.com/files/pdf/techpaper/Timekeeping-In-VirtualMachines.pdf
8. Chen, H., Jin, H., Hu, K.: XenHVMAcct: Accurate CPU Time Accounting for Hardware-Assisted Virtual Machine. In: Proc. of PDCAT 2010 (2010)
9. Broomhead, T., Cremean, L., Ridoux, J., Veitch, D.: Virtualize Everything But Time. In: Proc. of OSDI 2010 (2010)
10. El-Khamra, Y., Kim, H., Jha, S., Parashar, M.: Exploring the Performance Fluctuations of HPC Workloads on Clouds. In: Proc. of CloudCom 2010 (2010)
11. Schad, J., Dittrich, J., Quiané-Ruiz, J.: Runtime Measurements in the Cloud: Observing, Analyzing, and Reducing Variance. In: Proc. of the VLDB Endowment, vol. 3(1–2), pp. 460–471 (2010)

A UML Profile for Modeling Multicloud Applications

Joaquín Guillén[1], Javier Miranda[1], Juan Manuel Murillo[2], and Carlos Canal[3]

[1] Gloin, Calle de Las Ocas 2, Cáceres, Spain
{jguillen,jmiranda}@gloin.es
[2] Department of Information Technology and Telematic Systems Engineering,
University of Extremadura, Spain
juanmamu@unex.es
[3] Department of Computer Science, University of Málaga, Spain
canal@lcc.uma.es

Abstract. The benefits of counting with a high number of providers for developing cloud applications are overshadowed by the vendor lock-in issue, which makes it difficult for service-based applications to be migrated and replicated in new platforms. The MULTICLAPP framework tackles this issue by providing a three stage development process for building multicloud applications where developers do not require specific expertise on cloud technologies. The application modeling stage is described in this paper, where a UML profile is used for modeling applications in a platform independent manner. Multicloud applications are modeled as a composition of software artefacts, where each can be assigned to a different platform. This provides an intuitive way of modeling applications, and when integrated in the MULTICLAPP framework, makes it easier for them to be developed, maintained and redeployed in different platforms.

1   Introduction

Cloud Computing has gained a great acceptance over the past years thanks to the utility computing business model with which it is commercialized and the wide range of services it provides to simplify the construction and management of applications. However, the use of cloud services couples user applications to vendor specific service definitions. Hence, the so called vendor lock-in [3] issue becomes one of the main challenges that users have to cope with in the process of adopting cloud technologies.

Vendor lock-in is not the only issue to consider whilst developing software that will be deployed in a cloud platform. Software systems are sometimes comprised of different components which are subject to different sets of requirements that are only satisfied if a multicloud deployment scenario is considered. However developing those types of applications is currently a big challenge since the development tools and IDEs distributed by providers do not consider this as an option. Furthermore, the need for developing cloud applications is growing and this issue must be confronted.

K.-K. Lau, W. Lamersdorf, and E. Pimentel (Eds.): ESOCC 2013, LNCS 8135, pp. 180–187, 2013.
© Springer-Verlag Berlin Heidelberg 2013

In order to tackle each of these problems the MULTICLAPP Framework has been designed for developing multicloud applications in three stages. The two final stages were described in [7][4], and the initial stage is described in this paper with the inclusion of a UML profile for modeling multicloud applications.

The remainder of this paper is structured as follows. In Section 2 we present the motivations of our work, and more particularly the limitations of current proposals. A UML profile for modeling multicloud applications is described in Section 3. Section 4 provides a brief description of the MULTICLAPP framework and describes how the UML profile has been integrated in the framework. Section 5 presents a real case study where an application was modeled using MULTICLAPP. In Section 6 the related works are discussed and their differences with our solution are analysed. Finally, Section 7 contains the conclusions extracted from our work.

2   The Fine Print of Cloud Computing

Most people think of cloud computing as an extremely powerful and innovative technology that allows their organizations to actively compete against corporations with higher technological infrastructures, thanks to its affordable costs and its flexible business model. However this is only a biased view of the picture, which may turn out misleading if all of the factors related to cloud computing are not taken into account. Its adoption is often characterized by the vendor lock-in and by the difficulties that must be confronted if users wish to develop multicloud applications.

In order to mitigate the vendor lock-in issue the industry is currently working on different standardization initiatives that aim to homogenize the services provided by the existent providers. These were summarised in [7], where we outlined that neither of them have been adopted by the industry, and that their success can only be considered in a long-term basis. Therefore we consider that standardization initiatives must not be taken as the only means of combating vendor lock-in.

An alternative to standardization, which is commonly used for developing multicloud migratable applications, is the use of middleware platforms that create an abstraction between the applications and the cloud infrastructure. They constitute valid and robust solutions which are very popular both at academic [6][10] as well as at industrial [5][9] levels. Nevertheless these solutions shift the lock-in issue from the cloud to the middleware platforms.

As an alternative, model driven development (MDD) provides the means for constructing single and multicloud applications which are not coupled to any specific platform. The use of models allows system architects and developers to abstract their applications from specific cloud platforms. Applications are modeled and transformations are applied upon them in order to generate source code that complies with the requirements and services of the targeted platforms. However the existent approaches based on MDD do not generate the complete source code of the modeled applications and thereby require developers to enrol themselves in the complex task of working with generated source code that is tightly coupled to specific platforms.

To sum up, our motivations for the development of the UML profile presented in this paper, and for its integration in the MULTICLAPP framework, are based on the great number of difficulties that must be faced in order to model and develop multicloud applications and at the same time mitigate the risks associated with the adoption of cloud computing; i.e. those related to vendor lock-in and interoperability issues.

3 Design of the UML Profile

The UML profile that has been designed for modeling multicloud applications is illustrated in Figure 1.

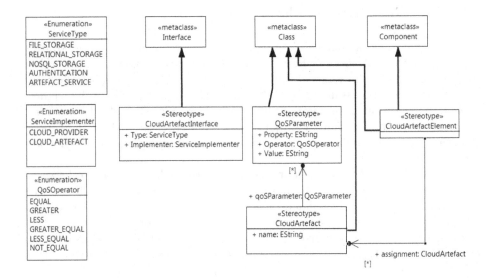

Fig. 1. MULTICLAPP UML Profile

Since we seek to model applications that can be deployed across multiple clouds without including platform specific information into the models, partitions of the applications have to be identified. Each of these partitions have been denominated *cloud artefacts* and are represented in the profile with the *CloudArtefact* stereotype. A cloud artefact is a software component that can be deployed in a cloud platform and that interoperates with other artefacts as well as with the services that it requires from the platform in which it is deployed. Artefacts are not assigned to cloud platforms whilst applications are being modeled in order to guarantee that the models are fully cloud agnostic.

All the classes and components that make up an application are stereotyped as *CloudArtefactElement*. This allows them to be assigned to at least one artefact, such that elements found within an artefact are deployed in the same platform, and therefore interoperate with one another locally, whereas those found in different artefacts interoperate with one another remotely.

Application models also include all the information required for artefacts to interoperate with one another and with the services provided by the cloud platform. Therefore the services required and provided by each artefact must be stated. This is achieved by establishing *use* and *extends* relationships with the *CloudArtefactInterface* stereotype, respectively.

Notice that since artefacts are not mapped to any specific platform during the modeling stage, it is only the *Type* of service required by each artefact that is identified. These types can be mapped to specific cloud service instances in subsequent development stages. Similarly, models also represent the dependencies that exist between artefacts and specify the interfaces through which interoperability between dependent artefacts is carried out.

Finally, the interest to develop multicloud applications is commonly motivated by the different non-functional requirements that each part of an application may be subject to, such as the response time of certain components or the physical location where they can be deployed. This information is present in the models for each cloud artefact through the use of the *QoSParameter* stereotype which contains three tagged values (*Property*, *Operator* and *Value*) that allow simple expressions to be formulated. Such expressions are interpreted during model transformations by a decision support system that assists the architect in the process of choosing the most suitable platform for a given artefact based on the platform's SLA offering.

4 The MULTICLAPP Framework

MULTICLAPP allows applications to be constructed in three stages: cloud applications are modeled in the first stage, the applications' functional behaviour is coded in the second stage, and specific cloud compliant artefacts are generated through an automated procedure in the third stage. An overview of the framework's development process is provided in [7]; the second and third development stages are detailed in [4].

During the application modeling stage, the UML profile presented in this paper is used to model multicloud applications. These models are then processed by a Model Transformation Engine that allows artefacts to be assigned to specific cloud platforms. The model transformations generate software projects composed of class skeletons and a XML-coded deployment plan that contains all cloud-related information. This allows the source code to be independent from any cloud platform and makes it easier for developers to code the application's functional behaviour without having to be familiarized with the peculiarities of any cloud.

Applications that have been fully coded and for which a deployment plan has been generated are processed by a Source Transformation Engine, which generates each of the cloud artefacts identified in the deployment plan [8].

Each artefact complies with the specifications of its assigned platform. It contains automatically generated adapters that allow it to interoperate with its dependant artefacts and with the cloud specific services that it requires. Once they are generated, the artefacts can be deployed in their cloud platforms.

5   Modeling a Multicloud Application

The MULTICLAPP framework described in this paper has been used in some of the projects carried out by Gloin to model and develop applications hosted in multicloud environments. In this section an excerpt of a cloud application model designed for one of those projects is presented in order to illustrate how the profile described in Section 3 was applied.

The project from which the application model has been taken consisted of a data quality project that was developed in the scope of the author rigths business. Its goal consisted on analysing large heterogeneous data sets in order to produce statistics and metadata about the analysed information. The numerous data sources that had to be analysed, the high volume of information that they contained, and the large number of use cases that had to be implemented, were factors that greatly increased the complexity of the project. Multiple components had to be constructed and integrated with one another, preferably using cloud environments to deploy the software in order to benefit from its low start-up costs and its high potential for scalability.

Each of the project's stakeholders imposed their own requirements regarding the platform and location in which certain components had to be executed, such that components had to be distributed across different platforms. Furthermore, building software that was decoupled from the cloud was a critical factor since some of the software components of the project had to be replicated in different platforms for performance reasons.

Figure 2 presents an excerpt of a model where the profile presented in Section 3 was applied to two interdependent software components developed in the project: an administration panel that provides a centralized interface from which to monitor and control the remaining components, and a data processing module that generates statistics and metadata that is sent out to other components. The data processing module is also responsible of authenticating and validating incoming requests from the administration panel; this is done through a security management module that validates the permissions of each user. Furthermore, the data processing module also provides the administration panel with monitoring information about its execution.

The QoS requirements of each of these components also differed from one another. Whilst the administration panel was not subject to any particular non-functional requirements, legal restrictions enforced the data processing component to be physically deployed in Spain since it managed sensible data that included the users' roles and permissions. An additional non-functional requirement of the data processing component was that it required a storage space greater than 1GB in order for its security management module to save all user related information.

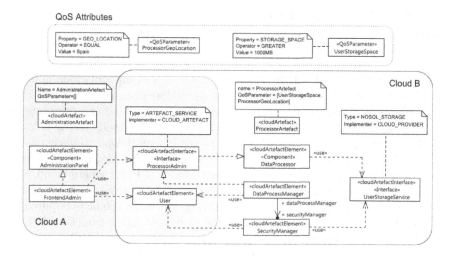

Fig. 2. Cloud application model excerpt

These requirements led to the decision of splitting the application into two direrent artefacts, containing the administration panel on one hand, and the data processor and security manager on the other. All elements assigned to *AdministrationArtefact* could potentially be deployed in a specific cloud which has been illustrated as *Cloud A*, and those assigned to *ProcessorArtefact* could potentially be assigned to a different one, illustrated as *Cloud B*. In this case the architect assigned *AdministrationArtefact* to Amazon's EC2 platform where other administration components were also hosted. On the other hand *ProcessorArtefact* was assigned to a private OpenNebula[1] instance in which a MongoDB database was installed; such configuration satisfied the data processor's storage and geographic deployment restrictions.

6   Related Work

Amongst the existent approaches for modeling cloud applications, CloudML[2] is currently one of the most mature works in this area. It lies under the scope of the FP7 REMICS project[2] and it proposes an extension of SoaMl for incorporating information into the models about the hardware and network resources that are required by the applications from their correspondent platforms. This allows cloud instances to be automatically generated with the modeled configurations through the use of an engine (CloudML Engine). It differs from the approach presented in this paper since it is mainly focused on managing how instances are provisioned. Furthermore, whilst the CloudML approach generates source code that can be deployed in the supported platforms using the JClouds API

---

[1] http://opennebula.org/
[2] http://www.remics.eu/

abstraction, MULTICLAPP follows an alternate approach that relies on the use of software adaptation techniques to allow the artefacts to interoperate with platform specific services.

MODAClouds[1] is another European FP7 project which shares some of the motivations of the MULTICLAPP framework for developing muticloud applications. The project is currently at an early stage of development and its goal consists on allowing system developers to design software in a cloud agnostic manner, allowing it to be instantiated and deployed across mutiple clouds. MODAClouds uses three different levels of abstraction to model multicloud applications: a Computation Independent Model (CIM) in which non-functional requirements are modeled, a Cloud-Provider Independent Model (CPIM) where cloud concepts are introduced into the model but kept away from any specific platform, and a Cloud-Provider Specific Model (CPSM) in which the artefacts required by each specific platform are introduced into the models. It differs from the MULTI-CLAPP approach in the generation of cloud dependent models (CPSM), whereas MULTICLAPP transforms the cloud independent models into software projects that contain a deployment plan in which all cloud related information is found. Furthermore it is yet unknown whether the proposal will be complemented with tools that allow developers to work with the generated source code.

Both of these works rely on model transformations to generate software artefacts that can be deployed in their supported platforms and consume the services provided by each platform. Nevertheless, considering that applications can be of any functional nature and that therefore do not belong to any particular domain, in their current state of work, none of these proposals generate the complete source code of an application directly from the models. Instead they require developers to code the applications and integrate this source code into the artefacts generated from the model transformations. Managing this source code can be quite complex and in most cases will require developers to be familiar with the peculiarities of the targeted cloud platforms.

7   Conclusions

MDD applied to cloud computing is currently a topic of interest for academics due to its great potential for combatting vendor lock-in. Furthermore, it becomes a lot more interesting when applied to multicloud applications since the increased complexity of their source code is largely simplified through the use of models. Nevertheless MDD applied to cloud and multicloud applications is still at a very early stage, and proof of this is that no proposal has yet been widely undertaken by the industry.

The MULTICLAPP framework's approach for modeling cloud applications has been engineered such that developers can code applications as if they were hosted in in-house environments, thereby favouring the software's independence and maintainability. Special attention has been put into designing a development process under which developers are not required to modify cloud dependent source code.

The framework is currently under development and work is being done in order to enhance its capabilities. More specifically, we are looking to replace the current approach for modeling non-functional requirements by an existent QoS modeling standard. Different alternatives have been analysed and the QFTP UML profile has been chosen as the most suitable solution since it consists on an OMG standard for modeling QoS requirements on software components and services, which can be publicly accessed and used in any UML profile.

Acknowledgments. This work has been partially funded by the Spanish Government under Projects TIN2011-24278, TIN2012-34945 and TIN2012-35669. It has also been funded by the Government of Extremadura and FEDER funds.

References

1. Ardagna, D., Di Nitto, E., Mohagheghi, P., Mosser, S., Ballagny, C., D'Andria, F., Casale, G., Matthews, P., Nechifor, C.-S., Petcu, D., Gericke, A., Sheridan, C.: Modaclouds: A model-driven approach for the design and execution of applications on multiple clouds. In: 2012 ICSE Workshop on Modeling in Software Engineering (MISE), pp. 50–56 (2012)
2. Brandtzaeg, E., Mosser, S.: Towards CloudML, a Model-based Approach to Provision Resources in the Clouds. In: Proceedings of the Model-Driven Engineering for and on the Cloud workshop (co-located with ECMFA 2012)(CloudMDE 2012) (257793) (2012)
3. Chow, R., Golle, P., Jakobsson, M., Shi, E., Staddon, J., Masuoka, R., Molina, J.: Controlling Data in the Cloud: Outsourcing Computation without Outsourcing Control. In: Security, pp. 85–90 (2009)
4. Guillén, J., Miranda, J., Murillo, J.M., Canal, C.: A service-oriented framework for developing cross cloud migratable software. Journal of Systems and Software (currently in print, 2013)
5. JClouds. JClouds (2011), http://www.jclouds.org/
6. Di Martino, B., Petcu, D., Cossu, R., Goncalves, P., Máhr, T., Loichate, M.: Building a mosaic of clouds. In: Guarracino, M.R., Vivien, F., Träff, J.L., Cannataro, M., Danelutto, M., Hast, A., Perla, F., Knüpfer, A., Di Martino, B., Alexander, M. (eds.) Euro-Par-Workshop 2010. LNCS, vol. 6586, pp. 571–578. Springer, Heidelberg (2011)
7. Miranda, J., Guillén, J., Murillo, J.M., Canal, C.: Enough about standardization, let's build cloud applications. In: Proceedings of the WICSA/ECSA 2012 Companion Volume on - WICSA/ECSA 2012, p. 74 (2012)
8. Miranda, J., Murillo, J.M., Guillén, J., Canal, C.: Identifying adaptation needs to avoid the vendor lock-in effect in the deployment of cloud sbas. In: Proceedings of the 2nd International Workshop on Adaptive Services for the Future Internet and 6th International Workshop on Web APIs and Service Mashups, WAS4FI-Mashups 2012, pp. 12–19. ACM, New York (2012)
9. Rightscale. Multi-cloud platform (2006)
10. Tsai, W.-T., Sun, X., Balasooriya, J.: Service-Oriented Cloud Computing Architecture. In: 2010 Seventh International Conference on Information Technology: New Generations, pp. 684–689 (2010)

Towards Cross-Layer Monitoring
of Multi-Cloud Service-Based Applications

Chrysostomos Zeginis, Kyriakos Kritikos, Panagiotis Garefalakis,
Konstantina Konsolaki, Kostas Magoutis, and Dimitris Plexousakis

Institute of Computer Science
Foundation for Research & Technology – Hellas
Heraklion 70013, Greece
{zegchris,kritikos,pgaref,konsolak,magoutis,dp}@ics.forth.gr

Abstract. Cloud computing is becoming a popular platform to deliver *service-based applications* (SBAs) based on service-oriented architecture (SOA) principles. Monitoring the performance and functionality
of SBAs deployed on multiple Cloud providers (in what is also known as
Multi-Cloud setups) and adapting them to variations/events produced by
several layers (infrastructure, platform, application, service, etc.) in a
coordinated manner are challenges for the research community. This paper proposes a monitoring framework for Multi-Cloud SBAs with two
main objectives: (a) perform cross-layer (Cloud and SOA) monitoring
enabling concerted adaptation actions; (b) address new challenges raised
in Multi-Cloud SBA deployment. The proposed framework is empirically
evaluated on a real-world Multi-Cloud setup.

Keywords: Cloud computing, service-oriented architecture, monitoring, modeling, event processing, service dependencies.

1   Introduction

Cloud computing emerges as a dominant IT services paradigm that enterprizes
increasingly acknowledge for its ability to flexibly host applications over managed virtualized infrastructures. As in any distributed application hosting environment, Clouds must support extensive monitoring mechanisms to aid in
controlling application performance and adapt to infrastructure variations.

Considering the close relations between Cloud (IaaS, PaaS and SaaS) and
SBAs layers (Business Process and Management (BPM), Service Composition
and Coordination (SCC) and Service Infrastructure (SI) [9]), it is essential to
perform and correlate monitoring across all layers. While it is hard to overesti-
mate the value of effective monitoring (strong infrastructure control, support for
elasticity policies and quality of service (QoS)), most related approaches are fragmented (confined within a specific Cloud provider or service layers) and not ap-
plicable/aligned across layers. Multi-Cloud SBA deployment further complicates
this due to lack of cross-platform support for uniform monitoring solutions [3].

This paper addresses the cross-layer Cloud SBA monitoring by exploiting the
dependencies among layers and using the *event patterns* concept. It supports

K.-K. Lau, W. Lamersdorf, and E. Pimentel (Eds.): ESOCC 2013, LNCS 8135, pp. 188–195, 2013.
© Springer-Verlag Berlin Heidelberg 2013

Multi-Cloud SBA deployment by distributing a monitoring mechanism across Cloud providers. Our monitoring framework relies on an event model to specify the possible monitored SBA events in a Cloud environment, and a component model to describe component dependencies [8] and capture system snapshots at any particular time point. Our evaluation indicates that collecting monitored events can be effectively distributed across Cloud providers. Event retrieval and publication towards a rule engine can be efficiently performed from any location.

The paper is structured as follows. Section 2 describes the architecture of our monitoring engine and implementation details. Section 3 introduces the event model. Section 4 evaluates aspects of our monitoring system. Section 5 describes related work. Finally, section 6 draws conclusions and future work directions.

2 Architecture Overview

The architecture presented in this paper builds upon our previous work [10] on cross-layer SBA monitoring and adaptation, extending it to a Multi-Cloud setting. It comprises a Monitoring Engine, collecting cross-layer events during SBA execution, and an Adaptation Engine, performing cross-layer adaptation actions, which communicate events via a publish/subscribe mechanism (Figure 1). A Model Repository provides various information, such as service descriptions, Multi-Cloud deployment models, layer dependencies, and metric/SLA models.

In this Multi-Cloud setting, SBAs are deployed on various Clouds based on the provided requirements. Three monitoring components are used to perform monitoring at the SaaS, PaaS, and IaaS layers, while a manager retrieves their monitoring results, stores them at a time-series database, and reports detected violations via the publish/subscribe mechanism to Adaptation Engine instances.

This paper focuses primarily on the Monitoring Engine and Model Repository implementation in Multi-Cloud setups. We define monitored events using OWL-Q [6], a semantic and extensible QoS description model for SBAs. It is designed modularly, incorporating several independent QoS-based SBA description facets, such as QoS offers, requests, metrics, attributes and constraints (requirements/capabilities). The SaaS monitoring component uses the Astro monitoring

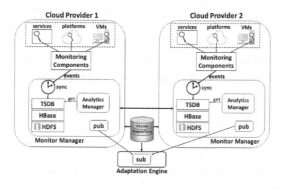

Fig. 1. Multi-Cloud deployment

tool [2] to collect events at the BPM and SCC layers. The supported QoS attributes (metrics) include service/SBA execution time (min, max), throughput (min, max, average) and availability.

The PaaS monitoring component exploits an existing cross-PaaS application management solution [11] which offers a Cloud technology-agnostic PaaS monitoring functionality and an SLA management layer, unifying diverse, provider-specific resource-level metrics. Supported metrics include application load, application and DB response time, and application container response time.

The IaaS monitoring component distinguishes between direct infrastructure monitoring and monitoring services offered by Cloud providers. We use Nagios (http://www.nagios.org) for direct monitoring of user-specified system resources and services via periodic checks on them. Monitored resources include memory usage, disk usage, and CPU load. We also use Amazon Cloudwatch as a Cloud monitoring service instance providing comprehensive monitoring for Cloud resources and applications run by customers on Amazon Web Services. To gain system-wide visibility of running EC2 VMs we enable a variety of metrics via the Cloudwatch API, including CPU utilization, disk read/write rate and volume of incoming/outgoing network traffic. Each Cloudwatch API request returns a datapoint that is handled as a monitored entity. Our requests are issued every few seconds to ensure that collected data are valid and can be reacted on at a reasonable latency.

Regarding event storing, standard solutions include stream processing engines and time-series databases (TSDBs). The former aim to meet stringent latency requirements when performing continuous queries on streaming data and minimize processing cost for large data sets. TSDBs differ as they focus more on persistent event storage and in performing *rollups* (e.g., aggregated metrics such as average, max, min) for user-specified intervals. Complex event processing (CEP) could also be exploited to aggregate events, but since we are interested to store both the raw events (even for a short period) and the rollups, our architecture uses (per-Cloud, federated) TSDBs. A variety of commercial and open source TSDBs can be used to handle timestamped events. We decided to use open-source OpenTSDB, a TSDB especially designed for distributed systems with high scalability requirements, to store monitored events.

A publish/subscribe mechanism handles transferring raw monitored events and TSDB rollups to the Adaptation Engine. Different adaptation engine instances may be deployed to distribute adaptation load across applications/ Clouds, each interested only in relevant events and rollups. We use the Siena (http://www.inf.usi.ch/carzaniga/siena) pub/sub event notification service for communicating events and rollups between TSDB and Adaptation Engine. Siena is expressive enough to capture all appropriate event information via an extensible data model without sacrificing scalability and performance during event delivery.

One of our approach's main goals is to identify particular *event patterns* occurring during SBA execution that lead to critical violations so as to enable selecting the appropriate cross-layer adaptation actions. Since the publishing order of events is significant, the Monitor Manager must time-synchronize them before being sent to the Adaptation Engine. Time synchronization is particularly important in Multi-Cloud settings as standard time synchronization solutions are rarely deployed across Cloud providers. Synchronized events are stored on a repository for post-processing to discover new patterns of interest in event streams. Various clock synchronization algorithms have been proposed to achieve temporal ordering of events produced by concurrent processes. The main approaches are those using logical clocks to create event sequence numbers and those using physical clocks to synchronize events. Physical clock-based algorithms, adjust the system components clocks based on server time or master machine time. As such algorithms are intended for use within intranets and require systematic adjustment of the machines' physical clock, a logical-clock algorithm seems more appropriate in a Multi-Cloud setting. We thus use Lamport's algorithm [7] to efficiently establish event ordering.

Finally, regarding monitor manager functionality, monitored events from within each Cloud are directed to local TSDB, which uses HBase (`http://hbase.apache.org`) (a non-relational, distributed database) to organize the event time-series. HDFS (`http://hadoop.apache.org`), a distributed file system replicating data across all Cloud providers, handles time series storage. For high performance during event collection, each Cloud's local replica is updated eagerly; remote replicas are updated in a relaxed (asynchronous) manner. Reads are performed from local copies when available. The monitor manager includes the synchronize and publish mechanisms on top of OpenTSDB. An analytics manager queries OpenTSDB to retrieve row and aggregated data to perform analysis for the adaptation engine. Stored events are tagged with other source information (service/software component, hosting resource, Cloud provider).

3   Event Model

This section presents an event meta-model describing the most common monitored event types and patterns that occur during the Cloud SBA execution. This model (Figure 2) is generic enough and extensible to incorporate any other event type defined by domain-specific service providers. A respective XML schema was designed to guarantee the validity of concrete event models defined in XML.

The main model class is *Event*. Its *CompositeEvent* and *SimpleEvent* subclasses represent simple and composite events, respectively. Composite events comprise two other (simple or composite) events (the *first* and *second*) which map to a particular *ordering*. For instance, consider a hardware event comprising a CPU overload and low available memory events. Simple events has a source component (defined in a component model not provided in this paper due to space limitations) and belong to a specific Cloud layer (SaaS, PaaS, IaaS). SaaS events can be further located at the BPM or SCC layers. Events are also characterized by their criticality as warning, critical or successful. A simple event can either be *Functional* or *Non-Functional*. Functional events refer to operational

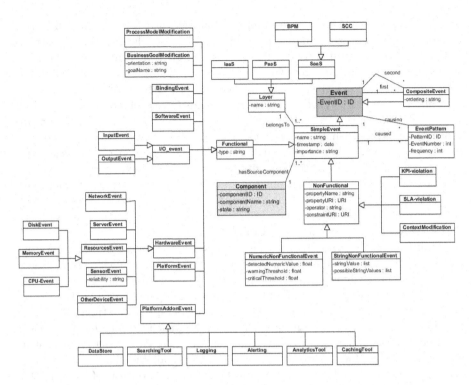

Fig. 2. The Event model

characteristics defining the overall SBA behavior, while non-functional events refer to quality attributes that are either measurable or get distinct qualitative values. Two additional and different classifications exist for non-functional events: (a) they can be classified as *KPI-violations*, *SLA-violations* or *contextModification* events, and (b) as numeric or string events. Sub-classes defined for functional events include: (a) *Process Model Modification*, (b) *Business Goal Modification*, *Software Event*, *I/O event*, *Hardware event*, and *Platform event*. Finally, the *EventPattern* class represents event pattern appearing during Cloud SBA execution and leading to critical violation events. Each event pattern has a (composite or simple) *causing event* and a simple *caused event*.

4   Evaluation

This section describes an experimental evaluation of our monitoring architecture under three deployments: single TSDB server in single Cloud provider (simple setup *1-1*); three TSDB servers in the same Cloud provider (scalability setup *3-1*); three TSDB servers in three different providers (one TSDB server in each Cloud, Multi-Cloud setup *3-3*). We use a monitored events dataset consisting of one million (1M) events comprising six metric types provided by the following sources: a service-level middleware based on the Astro monitoring tool

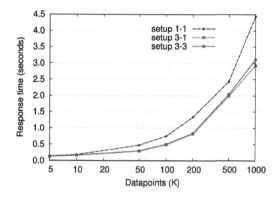

Fig. 3. TSDB read-query response time with varying scope under different setups

(Web service availability, execution time, and throughput); the Amazon Cloud-watch service (CPU utilization, data transfer, and disk usage metrics for under-lying VMs). In our experiments, the Siena pub/sub mechanism retrieves events of interest from the 1M event TSDB dataset via HTTP queries reflecting Siena filters (e.g., with interest on specific metrics and/or event sources). Retrieved events are then passed to an adaptation engine (where no further action is taken).

Our first experiment evaluates the three setups in terms of TSDB query completion time with increasingly broader scope. The query ranges from returning 5K to 1M events out of the 1M event dataset. In the *1-1* setup, TSDB, HBase, and HDFS run on a single VM. In the *3-1* setup, the same software stack (TSDB, HBase, HDFS) is deployed on three VMs in a single Cloud provider (Flexiant). HDFS is configured with two data nodes (single replica per block) and a single name node (responsible for metadata). HBase is configured with two region servers and a single master. In the *3-3* setup the three VMs reside on different providers (one VM in Amazon, Microsoft Azure, and Flexiant) using the same HBase and HDFS configurations. In the *3-1*, *3-3* setups, the 1M event dataset is created on all three servers (each creates a different third of the dataset) and thus events are spread over the HBase region servers and HDFS data nodes.

Figure 3 summarizes our results. Queries with smaller scope (returning 5-10K events out of 1M examined) perform similarly on all setups. As the scope increases, setups *3-1* and *3-3* outperform *1-1* due to simultaneously involving two HBase/HDFS servers for data retrieval. *3-1* seems to outperform *3-3* only for the 1M query due to cross-Cloud communication starting to impact overall time. Although that impact is small, replication will reduce it further since local-copy reads will mask the network latency of cross-Cloud communication.

Our next experiment measures the integrated (TSDB plus publish/subscribe engine) system performance focusing on end-to-end latency (time to complete one or more queries over 1M data points) and throughput (publish ops per second). Table 1 reports our results focusing on a single query going over 1M data points with increasing scope. Our results show that latency and throughput increase with an increasing number of publish-event operations. In practice such

Table 1. End-to-end (TSDB+Siena) response time, throughput under different setups

Number of events published (K)	5	10	50	100	200	500	1000
Single query latency (sec)	0.59	0.82	1.5	2.21	3.68	7.65	11.88
Single query throughput (Kops/sec)	8.5	12.2	33.3	45.2	54.3	65.4	84.2

large queries are expected to hurt responsiveness. Smaller, more frequent queries should result into longer end-to-end latencies (although response time of individual event publish operations will improve) and lower aggregate throughput. Experiments with 100 consecutive queries over 10K data points each, publishing a total of 1M events, take 15 sec (compared to 11.88 sec with a single query) and result in a 67 Kops/sec throughput (compared to 84.2 Kops/sec for one query).

5   Related Work

While several Cloud monitoring approaches have been proposed, few comprehensively consider cross-layer issues. Alcaraz Calero et al. [1] present an analysis of a wide distributed monitoring solution set analyzing the features, requirements, and topology of a cross-layer monitoring system for Cloud computing. A number of EU-funded research projects are currently examining Cloud monitoring solutions: IRMOS (http://www.irmosproject.eu) offers a Cloud infrastructure, comprising a service management system acting as a link between SaaS and IaaS to manage the application service component negotiation, reservation, execution and monitoring. RESERVOIR (http://www.reservoir-fp7.eu) introduces the Lattice non-intrusive monitoring framework for Cloud applications. Lattice features probes to collect and transmit data to the service management part. VISION Cloud (http://www.visioncloud.eu) proposes a monitoring framework able to aggregate events, apply rules on them, and generate new events, representing complex system states. Cloud4SOA (http://www.cloud4soa.eu) proposes a cross-PaaS management and monitoring system for applications hosted on multiple Clouds, to ensure that their performance consistently meets expectations and Cloud resources are being effectively utilized. In terms of cross-layer SBA monitoring, Guinea et al. [5] present an integrated approach for multi-layered SBA monitoring and adaptation which is based on a variant of MAPE control loops. Gjørven et al. [4] propose a coarse-grained approach exploiting mechanisms across SCC and SI layers in a coordinated fashion to support both monitoring and adaptation. All these related approaches do not consider all layers (Cloud and SOA) as well as Multi-Cloud setups (see [3] for an overview), while their main target is on non-functional properties. Our approach's main strength is that it deals with both service and Cloud-based applications while considering challenges raised in a Multi-Cloud environment.

6   Conclusions and Future Work

We have presented a cross-layer monitoring framework for Multi-Cloud SBAs. The framework integrates monitoring mechanisms within each Cloud layer and across Cloud providers. Our architecture uses an event and a component model (not analyzed due to space limitations) to describe monitored events and their source Cloud components. Evaluation of the cross-layer monitoring framework in different deployment settings shows that TSDB performance scales with the number of storage servers and minimally impacts a Multi-Cloud setup. Our next step is to complete developing the adaptation engine and performing larger-scale end-to-end Multi-Cloud experiments involving long-running SBAs.

Acknowledgements. We thankfully acknowledge the support of the PaaSage (FP7-317715) EU project.

References

1. Alcaraz Calero, J., König, B., Kirschnick, J.: Cross-layer monitoring in Cloud computing. In: Using Cross-layer Techniques for Communication Systems, Premier reference source. Igi Global (2012)
2. Barbon, F., Traverso, P., Pistore, M., Trainotti, M.: Run-time monitoring of instances and classes of web service compositions. In: ICWS, pp. 63–71 (2006)
3. Baryannis, G., Garefalakis, P., Kritikos, K., Magoutis, K., Papaioannou, A., Plexousakis, D., Zeginis, C.: Lifecycle Management of Service-based Applications on Multi-Clouds: A Research Roadmap. In: MultiCloud (2013)
4. Gjørven, E., Rouvoy, R., Eliassen, F.: Cross-layer self-adaptation of service-oriented architectures. In: MW4SOC, pp. 37–42. ACM (2008)
5. Guinea, S., Kecskemeti, G., Marconi, A., Wetzstein, B.: Multi-layered monitoring and adaptation. In: Kappel, G., Maamar, Z., Motahari-Nezhad, H.R. (eds.) ICSOC 2011. LNCS, vol. 7084, pp. 359–373. Springer, Heidelberg (2011)
6. Kritikos, K., Plexousakis, D.: Semantic QoS Metric Matching. In: IEEE European Conference on Web Services, Zurich, Switzerland (2006)
7. Lamport, L.: Time, clocks, and the ordering of events in a distributed system. Commun. ACM 21(7), 558–565 (1978)
8. Magoutis, K., Devarakonda, M.V., Joukov, N., Vogl, N.G.: Galapagos: Model-driven discovery of end-to-end application - storage relationships in distributed systems. IBM Journal of Research and Development 52(4-5), 367–378 (2008)
9. Zeginis, C., Konsolaki, K., Kritikos, K., Plexousakis, D.: ECMAF: An Event-Based Cross-Layer Service Monitoring and Adaptation Framework. In: Pallis, G., et al. (eds.) ICSOC 2011. LNCS, vol. 7221, pp. 147–161. Springer, Heidelberg (2012)
10. Zeginis, C., Konsolaki, K., Kritikos, K., Plexousakis, D.: Towards proactive cross-layer service adaptation. In: Wang, X.S., Cruz, I., Delis, A., Huang, G. (eds.) WISE 2012. LNCS, vol. 7651, pp. 704–711. Springer, Heidelberg (2012)
11. Zeginis, D., D'Andria, F., Bocconi, S., Gorronogoitia Cruz, J., Collell Martin, O., Gouvas, P., Ledakis, G., Tarabanis, K.: A user-centric multi-PaaS application management solution for hybrid Multi-Cloud scenarios. Scalable Computing: Practice and Experience 14(1), 17–32 (2013)

A Reliable and Scalable Service Bus
Based on Amazon SQS

Sergio Hernández, Javier Fabra, Pedro Álvarez, and Joaquín Ezpeleta

Aragón Institute of Engineering Research (I3A)
Department of Computer Science and Systems Engineering
University of Zaragoza, Spain
{shernandez,jfabra,alvaper,ezpeleta}@unizar.es

Abstract. Cloud computing infrastructures are becoming a very powerful mean for the implementation of reliable and extensible computing systems. In this paper, we evaluate the viability of migrating a framework for the execution of (scientific) workflows from a cluster-based to a cloud-supported implementation. As a first step, we focus on the viability of adapting the framework message bus (which has a Linda semantics) to the use of the Amazon Simple Queue Service (Amazon SQS). The paper evaluates the performance of the cloud-based bus and studies the influence of the network latency, depending on different geographical locations and configurations. It also compares the cloud-based bus with DRLinda, our former implementation, in terms of economic cost and performance. This comparison allows us to conclude that, under the same conditions, the cloud-based message bus is faster, more scalable and more reliable.

Keywords: Cloud based interoperation, Cost evaluation, Web service based coordination.

1 Introduction

Scientific computing requires more and more computing resources to solve increasingly complex problems. Traditionally, computational clusters and grids have been used to meet the needs of scientists. Recently, the appearance of cloud computing as an environment able to provide users with infinite on-demand resources in a pay-per-use model promises new opportunities [1]. However, although different cloud services have been proven to be valid for scientific applications [2,3], in general, cloud infrastructures are still unable to meet the needs of the scientific community due to their high network latencies [4] and lack of performance [5]. Therefore, their use has been limited to dealing with bursts of jobs and to meeting deadlines. Meanwhile, different frameworks able to integrate several heterogeneous computing infrastructures have been proposed [6,7].

In [8], we introduced a framework for the flexible deployment and execution of scientific workflows in cluster, grid and cloud environments. Figure 1 shows a high-level view of the framework, which is composed of three different layers. At the top, the *User interface layer* allows users to program workflows using different

K.-K. Lau, W. Lamersdorf, and E. Pimentel (Eds.): ESOCC 2013, LNCS 8135, pp. 196–211, 2013.
© Springer-Verlag Berlin Heidelberg 2013

paradigms and widespread tools in the scientific community (Taverna, Triana, Kepler, Pegasus, etc.). Developed workflows are submitted to the framework for their execution via a Web Services interface. The *Execution layer* is responsible for managing the life-cycle of jobs composing the workflow. Internally, *a message bus* is used to exchange messages between users and the framework components that provide the core functionalities. Finally, at the bottom of the infrastructure, several heterogeneous infrastructures form the *Computing infrastructures layer.* Specifically, we have integrated: the HERMES cluster hosted by the Aragón Institute of Engineering Research (http://i3a.unizar.es/, I3A), which is managed by the HTCondor middleware (http://research.cs.wisc.edu/htcondor/); two research and production grids hosted by the Institute for Biocomputation and Physics of Complex Systems (http://bifi.es/en/, BIFI) and managed by the gLite middleware (http://glite.cern.ch/), namely AraGrid (http://www.aragrid.es/) and PireGrid (http://www.piregrid.eu/); and the Amazon Elastic Compute Cloud (Amazon EC2) [9]. A more detailed description can be found in [8,10].

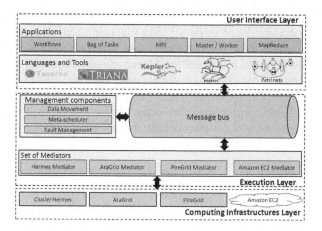

Fig. 1. Layered architecture of the framework for the deployment and execution of scientific workflows in heterogeneous computing infrastructures

The cornerstone of the proposed approach is the use of a *message bus*-based integration model. The message bus was based on the Linda coordination model [11] (more details are provided in Section 3). In [12], we described DRLinda, a distributed message bus built using high-level Petri Nets. The approach has proven to be effective in solving a variety of computationally complex scientific problems such as the First Provenance Challenge [8] or the LIGO Inspiral analysis workflow [10], for instance. However, the DRLinda-based message bus suffers from two major problems. On the one hand, the message bus is not fault-tolerant. Therefore, a machine failure can cause message loss or service interruption. On the other hand, scalability is achieved by using a large number of machines to host DRLinda distributed nodes. Hence, too many resources are required in order to ensure a good Quality of Service, which implies high economic costs [13].

As a consequence, the approach is not reliable enough to support long-term experiments, where the framework must work without errors and uninterruptedly, and a large number of users submitting jobs and recovering results at the same time. To deal with these issues, in this paper we explore the use of cloud computing to implement the message bus. As shown in Section 4, we propose a flexible design where the message bus interface and implementation are decoupled. On the one hand, elasticity, load balancing and replication mechanisms are key to address performance, scalability and fault-tolerance issues in the interface. On the other hand, the use of the Amazon Simple Queue Service (Amazon SQS) [9], a highly reliable (messages are stored redundantly across multiple data centers and servers), available (Amazon SLA guarantees a 99.95$ availability) and scalable (an unlimited number of clients can read and write an unlimited number of messages at any time) asynchronous message queueing service, represents the core of the proposed design. Finally, we evaluate the performance and scalability of the new message bus and we compare it with our former DRLinda-based implementation showing the goodness of the cloud-based design.

The remainder of this paper is organized as follows. Section 3 discusses the advantages and drawbacks of using a Linda-like communication model versus a queue-based paradigm for the implementation of a message-based coordination system. Section 4 explores the benefits of using cloud computing services to improve the message bus capabilities and proposes a design based on the Amazon SQS service. Section 5 analyses the performance and scalability of the proposed implementation, comparing it with the former Linda-based implementation. Finally, some conclusions and future work directions are presented in Section 6.

2   Related Work

The usefulness of Amazon services for scientific computing has been previously analysed. [14] extends the capacity of a private grid integrating Cloud resources on-demand. By means of some experimental executions of real-world applications, the authors show the benefits of adding external Cloud-based resources to improve computing capabilities of grids and deal with load peaks. In [15], the viability of Amazon S3 as the storage option for large scale science projects is analysed. Performance, cost and availability are the targets of the study. As a result, the study provides some recommendations that any storage service for the scientific community should provide and concludes that, although Amazon S3 is a good option for many usual applications, its security is not adequate for supporting complex collaborative scenarios, which are usual in scientific environments. Studying the impact of several configuration in the use of Amazon EC2 and Amazon S3 is the goal of [16]. The configurations are established in terms of computing and storage resources and are analysed via simulation. As a result, the experiments proved that the provisioning technique can have a significant impact in the total execution cost.

Regarding Amazon SQS, some research evaluate its performance and capabilities. In [17], the author evaluates the throughput of different Amazon services including Amazon SQS. The author concludes that the performance is sufficient to schedule a few long tasks (tasks that last minutes or hours) but it is necessary to group tasks into batches in scenarios with many short tasks (a few seconds). However, these experiments are performed in 2007 when the service was in its first steps and they do not exploit the parallelization capabilities of the service. More recent research shows Amazon SQS as a suitable environment for high performance scenarios [3]. To test it, they propose the use of a process with three threads: a sender, a receiver and a deleter, which manage share data structures to deal with duplicate messages and to delete read messages. As a result, they observed that Amazon SQS is able to provide the performance required for scientific computations. Also, they analyse the importance of the configuration of the message visibility timeout to prevent the appearance of duplicate messages when messages are not processed within the specified timeout. In [2], Amazon SQS is used as part of a fault-tolerant MapReduce implementation able to work with spot instances and massive machine terminations. Amazon SQS is key to provide the required flexibility to the implementation by decoupling sending messages between master and worker processes. Workers dequeue messages, process the corresponding split and then delete the message. Thus, if the worker machine fails or terminates while it is processing a split, the message visibility timeout will eventually expire and another worker will retrieve and process that split.

3   Linda-Based versus Queue-Based Bus

The proposed framework is based on the use of a bus implemented according to the Linda coordination model proposed in [11]. Linda coordination is based on the use of a data space shared by the processes that must communicate, which is known as the tuple space. Processes communicate by introducing tuples into the tuple space, in an asynchronous way, and removing them by using a blocking pattern-based matching function. This blocking operation provides the necessary synchronization mechanism. Two different implementations of the Linda-based message bus, called RLinda [18] and DRLinda [12] were developed by the authors. RLinda is a centralized implementation whereas DRLinda is a distributed version that uses several RLinda nodes to host messages in a distributed way.

We adopted Linda as the coordination model because it is specially adapted for the flexibility required by evolving systems. The fact of using a unique point for information exchange allows processes to enter or leave the coordination space in a dynamic way. In this sense, alternative asynchronous communication systems, which require processes to know the communication topology in order to send the appropriate messages to the appropriate channels (queues), are not flexible enough. This is so because no selective reading of messages is allowed in queue systems: just take the next message. A way of alleviating this constraint is to use as many queues as message types.

Despite the fact that the Linda implementations we used have proven to be effective and valid in terms of system performance, they present some drawbacks. Firstly, they are not fault-tolerant: messages (tuples) are stored in memory and, hence, a host failure will cause message loss. This is especially problematic for the non-distributed version. Otherwise, scalability (in the sense of being able to deal with an increasing number of message exchanges) is achieved by increasing the capabilities of the Linda implementation. In the case of the distributed version this is easier, since it can be done by increasing the number of nodes. Secondly, the number of used distributed Linda nodes could not be decreased in an easy way, since that would require some mechanisms to efficiently move tuples among nodes, which can be a time consuming task. As a consequence, DRLinda is able to deal with bursts of requests but it remains oversized when the load drops, making the message bus more prone to failures and increasing the economic costs of the solution.

Even if, as stated before, the use of a queue system can be expensive in terms of the number of required queues, the question of evaluating the possibility of implementing a queue-based bus version appeared as a plausible solution to deal with the drawbacks of the Linda-based implementations used by the framework. One of the main reasons is that developing a service oriented architecture based on asynchronous service invocations, as in this the case, is not difficult.

4   A Highly Scalable and Reliable Cloud-Based Message Bus

To improve the scalability and reliability of the message bus, cloud computing provides new opportunities. Public cloud providers supply on-demand resources and a great variety of services in a pay-per-use model. This view of infinite resources along with other cloud capabilities such as elasticity, flexibility, reliability, auto-scaling, or self-management make cloud computing an ideal environment to support applications with high scalability and reliability requirements [1].

In [13], we first explored the use of cloud computing to improve the performance of the message bus. Specifically, we proposed an elastic design of DR-Linda that combines the use of local machines and cloud resources, and also auto-scales the number of distributed nodes used at each moment depending on different performance parameters. Thereby, nodes are reserved and released dynamically according to a defined scaling policy. The goal was to reduce the cost while maintaining the performance and the Quality of Service. However, despite of solving the scalability problem (performance degradation experienced when multiple clients use the message bus at the same time), this solution is still not fault-tolerant, suffering the same reliability issues as the original (non cloud-based) DRLinda implementation.

Let us now describe how the service has been designed and implemented using the Amazon Simple Queue Service (Amazon SQS) [9].

4.1   An Elastic, Scalable and Reliable Bus Entry Point

The message bus entry point (the view processes have of the bus) and implementation (where messages are stored and how they are accessed) have been developed in a decoupled way. This approach makes the bus much more flexible and adaptable. The main advantage is that different implementations can be easily deployed, keeping the interface simple with the users unaware of the specific implementation used. Thus, different implementations can be used depending on the desired Quality of Service, the application domain, and performance and reliability requirements, for instance. Besides, this design makes it possible to completely change the bus implementation at run-time transparently to users.

On the other hand, decoupling the actual implementation of the message bus and the entry point do have some drawbacks. As the implementation and the entry point are decoupled, and probably hosted in different distributed machines, the entry point could represent a single point of failure and a bottleneck.

Figure 2 depicts the bus entry point design. First, the *DNS Server* is responsible for routing requests to active *Load Balancers*. Obviously, it must be highly reliable and scalable since it represents a potential bottleneck and a single point of failure. It must also provide with a mechanism (for instance, DNS Failover) to route traffic to alive *Load Balancers* and make sure all requests are served.

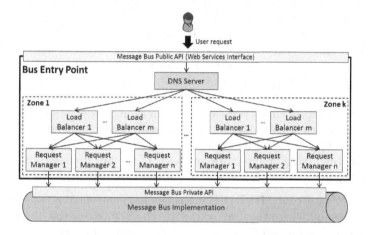

Fig. 2. A high-level view of the bus access component

Next, *Load Balancers* are responsible for balancing requests between the *Request Managers*. Multiple load balancers can be used to ensure the component is not a bottleneck and all requests are served without unnecessary delays. With regard to reliability, several Load Balancers can be used and the DNS Server only uses active Load Balancers.

Finally, *Request Managers* handle specific requests by interacting with the private interface of the specific message bus implementation used. Depending on the implementation, a request could correspond to a direct request or a complex chain of multiple interactions. In any case, these interactions are managed in a completely transparent way to users. To ensure the scalability of the component, *Request Managers* are deployed elastically: the number of machine instances used is automatically scaled depending on system load and number of requests, while faulty machines are transparently replaced by new ones.

Related *Load Balancers* and *Request Managers* are deployed as part of the same zone to reduce network latency. Thus, in order to prevent loss of service if an entire zone goes down, the bus entry point consists of several zones. Then, different configurations can be used: all zones can be active, just one zone can be active while the remaining are used as backup, or some hybrid alternative.

4.2   An Implementation of the Message Bus Based on Amazon SQS

For the implementation of the message bus we have chosen the Amazon Simple Queue Service (Amazon SQS) [9]. Amazon SQS is a highly reliable and scalable message queueing service for storing messages in queues and sharing information between different components of a distributed system in an asynchronous way. The service is particularly simple to use thanks to its REST-based API and the high-level development kits provided by Amazon. Amazon SQS is built to be highly reliable and to provide high availability. Messages are highly durable: each message is redundantly stored across different computation nodes and different availability zones in the defined region. In the presence of node failures or problems in some zone, the service is still available, with the guaranty of no message loss. Also, Amazon SQS has been designed to be extremely scalable. It supports an unlimited number of queues, an unlimited number of messages in each queue, an unlimited number of clients reading and writing messages and concurrent access to each queue at any time and without performance degradation [9]. Therefore, its characteristics make Amazon SQS a very suitable choice for the message bus implementation. Furthermore, using Amazon SQS to implement the message bus allows us to use other Amazon services in the deployment.

Figure 3 sketches an architectural overview of the bus implementation. From a structural point of view, it is composed of the following elements:

The Bus Entry Point (BEP). The bus has a unique entry point where messages are sent and where they are retrieved. The BEP parses the message information and acts accordingly to the message content and the type of request: out (write operation) and in (destructive read operation or *take* operation). If the message corresponds to a job invocation, it sends the message to the Job Meta-scheduler (JMeta) component, returns the Amazon unique message identifier to the calling process and creates a queue in the Results Queues Pool (RQP) using that identifier. Also, the message identifier is stored into the own message to be used later by different components. If the message is a request of a job result, it reads the message from the specified queue (using the provided identifier) until a new message is available (so the client is in a synchronous waiting status), deletes it and destroys the queue. There is a queue collection process which is on charge of destroying the queues, so the request returns as soon as the result message is available, and no further delay is required.

Job Meta-Scheduler (JMeta). The Job Meta-scheduler has a queue in which receives job invocation messages. If there is a specific infrastructure set as the target for the invocation, the JMeta routes it to the appropriate Mediator.

Otherwise, all Mediators compete for the message, which means that the JMeta component will dispatch it according to certain rules and QoS parameters [10].

Mediators. There is a mediator for each component able to provide any service. Mediators can correspond to computing resources, in which case they are in charge of invoking resource services and dealing with the results, or they may correspond to any alternative software module. Any mediator is composed of an input queue, where messages for the mediated component are sent, as well as the Message Processing Unit (MPU). Also, each mediator contains a local job response handler, a component that processes the result of the computing infrastructure and takes certain decisions depending on the termination status, such as resubmitting the job or sending it to the Fault Handler (FH) component. In case the job finishes successfully, the results are sent to the queue specified by means of the queue identifier contained in the job invocation message, and stored in the Results Queues Pool component.

Fault Handler (FH). Messages that are returned from a computing infrastructure in a faulty error are processed by the Fault Handler component. The FH takes certain decisions depending on the error status of the job, such as getting another target infrastructure to succeed in the job execution or discard its execution [13], for instance. For such purposes, it can modify the target of the job invocation and then route the message back to the JMeta. In case the job has been executed several times without succeed, it can return an error status to the original sender, so it will return the message to the corresponding queue in the Results Queues Pool.

Results Queues Pool (RQP). As was previously stated, the BEP creates a new queue for each incoming job invocation. Every queue can be accessed twofold. On the one hand, an external process can access a specific queue by means of the identifier returned when it originally sent the job invocation through the BEP. On the other hand, internally, both Mediators and the Fault Handler component can access each queue by means of the corresponding identifier stored in the messages that are exchanged among the framework components.

Let us now briefly describe the life-cycle of a service invocation by means of a case in which a process requests the execution of a job in the HERMES cluster and it is performed without errors. Figure 3 shows the messages exchanged and their order. First, the process sends the request to the BEP (step 1), which routes the message to the JMeta (step 2). Next, the message identifier provided by Amazon is returned to the invoking process (step 3) and used to create a queue in the RQP (step 4). The JMeta reads the message from its queue and sends it to the HERMES Mediator (step 5), which invokes the computing service (step 6). Once the result is received, the HERMES Mediator sends it to the previously created queue in the RPQ (step 7). On the other hand, the process eventually requests the job result to the BEP (step 8), who routes the request to the appropriate queue in the RQP (step 9). Finally, when the message is read from the queue (step 10), the BEP provides the invoking process with the message (step 11).

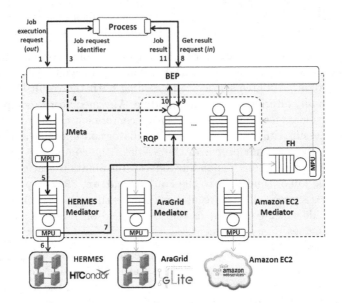

Fig. 3. High-level view of the bus architecture. The arrows indicates the messages exchanged between the framework components. The bold arrows show a use case where a process request the execution of a job in the HERMES cluster and it is performed without errors. The numbers indicate the order of operations in the use case.

4.3   Dealing with Some SQS Constraints

Let us now discuss how the constraints imposed by Amazon SQS affect us and how we deal with them in order to make the bus implementation viable.

Amazon SQS only guarantees at-least-once message delivery. This means that the same message can be read from the same queue more than once. In the case of messages sent by the computing infrastructure mediators to invoking processes (depicted with number 7 in Figure 3), this is not a problem: after the first copy is read, the queue is destroyed. But the problem is real when the message corresponds, for instance, to a job invocation (depicted with number 5 in Figure 3), since it would be possible to execute more than once an expensive computation. To prevent these problems, the framework components save the identifier of each read message and, when a new message is received, they check the new identifier and discard duplicate messages. In future, we plan to analyse other more elaborate solutions to manage duplicate messages transparently.

Amazon SQS imposes a message visibility timeout. This timeout defines a time period during which a message cannot be read more than once. As shown in [3], a bad set of this timeout may cause a significant performance degradation. This is because if an already read message is not deleted before its visibility timeout expires, the message becomes available and can be read again, increasing the number of messages handled and degrading the bus performance. Furthermore, setting a long visibility timeout could cause some messages to be inaccessible if there is an error between the receive and delete operations. Therefore, a proper configuration of the visibility timeout is required. In our tests, we have checked that the standard 30-second timeout is enough to handle any message. This value could change depending on the application context.

Amazon SQS does not guarantee a FIFO message delivery policy, but a best-effort FIFO policy. Therefore, if an application requires message ordering, clients are responsible for handling this. In our case, message ordering is not an important feature and the best-effort FIFO policy is sufficient for our needs.

Amazon SQS imposes a maximum size of 256 KB for messages. In our framework, the larger messages are those that describe jobs to be executed. Their size depends on the complexity of the job (arguments, input files, output files, etc.) and it can vary from a few bytes to hundred of kilobytes. To support any size messages, we follow the next approach. If the message is over 256 KB, it is compressed in GZIP format and encoded in Base64 (Amazon SQS only supports a small range of printable characters). If the compressed message is still too large, the message is stored in Amazon S3 [9] and a pointer to the message is sent to the corresponding queue. To detect whether a message has been compressed or whether it is a pointer, a header is added to the beginning of the message.

Message reception is a non-blocking operation. By default, reading messages from a queue is a non-blocking operation even when the queue is empty. However, Amazon provides a long polling feature that allows a read request to wait up to 20 seconds for a new message before returning an empty response. Besides, there is no delay when messages are available. Therefore, we chain consecutive reads until a new message is received.

Amazon SQS imposes a deadline of 14 days for a message to stay in a queue. When this retention period is exceeded, the message is automatically deleted. This situation may occur in two different ways: a user does not get the execution result of a job or a framework component does not get a job request. In the first case, we assume that the user is not interested in that job, whereas in the second case, there is no component able to handle that message so it may be discard. Therefore, the message retention period is not an actual limitation.

5   Evaluation

In this section, we detail the experiments performed in order to measure the scalability of the Amazon-based bus and to compare it to the previous one.

The experiments aim to measure the performance and the scalability of the proposed cloud-based message bus. They were performed in the Oregon region because it provides better performance than the other regions, as we show below. Regarding the message bus deployment, a single *Amazon Elastic Load Balancer* was used because this is sufficient for our needs. *Request Managers* were deployed using *t1.micro* instances since they do not need high performance capabilities as the scalability is achieved using several instances. In the *Request Managers* implementation, we used the sequential Amazon SQS client provided by Amazon because we wanted to measure the individual economic cost of each user request (one request consists of multiple interaction with the Amazon SQS). In the future, we will experiment with the Amazon batch client to increase the performance and reduce the cost. Regarding clients, the messages used are extracted from our previous experiments presented in [8], their average size is 40 KB. Finally, each experiment was carried out five times. Therefore, the results presented below show the average values obtained from these experiments.

Influence of the Amazon Region. Amazon divides its cloud into different regions distributed around the world. They have different prices and, depending on where the clients and the bus are being executed, this can also influence the access latency. The first experiment tries to achieve an insight into how influential this may be. With this purpose, an experiment where a unique client puts 5000 messages into a SQS queue (send message operation) and then get them (read message and delete message operations) was performed. Both client and bus were placed in every Amazon region available and all possible combinations were tested. Table 1 shows the average performance of the *write* operation, the same results can be extrapolated for the *destructive read* operation. Each value in the table shows the time, in milliseconds, required for the client in this column to write a message in the queue managed by the bus hosted in that row.

Table 1. Performance of write operation through different Amazon regions. Times in the table are expressed in milliseconds.

	Singapore	Sydney	Tokyo	Ireland	Sao Paulo	N.California	N.Virginia	Oregon
Singapore	**86**	1059	462	1438	1751	914	1300	1134
Sydney	971	**56**	697	1577	1810	814	1389	971
Tokyo	478	659	**72**	1218	1557	593	987	784
Ireland	1475	1473	1480	**94**	1282	898	581	899
Sao Paulo	1721	1448	1558	1225	**55**	835	822	1080
N.California	817	1007	582	838	1047	**58**	491	142
N.Virginia	1203	1292	1017	555	820	410	**110**	487
Oregon	1111	978	695	715	1143	137	443	**49**

The results show the importance of the client and the message bus being close together. When the client and the message bus are located in the same region, the average time is between 49 milliseconds (Oregon) and 110 milliseconds (N. Virginia). However, if the client and the message bus are located in different regions, the time required for each operation increases substantially to around 1 second. Also, there is a significant performance variation between different regions, even twice in same cases. Additionally, the results show that to offer a worldwide service, it is important to analyse the different latencies obtained by several clients distributed along the world. Finally, the results allow us conclude that the developed Amazon-based message bus is viable for our purpose because the time required for *read* and *write* is much less than the time required for the execution of scientific computations.

Influence of the Number of Clients. In this experiment, we measured how the number of concurrent clients accessing the bus described in Section 4 can influence the bus performance. For this purpose, up to 100 clients accessed the unique bus entry point, introducing and recovering 1000 messages, with a random delay between [200, 250] milliseconds among each **out** (write) and its corresponding **in** (destructive read or *take*) operation. The entry point was deployed with a single *t1.micro* machine during the whole experiment. Figure 4 shows the experiment results. They show the average time observed by clients in the performed operations (by solid lines in Figure 4) and the time required for the different Amazon SQS requests involved (dashed lines in Figure 4).

The results point towards the importance of a correct configuration of the Bus Entry Point. Up to 25 concurrent clients, the performance observed by clients remains within acceptable bounds. It varies from 253.26 ms to 410.61 ms for the **out** operation and from 124.94 ms to 233.40 ms for the **in** operation when the number of clients is increased from 5 to 25. However, when 50 clients access the bus at the same time, we observe an exponential performance degradation. In this case, the average time required to complete the **out** and **in** operations becomes 2262.44 ms and 1956.98 ms respectively. Finally, when the number of clients reaches 75 clients, the entry point is unable to manage so many connections and becomes inaccessible.

Influence of the Number of Machines Used for the Deployment of the Bus Entry Point. In this experiment, we varied the number of t1.micro instance machines used for the deployment of the Bus Entry Point and measured the influence of the number of instances used when the number of concurrent clients accessing the bus increases. Figure 5 shows the experiment results. Each curve shows the performance of the **out** and **in** operations for a fixed number of instances forming the Bus Entry Point.

The results show that when there are few concurrent clients, there is no benefit in having several instances and a single one may be sufficient. However, as the number of clients increases, more and more instances are required in order to maintain the bus performance and prevent service loss. Good performance can be

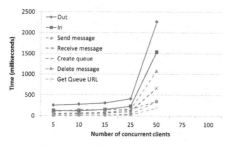
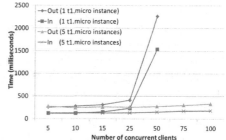
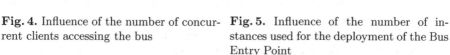

Fig. 4. Influence of the number of concurrent clients accessing the bus

Fig. 5. Influence of the number of instances used for the deployment of the Bus Entry Point

achieved by using five *t1.micro* instances to form the Bus Entry Point. Therefore, these results show the importance of an elastic design of the BEP, as we propose in Section 4. In any case, it will be necessary to explore scenarios with a large number of clients and different configurations of the Bus Entry Point in order to establish the number of requests that each machine can handle, and use this information to define autoscaling policies in the elastic design.

Amazon-Based Bus versus DRLinda Bus. In this experiment, we compared our former DRLinda (*Distributed Reference-nets based Linda*) implementation of the message bus [12] with the cloud-based approach presented in this paper. The comparison was performed in terms of the average performance of an operation and by varying the number of concurrent clients accessing the bus (25, 50, 75 and 100 clients). Each client repeat the previous experiments behaviour, but at this stage we ran the experiment for an hour.

First, we performed the experiment using the Amazon-based message bus with five *t1.micro* instances for the Bus Entry Point, because this configuration gave good enough performance in the previous experiments. After that, we calculated the cost of this approach in terms of dollars per hour, and the corresponding number of *t1.medium* and *t1.large* instances needed in order to match that cost. Table 2 summarizes this information. Note that depending on the number of clients accessing the bus, the cost of the Amazon-based approach increases, this is because the Amazon SQS charges according to the number of requests and the Amazon Elastic Load Balancer charges according to the amount of data processed.

Table 2. Approximate cost of the Amazon-based approach and the corresponding number of *t1.medium* and *t1.large* instances needed to match that cost

	25 clients	50 clients	75 clients	100 clients
Approximate cost ($/hour)	0.58	1.04	1.50	1.96
Number of *t1.medium* instances	4.86	8.67	12.49	16.30
Number of *t1.large* instances	2.43	4.34	6.24	8.15

In order to make a fair comparison of both implementations, DRLinda was deployed in order to have the same cost as the Amazon-based message bus. For each experiment, two different configurations were explored, using *t1.medium* and *t1.large* instances. The number of instances that appear in the table have been rounded up. Figure 6 depicts the experiment results.

The results show that, for the same cost, the Amazon-based bus is approximately 50% faster than the DRLinda bus. If we try to get the same performance for both implementations, the Amazon-based message bus is a much cheaper approach than DRLinda. Therefore, we can conclude that the Amazon-based bus approach outperforms the performance of the DRLinda bus for the same cost. The Amazon-based bus is faster but also is much more reliable and scalable than DRLinda because Amazon SQS (the actual implementation used for storing messages) is highly reliable and scalable. The Bus Entry Point has been designed to be fault-tolerant and it can be deployed elastically to fit the load

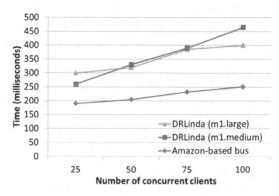

Fig. 6. Performance comparison between the DRLinda bus and the Amazon-based bus

experienced at each moment, which turns our proposal into a very suitable solution for a high variety of environments and scenarios.

6   Conclusions and Future Work

In this paper, we have proposed a new cloud-based design for the message bus of a framework for the execution of scientific computations in cluster, grids and clouds. The proposed approach is based in a flexible design where the Bus Entry Point and the specific implementation are decoupled. On the one hand, the Bus Entry Point is designed elastically in order to be scalable and fault tolerant. On the other hand, the Amazon Simple Queue Service (Amazon SQS), a highly scalable and reliable Amazon service, is used for the actual message bus implementation. Our experiments show the importance of placing clients and the message bus close together due to the high latencies observed between different regions. Also, they show the need for an elastic design capable of autoscaling the number of instances used to form the Bus Entry Point depending on the number of client requests. Finally, the comparison between the new Amazon-based bus and the former DRLinda bus shows that, for the same cost, the new message bus is also faster.

As future work, we will improve the statistical quality of the presented results by increasing the size and scale of the experiments performed. New experiments aimed at improving our knowledge of the Amazon Simple Queue Service, testing the proposed elastic design of the Bus Entry Point and understanding the impact of using different instance types in the Bus Entry Point will be performed. Also, we will study in detail the economic cost of the proposed bus and explore techniques for reducing it. Regarding duplicate messages, we will analyse their impact and we will explore solutions for minimizing it. Finally, we will also explore the use of other alternatives to Amazon SQS such as RabbitMQ (http://www.rabbitmq.com/), a highly reliable enterprise messaging system.

Acknowledgment. This work has been supported by the research project TIN2010-17905, granted by the Spanish Ministry of Science and Innovation, and the regional project DGA-FSE, granted by the European Regional Development Fund (ERDF).

References

1. Vaquero, L.M., Rodero-Merino, L., Caceres, J., Lindner, M.: A break in the clouds: towards a cloud definition. SIGCOMM Comput. Commun. Rev. 39(1), 50–55 (2008)
2. Liu, H.: Cutting mapreduce cost with spot market. In: The 3rd USENIX Conference on Hot topics in Cloud Computing, HotCloud 2011 (2011)
3. Yoon, H., Gavrilovska, A., Schwan, K., Donahue, J.: Interactive use of cloud services: Amazon sqs and s3. In: The 12th IEEE/ACM International Symposium on Cluster, Cloud and Grid Computing, CCGRID 2012, pp. 523–530 (2012)
4. Jackson, K.R., Ramakrishnan, L., Muriki, K., Canon, S., Cholia, S., Shalf, J., Wasserman, H.J., Wright, N.J.: Performance analysis of high performance computing applications on the amazon web services cloud. In: The 2010 IEEE Second International Conference on Cloud Computing Technology and Science, CLOUD-COM 2010, pp. 159–168 (2010)
5. Losup, A., Ostermann, S., Yigitbasi, N., Prodan, R., Fahringer, T., Epema, D.: Performance analysis of cloud computing services for many-tasks scientific computing. IEEE Trans. Parallel Distrib. Syst. 22(6), 931–945 (2011)
6. Yu, J., Buyya, R.: A taxonomy of workflow management systems for grid computing. J. Grid Comput. 3(3-4), 171–200 (2005)
7. Rahman, M., Ranjan, R., Buyya, R., Benatallah, B.: A taxonomy and survey on autonomic management of applications in grid computing environments. Concur. Comput.: Pract. Exper. 23(16), 1990–2019 (2011)
8. Fabra, J., Hernández, S., Álvarez, P., Ezpeleta, J.: A framework for the flexible deployment of scientific workflows in grid environments. In: The Third International Conference on Cloud Computing, GRIDs, and Virtualization, CLOUD COMPUTING 2012, pp. 1–8 (2012)
9. Amazon Web Services (2012), http://aws.amazon.com (accessed May 1, 2013)
10. Hernández, S., Fabra, J., Álvarez, P., Ezpeleta, J.: A Simulation-based Scheduling Strategy for Scientific Workflows. In: The 2nd International Conference on Simulation and Modeling Methodologies, Technologies and Applications, SIMULTECH 2012, pp. 61–70 (2012)
11. Carriero, N., Gelernter, D.: Linda in context. Commun. ACM 32(4), 444–458 (1989)
12. Fabra, J., Álvarez, P., Ezpeleta, J.: DRLinda: A Distributed Message Broker for Collaborative Interactions Among Business Processes. In: Psaila, G., Wagner, R. (eds.) EC-Web 2007. LNCS, vol. 4655, pp. 212–221. Springer, Heidelberg (2007)
13. Hernández, S., Fabra, J., Álvarez, P., Ezpeleta, J.: Using cloud-based resources to improve availability and reliability in a scientific workflow execution framework. In: The Fourth International Conference on Cloud Computing, GRIDs, and Virtualization, CLOUD COMPUTING 2013, pp. 230–237 (2013)
14. Ostermann, S., Prodan, R., Fahringer, T.: Extending grids with cloud resource management for scientific computing. In: The 10th IEEE/ACM International Conference on Grid Computing, pp. 42–49 (2009)

15. Palankar, M.R., Iamnitchi, A., Ripeanu, M., Garfinkel, S.: Amazon s3 for science grids: a viable solution? In: The 2008 International Workshop on Data-Aware Distributed Computing, DADC 2008, pp. 55–64 (2008)
16. Deelman, E., Singh, G., Livny, M., Berriman, B., Good, J.: The cost of doing science on the cloud: The montage example. In: the International Conference for High Performance Computing, Networking, Storage and Analysis, SC 2008, pp. 1–12 (2008)
17. Garfinkel, S.L.: An evaluation of amazons grid computing services: Ec2, s3 and sqs. Technical report. Center for Research on Computation and Society (2007)
18. Fabra, J., Álvarez, P., Bañares, J.A., Ezpeleta, J.: RLinda: A Petri Net Based Implementation of the Linda Coordination Paradigm for Web Services Interactions. In: Bauknecht, K., Pröll, B., Werthner, H. (eds.) EC-Web 2006. LNCS, vol. 4082, pp. 183–192. Springer, Heidelberg (2006)

A Comparison of On-Premise
to Cloud Migration Approaches

Claus Pahl, Huanhuan Xiong, and Ray Walshe

IC4, Dublin City University
Dublin 9, Ireland
http://www.ic4.ie/

Abstract. While cloud computing has certainly gained attention, the potential for increased uptake of the technology is still large. As a consequence, how to move and migrate to the cloud is an unanswered question for many organisations. Gaining an understanding of cloud migration processes from on-premise architectures is our aim here. For this purpose, we look at three provider-driven case studies based on the common three layers of cloud computing: Infrastructure (IaaS), platform (PaaS) and software (SaaS) as a service. These shall be complemented by a fourth, independent systems integration perspective. We extract common migration process activities for the layer-specific processes and discuss commonalities, differences and open issues. The results presented are based on expert interviews and focus groups held with major international cloud solution providers and independent consultants.

Keywords: Cloud Migration, Cloud Migration Processes, On-premise to Cloud, Cloud Architecture.

1 Introduction

Software application hosting settings range from on-premise solutions to private clouds to public clouds [1]. The migration into the cloud or between these often hybrid scenarios or between offerings is a key concern and the determination and assessment of possible migration processes is important. We carried out research into migration scenarios in the form of migrations processes and patterns based on expert interviews and focus groups with major international cloud solution providers and independent consultants. The proposed processes document a range of different architectural settings. They highlight the concerns – like costs, skills and technologies – to be considered to deploy applications in various cloud scenarios and to migrate into these from on-premise architectures. Attention also needs to be given to hybrid solutions where parts of an application system remain on-premise and parts are migrated to the cloud, maintaining an efficient division of responsibilities and effective data flows.

In order to start the migration process determination and evaluation, an empirical investigation into migration processes was conducted at the Irish Centre for Cloud Computing and Commerce (IC4). A structured methodological approach

K.-K. Lau, W. Lamersdorf, and E. Pimentel (Eds.): ESOCC 2013, LNCS 8135, pp. 212–226, 2013.
© Springer-Verlag Berlin Heidelberg 2013

was followed, involving IC4 industry consortium members (`http:www. ic4.ie`) with background or experience in cloud migration. We conducted expert interviews to gain a broader understanding beyond individual cases than would have been possible through concrete projects observation alone. The experts would have had 15-20 years of industrial practice and a minimum of 3 years in cloud migration.

Our work has focused on determining the principle cloud migration processes. Our investigation has shown differences between the cloud deployment models IaaS, PaaS and SaaS, which we will reflect by model-specific migration processes based on a catalogue of common activities. We emphasise the differences and commonalities between the three layers, but also use an independent broker acting as a systems integrator (in contrast to the other more provider-based migration) to broaden the view and evaluate previous results.

We discuss some foundations for our study in Section 2, before detailing the results in Section 3. The observations are discussed in Section 4, before summarising related work in Section 5.

2   Assumptions and Background

The migration layers that we identified are mainly derived from the user-oriented service models SaaS, PaaS and IaaS [1, 10]. The concerns shall briefly be outlined:

- SaaS. Companies look for a migration solution to move their existing on-premises applications to a cloud environment. Application vendors frequently want to evaluate a cloud platform on which to deploy a new application or SaaS offering.
- PaaS. PaaS Migration is the process of moving from the use of one software operating and deployment environment to another environment. At this layer customers do not manage their virtual machines, but rely on the infrastructure layer's compute and storage resources. They merely create applications within an existing API or programing language.
- IaaS. IaaS migration is mainly offering virtual machines as a (compute) service to users, such as moving from one VM to another, or managing or interoperating the different VMs. In addition, storage or network capabilities can also be provided. Instead of purchasing servers or even hosted services, IaaS customers can procure and operate servers, data storage systems, or networking resources at will.

We define cloud migration as follows. Cloud migration is the process of partially or completely deploying an organization's digital assets, services, IT resources or applications to the cloud. The cloud migration process may involve retaining some IT infrastructure on-site. In such a scenario, the existing system may be fused with a partial cloud solution that can be hosted by a third party over the Internet for a fee. The cloud component of this hybridised system can transition between several cloud providers allowing businesses to choose the most cost-effective solution. However, the migration process involves the risk of accidentally exposing sensitive business critical information. Therefore, cloud migration requires careful analysis, planning and execution to ensure the cloud solution's compatibility with organizational requirements, while maintaining the availability and integrity of the organization's IT systems.

Our motivation is to determine common migration processes and decompose them into operational level activities in order to make the migration process more transparent, agile, and suitable for a variety of business models. Our research will provide an understanding of the core mechanism to assist SMEs (Small to Medium Enterprises) in particular with the migration of their IT infrastructure to the Cloud. We will concentrate particularly on the area of managing the transition of on-premises applications to the Cloud. Our ultimate aim (beyond the aims of this investigation here) is to develop a system to minimise the inherent complexities involved with the migration to a Cloud Computing environment.

3   Cloud Migration Case Studies

The three case studies SaaS, PaaS and IaaS, as well as the systems integrator case study shall now be looked at individually. The results presented here were extracted from interviews and focus groups held with migration experts. Primarily, on-premise to cloud migration was considered. A common understanding of cloud migration processes was assumed as follows:

> A cloud migration process is a set of migration activities carried to support an end-to-end cloud migration. Cloud migration processes define a comprehensive perspective, capturing business and technical concerns. Stakeholder with different backgrounds are involved.

Thus, initial requirements and expectation elicitations are part of the processes as are tools for automated migration of IT artefacts or plans for the deployment of new cloud services and decommissioning of old infrastructure.

We define typically three or four top-level activities that are performed as discrete, sequenced steps. For each activity, we describe the following concerns:

Concern	Concern of the Respective Activity
focus	a differentiation whether the focus is technical or business-oriented in nature
from-to	source and target of migration activity
vision & ignorance	a distinction of migration benefits amd expectations that potential users are aware of (their 'vision') and those overlooked (their 'ignorance')
cases	an identification of any distinguishable special cases
stakeholder	the stakeholder involved
artefacts	the IT artefacts involved
steps	the individual, smaller steps involved in the activity

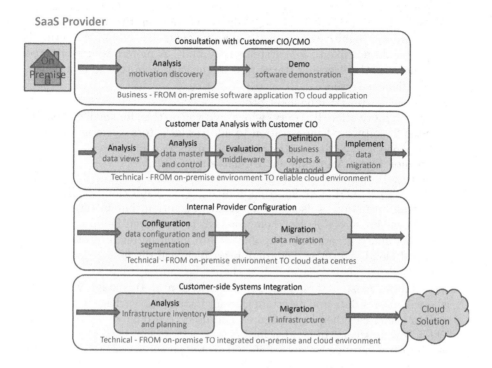

Fig. 1. SaaS Migration Processes

The top-level process activities and the individual steps will be summarised in respective diagrams. The discussion reflects the perspective of the solution providers, e.g. their aim to clarify benefits, but also potential problems.

3.1   SaaS-Level Migration

For SaaS-level migration (Fig. 1), the software applications under consideration here are classical ERP packages for accounting, HR management, CRM etc., but also domain-specific software for the retailing or engineering sector would apply.

1. **Consultation with Customer CIO (or CMO)**
   – Focus: Business
   – From-To: FROM on-premise software TO cloud software application
   Cloud application providers aim to sell their product, but also need to guide the process. An important element of the discussion with customers is to emphasise that a democratisation of software provisioning takes place, i.e. the same service is provided for everyone.

- Vision: more agility through a more declarative way of configuring and managing software and a drag & drop style of operating applications.
- Ignorance: cognitive dissidence, i.e. losing control, is often a concern. IT people do not like to lose systems they built. A more business-oriented concern is the licensing status that might vary from tool to tool, which is a financial issue.

The following steps can be identified:

- Step 1: motivation discovery (why would you do this) for small companies
- Step 2: software demonstration to address all actors concerns (meeting or phone call) as an additional step for midsize companies

2. **Customer Data Analysis with Customer CIO**
   - Focus: Technical
   - From-To: FROM on-premise environment TO reliable cloud environment

Data transformation is usually the technical solution, but in terms of expected benefits, a reliable cloud environment is the driver. Failure assurance (failover), analysis and audit capabilities are much better in professionally managed cloud solutions. This requires a technical discussion under these headings as to what data would or should be moved, what views and responsibilities exist. A first analysis and selection at this stage will define who will master data and ascertain that for instance no garbage is migrated. A data loader can then be configured and used accordingly.

The following steps can be identified:

- Step 1: what view on data: 180-360 degree perspectives
- Step 2: who will master data
- Step 3: evaluate middleware solutions: once-off, incremental or (full-blown) integration in the cloud
- Step 4: the customer MIS plan defines the application data model (model the business object such as a customer, an account, activities)
- Step 5: select core data for migration: segmentation if a data model exists

3. **Internal Provider Configuration**
   - Focus: Technical
   - From-To: FROM on-premise environment TO cloud data centres

The concern is the provider-side (internal) configuration and segmentation of data for transfer and storage. SaaS providers often provide data migration tools through sales infrastructures like app marketplaces.

Two cases can be distinguished. SMBs (small-mid business) have a customisation need arising from the B2B environment where efficiency and growth are the drivers. USBs (ultra-small business) require configuration for their B2C environment, targeting engagement, campaigns and loyalty as drivers.

4. **Customer-side Systems Integration**
   - Focus: Technical
   - From-To: FROM on-premise environment TO integrated on-premise and cloud environment

Rarely all on-premise IT infrastructure will be migrated into a cloud environment. Thus, an integration between different on-premise and (hybrid) cloud solutions is required. Larger solution providers offer these integration tools, the IBM Websphere Cast Iron cloud integration is an example.

An often observed problem concerns IT staff: they often feel overstretched due to recent virtualisation cycles in their organisations and do not like their own systems to be abandoned. Cooperation can consequently be reluctant.

Migration should be more than just redoing past activities in the cloud, i.e. cloud migration creates an opportunity to transform architectures and internal processes to some extent.

Success of the migration process is of importance for both providers and their clients. This can be measured in terms of different metrics such as headcount (a business concern for the provider) or fewer servers in use (a technical concern for the client).

Like any other process, cloud migration benefits from tools and proven techniques to be applied. The data loader is a tool example for most application software. In addition, a list of questions alone or better a template for discussions with questions, particularly for the first stage, is useful. As some of the software applications are common in organisations, so are migration, integration and deployment support. There is a noticeable differentiation between organisations of different size, only offering standard solutions for smaller clients.

3.2   PaaS-Level Migration

PaaS solutions provide support for the development and deployment of software. We will particularly focus on development (Fig. 2), with ISVs (independent software vendors) supporting other organisations with their development. This provides a more complex PaaS setting. Specifically, we consider here a PaaS solution by a multinational, providing a platform based on globally distributed datacentres. SDKs for different development languages are available.

1. **Consultation with ISV CEO**
   - Focus: Business
   - From-To: FROM classical licensing model TO SaaS
   The transfer is often forced by an ISV's end customers. As the latter are the ISV's PaaS customers, as a consequence, a SaaS/PaaS alignment is required where the ISV solution is made available as a SaaS, making the situation more complex than the previous SaaS case. Also, the PaaS providers as multinationals are companies that often work with partners (consultancies), which can be involved at all levels.
     - Vision: costs, sales and marketing are the drivers for an ISV to adopt cloud development. The value proposition is that hosting is outsourced, i.e. no more management of infrastructure is required.
     - Ignorance: while in general benefits and concerns such as security or failure are clear (and would be covered in SLA negotiations), some major changes result as implications that are not fully understood. This includes changed cash flow from a reliable up-front licensing model to a more unreliable pay-as-you-go or post-usage billing. Another major aspect overlooked is a necessary skills change. This applies to IT managers in particular, e.g. in relation to security technology like firewalls, but also the developers themselves, as we will discuss later on.

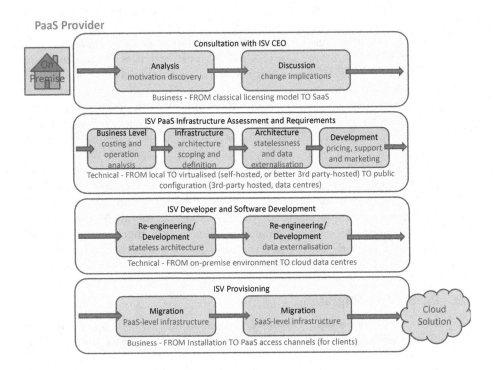

Fig. 2. PaaS Migration Processes

2. **ISV PaaS Infrastructure Assessment and Requirements**
   - Focus: Technical
   - From-To: FROM local TO virtualised (self-hosted, or better 3rd party-hosted) TO public configuration (3rd-party hosted, data centres)

The technology focus is on determining the elements of the existing IT development infrastructure and any dependencies between the components. A dependency analysis (using tools where possible, e.g. scanning networks to detect dependencies) needs to be carried out – this includes applications and machines. Already virtualised solutions are easier to move.

3. **ISV Developer and Software Development**
   - Focus: Technical
   - From-To: FROM Traditional OO/SC/Server Architectures TO cloud PaaS architecture

Development using a PaaS environment requires a number of major changes regarding the architecture design and software development approach.
   - Firstly, statelessness is a requirement for virtual machines (VMs) to be deployable without data.
   - Secondly, as a consequence, data externalisation is required to prepare for scale-out, which necessitates externalisation for an efficient management of elasticity requirements.

Consequently, this requires the developer to change development styles, possibly in a significant way depending on the current approach.

4. **ISV Provisioning**
   - Focus: Business
   - From-To: FROM Installation TO PaaS access channels (for clients)

The business focus reflects the transfer of cloud advantages from the ISV (at the PaaS-level) to its client (at the SaaS-level). Corresponding access channels to the new cloud deployment platform need to be provided.

As for SaaS, supporting techniques would be beneficial, but due to the increased complexity, these have less of an impact [7]. Commonly used are question catalogues (typical are 100 questions that help to capture current and envisioned development architectures) – used manually by PaaS provider consultants in the early stages of the migration process. Sometimes, these questions are organised into decision trees to guide and focus their application [6].

Some other observations are noteworthy. In contrast to the SaaS observations, the business side can be difficult to convince, while it is easier with IT staff. This indicates that changed cash flow is more of a problem than IT development re-skilling. Despite this observation, the architecture complexity (Stage 3) is often underestimated.

Success criteria that are applied here are expenditure-based and end-customer numbers (of ISVs) as metrics.

3.3   IaaS-Level Migration

At the IaaS level (Fig. 3), a number of different concerns including VM migration and big data migration emerge. We take a comprehensive view, i.e. migration of a full IT infrastructure is the setting.

1. **Business Case Determination**
   - Focus: Business
   - From-To: FROM on-premise installation TO IaaS solution

The key drivers are cost (reduction in operational expenditure is aimed at, but migration costs are often neglected), time (will almost always be incremental), impact (adding flexibility), strategy (what part of the operation or business would gain, which would suffer pain). Generally, given the normal scale, an incremental approach is taken. A testbed is defined and a migration strategy based on best-practice is selected where possible.

   - Vision: the drivers listed above have summarised the main concern, but cost reduction and increased flexibility are important expectations.
   - Ignorance: the 'pain versus gain' problem, i.e. negative aspects and the cost of required changes are sometimes neglected.

2. **Assessment and Planning**
   - Focus: Business
   - From-To: FROM on-premise installation TO IaaS solution

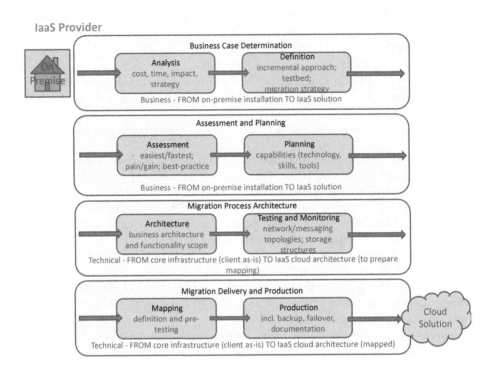

Fig. 3. IaaS Migration Processes

Input for this assessment stage includes a determination of the 'easiest/fastest' aspects (in order to start an incremental process), the pain/gain flow chart (gains versus costs) and, if possible, best-practice/reference cases. As part of a contracted process, success criteria are also determined.

The planning involves the determination of the required capabilities for the migration in terms of technology, skills and tools. Specifically, this could involve assessing the IaaS provider's own capabilities, i.e. tools available, the need to bring in contract partners. This results in building a migration project team, bringing together provider and customer. The project planning defines milestones, metrics, and role distribution for the project team.

3. **Migration Process Architecture**
   - Focus: Technical
   - From-To: FROM core infrastructure (client as-is) TO IaaS cloud architecture (to prepare mapping)

The technical focus starts with the business architecture and defines the functionality scope for the cloud architecture. Testing and monitoring are aspects that need to be addressed at this stage. The architecture concerns here are network, directory structures, the messaging topology and the application topology based on the identified business functions – there should be a cloud solution for each function as a guideline. Generally, the client's development methodology and processes and well as the operations processes need to be adapted. This follows our observations for the PaaS layer.

4. **Migration Delivery and Production**
    – Focus: Technical
    – From-To: FROM core infrastructure (client as-is) TO IaaS cloud architecture (mapped)

    The technical work includes the following steps: mapping definition and a pre-testing step before the new system is put into production. Despite some technical elements, the process is based on experience (past projects and general best-practice) are considered for migration projects as a whole.

    Production involves backup and documentation. Failover and other failure management need to be considered here as part of the migration of a production system.
    – an incremental approach plugs in components individually into the customer architecture and tests them,
    – a backup is to be kept both on-premise and in-cloud in operation while data are moved; only then can decommissioning of on-premise infrastructure start. Decommissioning needs a planned approach.

    Proper documentation and specification is, of course, a key concern.

Success criteria that can be applied here are the time frame or the metrics (by milestone) as discussed earlier.

Tool support is, as with the other cases, varied. On a higher level, reference case and best-practice approaches play an important role. Only in the technical context of virtualization technology, tools and automation are available. We can easily create virtual machines consisting of virtualized processor, communications, storage, networking, and I/O resources. Standards like OVF for VM packaging and exchange and OCCI as an example for VM lifecycle management or TOSCA for portability at the IaaS layer (and compliant tools) can be utilised.

Again, architecture emerges as critical concern. Specific to this level, networks, storage and messaging and application topology are the aspects.

3.4   Systems Integrator

This case study (Fig. 4) has a validating role as a number concerns already addressed above will reappear here. Again, the focus is on-premise to cloud migration. The company providing input for our study has acted as an intermediary/consultant supporting others to use a cloud service and as a service solution provider (another SaaS example), for instance an ISV-SaaS provider of accounting systems using a PaaS platform like Google Apps. Systems integration refers to the utilisation of infrastructure technologies to communication and processes to be supported [18].

1. **Customer - Business Analysis.** As in other cases, the main expected benefit is cost reduction. Another confirmation applies to the PaaS model. Cash flows change, but equally important, there is no hybrid between a software licence model and a SaaS model. A clear decision needs to be taken.

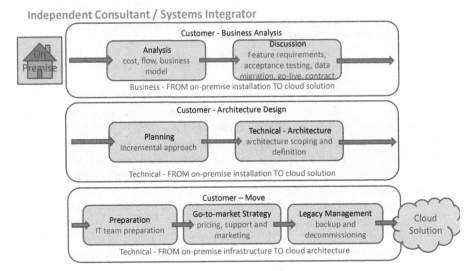

Fig. 4. Systems Integrator Migration Processes

The initial consultation with the client involves a discussion covering the following aspects and later steps of a migration process (a sample system type would be an accounting system moved to the cloud):

- Feature requirements determination
- User acceptance testing
- Data migration
- Go-live discussion
- Contract discussion

2. **Customer - Architecture Design.** The determination of the architectural scope is the aim. As in other complex cases, an incremental execution is the preferred solution. A lean startup solution would start with the top 5 out of 50 features as the first step, adding features in regular extensions. For a consultant, platform (and provider) selection is the first major decision.

   - At the SaaS layer, e.g. Salesforce is a leading provider of CRM software. The ecosystem can play a role here. Salesforce's App Exchange on top of its CRM provides additional benefits in terms of migration support and systems integration.
   - At the PaaS layer, e.g. MS Azure supports a variety of development languages such as Python and, of course, the .NET platform. However, Microsoft is less advanced in terms of marketplace solutions.

   Another dimension in choosing a provider are the different product lines, such as premium, standard and free, offering choice to the client.

3. **Customer - Move.** The final stage addresses business and technical concerns. This go-to-market stage needs an IT team preparation activity.
   Architecture emerges as a critical concern, what we have already noted. Architecture problems do occur and improperly architected solutions need to

be targeted. There is often a need (but also an opportunity) to redesign a cloud architecture solution (e.g. storage costs are often underestimated, which either requires unnecessary garbage data to be removed or a differently configured solution to be used). Possibilities for configuration that cloud solutions offer are often, at least initially, not considered. Changes in the cloud solution architecture would anyway require an agile approach to architectures.

Legacy management is another concern that needs to be looked at from the outset. Decommissioning needs to take place (as discussed for the IaaS layer). Backup systems are useful at early migration stages, but provide consistency problems later on and incur costs.

4 Analysis

A summary of the processes employed by the four different migration solution provider with their essential activities is given in Figure 5.

Our vision and ignorance discussion has demonstrated a good understanding of the benefits, but also that a number of concerns emerge that potential users and also providers do not properly understand and address – both business and technology issues.

- Technical: As a critical issue, the central role of the architecture emerges [19]. Stateless components and data externalisation are required if cloud advantages like elasticity are to be gained. Consequently, re-architecting is often necessary if more than data transfer into the cloud (for standard applications) is the migration scope.
- Business: Skills and cash flow emerge as two concerns. Particularly, for some IT staff, more emphasis needs to be put on integration, configuration and security. A cloud solution will not only facilitate the change from capital expenditure to operational expenditure as a positive aspect, but create different cash flow situations for users of infrastructure or platform solution who themselves become cloud solution providers.

The attitude of stakeholders varies, e.g. IT specialists can react in a positive, but also negative way to cloud migration plans. An understanding of the technical benefits exists, but can be counteracted by the fear to lose control and status as software is created and managed elsewhere.

Security, trust and data protection are all-encompassing issues that we have not covered here, due to their very different technical nature compared to the architecture concerns.

While we acknowledge that the processes presented here are limited to specific solution providers and might be not be considered as generalised, we have tried to alleviate this concern by specifically selecting experts with a long experience (often across companies) and by using the results obtained from the independent consultant to validate the other three case study results.

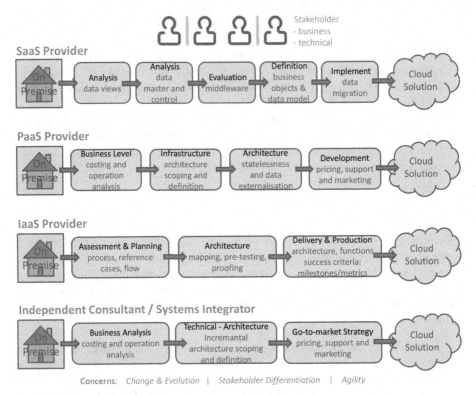

Fig. 5. Migration Processes Framework – Use Cases and Selected Activities

5   Related Work

Related research focuses for instance on an advanced model-driven methodology and tools for reuse and migration of on-premises applications to cloud. To support the migration, e.g. the REMICS project (EU FP7) enhances the OMG Architecture Driven Modernization (ADM) methodology with specific methods, meta-models and tool support, including knowledge discovery, patterns and transformations for SOA and Cloud Computing.

The REMICS project is looking at a model-driven solution to support migration [19–21]. Part of the work concentrates on the opportunity for software modernisation – a challenge, but also opportunity that we have also identified. Their architecture-driven modernisation extracts the legacy architecture in order for it to form the basis of the new cloud solution. Automated translation of business process, component and test specification preserves existing features, and will also allow weaving in new architectural elements in a coherent way. The SMART process governs the sequence of activities. However, our concern here was less to provide a concrete software architecture solution – rather to look at concerns from a broader management perspective.

A number of practical guidelines exist, published by cloud solution providers to aid the migration to their own products:

- Amazon provides whitepapers for its Amazon Web services solutions (including e.g. EC2) [14]. These AWS whitepapers outline the target architecture, their interfaces and also migration aspects.
- Similar documents are published by other companies, such as IBM [5], Salesforce [4] or Oracle [11, 12].
- Microsoft as another major provider in the PaaS space also provides whitepapers [2]. Additionally, technology evangelists like David Chappell provide material in various media types [3].

Data migration [9] emerges as a more mature migration concern. An aspect that can be tool-supported is cost estimation [8], which can alleviate initial concerns.

6 Conclusions

Migration to the cloud raises currently a range of questions. Common procedures do not exist and tool support is often not available. Migration experts rely on their own experience and some basic tools to facilitate the process. We have aimed to identify commonalities in the migration process in different context, using the cloud IaaS/PaaS/SaaS layers as the primary differentiation factor.

We have established core elements of a migration process toolkit like standard activities and steps, based on facets of (a here implicit) cloud migration ontology defining major concerns. The activities and steps across the different layers point to a common set of migration tasks that can be assembled to match the needs of the different deployment layers, but also provider and user types. The discussion has highlighted the immaturity in terms of established procedures and availability of tools to support the process. Important challenges arising from our observations include the importance of adequate architecture design for the cloud, but also the implications in terms of changed business models.

A plan arising from this discussion is a migration pattern catalogue. Patterns are templates that can be applied in a concrete situation. A migration pattern would be more specific than the processes described. In addition to cloud layers, which we have used to discriminate between different cloud migrations, a number of other factors arise from our discussion. The size of the organisation plays a role. It dictates the needs, but also the financial scope, which in turn limits the effort a provider will make to accommodate special configurations. Distinguishing between different SaaS application categories (e.g. ERP versus technical software) makes sense as well as distinguishing more clearly between PaaS development and deployment or IaaS compute, storage and networking.

Acknowledgements. The authors are greatly indebted to the participants of the IC4 migration studies.

References

1. Mell, P., Grance, T.: The NIST Definition of Cloud Computing. NIST Special Publication 800-145 (2010)
2. Server and Cloud Platform (2013), http://www.microsoft.com/en-us/server-cloud/default.aspx
3. Chappell, D.: How SaaS Changes an ISV's Business, Sponsored by Microsoft Corporation (2012), http://www.davidchappell.com/writing/white_papers/How_SaaS_Changes_an_ISVs_Business--Chappell_v1.0.pdf
4. Developerforce (2013), http://wiki.developerforce.com/page/Tools
5. IBM: Cloud Computing Reference Architecture 2.0 (2011), https://www.ibm.com/developerworks/mydeveloperworks/blogs/c2028fdc-41fe-4493-8257-33a59069fa04/entry/chapter_13_cloud_computing_reference_architecture1?lang=en
6. Skilton, M., Gordon, P.: Cloud Buyers' Decision Tree. The Open Group (2010)
7. In, H.: Conflict Identification and Resolution for Software Attribute Requirements. PhD dissertation. University of Southern California (1998)
8. RightScale: PlanForCloud (2012), http://www.planforcloud.com/
9. Mohanty, S.: Data Migration Strategy (2004), http://www.information-management.com/specialreports/20040518/1003611-1.html
10. Murtaza, S., Masud, R.A.: An Extended and Granular Classification of Cloud's Taxonomy and Services. International Journal of Soft Computing and Engineering 2(2), 278–286 (2012)
11. Oracle: SQL Developer Migration (2010), http://www.oracle.com/technetwork/products/migration/sqldevelopermigration21-wp-131240.pdf
12. Oracle: After Migrating or Upgrading the Database (2011), http://docs.oracle.com/cd/A87860_01/doc/server.817/a86632/migaftrm.htm
13. Rational Software Development Platform: Migrate from VisualAge Generator 4.5 to the Enterprise Generation Language (EGL). IBM (2012), http://www.ibm.com/developerworks/rational/library/egldoc.html
14. Varia, J.: Migrating your Existing Applications to the AWS Cloud: A Phase-driven Approach to Cloud Migration, AWS Cloud Computing Whitepapers (2010), http://media.amazonwebservices.com/CloudMigration-main.pdf
15. Email Migration Toolkit (2013), http://www.sitaas.de/fileadmin/data/Email_Migration_Toolkit.pdf
16. Pahl, C., Giesecke, S., Hasselbring, W.: Ontology-based modelling of architectural styles. Information and Software Technology 51(12), 1739–1749 (2009)
17. Wang, M.X., Bandara, K.Y., Pahl, C.: Process as a Service Distributed Multi-tenant Policy-Based Process Runtime Governance. In: IEEE International Conference on Services Computing (SCC), pp. 578–585. IEEE (2010)
18. Halvey, J.K., Melby, B.M.: Business Process Outsourcing: Processes, Strategies, and Contracts. John Wiley & Sons, Inc., Hoboken (2007)
19. Mohagheghi, P., Saether, T.: Software Engineering Challenges for Migration to the Service Cloud Paradigm. In: World Congress on Services 2011, pp. 507–514. IEEE (2011)
20. Mohagheghi, P., Berre, A.J., Sadovykh, A., Barbier, F., Benguria, G.: Reuse and Migration of Legacy Systems to Interoperable Cloud Services - The REMICS project. In: Mda4ServiceCloud 2010 Workshop (2010)
21. Orue-Echevarria, L., Alonso, J., Escalante, M., Benguria, G.: Moving to SaaS: Building a migration strategy from concept to deployment. In: Ionita, A.D., Litoiu, M., Lewis, G. (eds.) Migrating Legacy Applications: Challenges in Service Oriented Architecture and Cloud Computing Environments. IGI (2012)

Migration of an On-Premise Application to the Cloud: Experience Report

Pavel Rabetski and Gerardo Schneider

Department of Computer Science and Engineering
Chalmers University of Technology, and the University of Gothenburg
Gothenburg, Sweden
rabeckijps@gmail.com, gerardo@cse.gu.se

Abstract. As of today it is still not clear how and when cloud computing should be used. Developers very often write applications in a way that does not really fit a cloud environment, and in some cases without taking into account how quality attributes (like performance, security or portability) are affected. In this paper we share our experience and observations from adopting cloud computing for an on-premise enterprise application in a context of a small software company. We present experimental results concerning a comparative evaluation (w.r.t. performance and cost) of the behavior of the original system both on-premise and on the Cloud, considering different scenarios in the Cloud.

1 Introduction

Cloud computing refers to a utility-based provisioning of virtualized computational resources over the Internet. Even though *computing as a utility* is not a new concept [15], it has only recently become commercially available due to new technological shifts in virtualization, distributed computing and communication technologies. From a long-held dream cloud computing has turned into a new promising trend of the IT industry that is about to change the way computational resources and software are designed and purchased. Bottery et al [3] believe that the emergence of cloud computing will fundamentally transform the economics of the multi-billion dollar software industry. Strategy consulting firm AMI-Partners predicts that small business spending on cloud computing will hit $100 billion by 2014 [7]. Despite such promising predictions, there is a big confusion among potential adopters as cloud computing is not mature enough. Indeed, it is not clear what cloud computing is and when it is convenient to use it [1]. According to the Gartner report [6], cloud computing will become the preferred option for application development only around 2015, despite initial growth. Moreover, the lack of standards and keen competition on the new market has led to a variety of idiosyncratic cloud platforms. Cloud giants like Amazon, Google, Microsoft, and SalesForce are trying to establish their rules and promote their franchise. Choosing a proper cloud provider additionally complicates the migration planning, especially for smaller companies that do not have resources for extensive research on cloud computing.

K.-K. Lau, W. Lamersdorf, and E. Pimentel (Eds.): ESOCC 2013, LNCS 8135, pp. 227–241, 2013.
© Springer-Verlag Berlin Heidelberg 2013

The main objective of this work is to analyze what it means to migrate an on-premise application to the Cloud and what are the consequences of the migration. We perform our study on a specific industrial case study described in detail later in the paper. Our main contributions are: 1. The migration of an industrial enterprise web application to the Cloud; 2. Experiments concerning performance and costs of the migration. Based on our experimental results we draw conclusions on the consequences of the migration and provide suggestions on how to extrapolate our experience to other software systems.

The rest of the paper is organized as follows: Section 2 gives necessary background information. Sections 3 and 4 describe the migration of an industrial enterprise system to the Cloud, and our experimental results. Section 5 presents related work, and the last section summarizes the results.

2   Cloud Computing

In this section we give a definition of cloud computing along with its key characteristics, and we describe two existing cloud classifications.

Cloud computing usually refers to a utility-based provisioning of computational resources over the Internet. Widely used analogies to explain cloud computing are electricity and water supply systems. Like the Cloud, they provide centralized resources that are accessible for everyone. Also, in the Cloud you only pay for what you have used. And finally, resources are usually consumed by those who have difficulties to produce necessary amounts by themselves or just do not want to do that. Despite the description by analogy, it is difficult to give a unique and precise definition. The definitions proposed are often focused on different perspectives and do not have common baselines. Vaquero et al [20] gives a definition highlighting three features that most closely describe cloud computing: *scalability, pay-as-you-go utility model* and *virtualization* [20].

There are two widely used cloud computing classifications. The first one describes four cloud types depending on the *deployment location*: public, private, community, and hybrid clouds [13]. The second classification is a widely used cloud ontology describing three cloud models depending on the *provided capabilities* [22]: i) Infrastructure as a Service (IaaS), ii) Platform as a Service (PaaS), and iii) Software as a Service (SaaS). It is also called a *cloud stack* because they are somehow typically built on top of each other. They can exist independently or may co-exist. Due to the lack of standardization it is not very clear where the exact boundaries lie between the components of the cloud stack.

- *IaaS.* The infrastructure layer represents fundamental resources that are the basis for the upper layers. It is very similar to a regular virtual server hosting. IaaS is built directly on the hardware, providing virtualized resources (e.g. storing and processing capacities) as a service. Examples of public IaaS providers are Amazon Web Services and GoGrid.
- *PaaS.* This layer is usually built on top of IaaS. The platform layer provides a higher level software platform with extended services where other systems can run. It delivers a programming-language-level environment with a set of

language-integrated APIs for implementing and deploying SaaS applications. Microsoft Azure and Google App Engine are examples of PaaS.

– *SaaS.* The services exposed in this layer represent alternatives to locally running end-user applications. They are usually interesting for a wide market, compared to IaaS or PaaS. They can also be composed from other services available in the Cloud. Normally, SaaS applications are accessed through web-portals for some fee. Microsoft Office365 or Gmail are examples of SaaS.

3 Case Study: Migrating DC System to the Cloud

We describe here the migration of an enterprise system to the Cloud. We follow the migration process suggested in [19]. First, we describe the current system implementation. Then, we describe the new cloud architecture for the migrated application along with identified compatibility issues. We also suggest several system improvements to further leverage the cloud environment.

3.1 Preliminary Analysis

Before doing the migration we have done a careful analysis of advantages and disadvantages of cloud computing. A summary of the results is presented in Table 1. In addition to that, we have studied existing public cloud platforms, namely, Amazon Web Services, Google App Engine, and Microsoft Azure in order to find the most suitable one. See [16] for a more detailed description.

3.2 Current DC Implementation

InformaIT Company. *InformaIT* is a small independent software vendor (ISV) that focuses on document management systems. Most of the systems are based on Microsoft products and technologies. Being an innovative company, InformaIT is very interested in modern IT trends. The *Document Comparison system* (DC) was selected as a candidate for experimenting on the migration of applications to the Cloud. DC is a small web-based enterprise solution that enhances document management processes. The main purpose is to provide a fast and easy way to compare textual and graphical content of different digital documents.

Table 1. Summary of advantages and challenges of cloud computing

Advantages:	no upfront investments; on-demand capacity; focus on core applications; potential for more sales; easier customer maintenance; platform-provided features
Challenges:	security and privacy; availability; performance; compliance requirements; vendor lock-in; environment limitations (e.g. sandbox); multi-tenancy and licensing

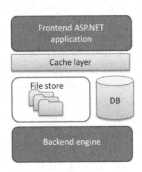

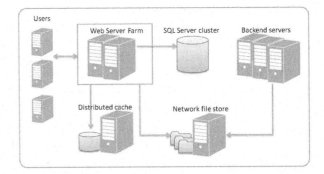

Fig. 1. DC components   **Fig. 2.** On-premise distributed deployment model of DC

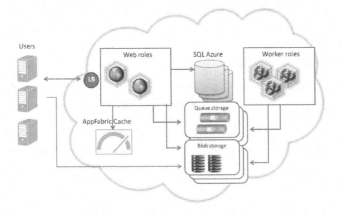

Fig. 3. Cloud deployment model of DC

DC Architecture. The system is implemented using Microsoft .NET 2.0 framework and various programming languages including server-side C# and C++, and client-side JavaScript. DC contains five main components: i) frontend web application, ii) backend engine, iii) distributed cache, iv) database, and v) shared file store (see Fig. 1).

The frontend is a simple ASP.NET web application running under IIS on Windows OS. It provides web interfaces for end-users, so they can upload digital documents, change configuration settings, analyze the result, and generate reports. The frontend extensively uses ASP.NET session state to track processed information and a current user status.

The backend is implemented as a Windows service (.NET based). It performs long running computational tasks e.g. the rasterization of digital documents. A special commercial library is used to fasten this process which accesses the files via regular file system API. It also requires the registration of a COM component.

The file store serves as a shared storage for system components. It keeps persistent data and organizes asynchronous communication between the frontend and the backend.

The cache layer keeps frequently used data, which increases the performance of the system. For example, the frontend stores the latest document comparison result there.

Unlike many document management systems, DC is not database-centric. The amount of data in the database is quite small and is used infrequently.

Deployment Model. DC is deployed on servers located in the data centers of customer organizations. This means customers have to take care of the infrastructure, and have technical personnel to maintain it. The amount of required hardware depends on the amount and the complexity of processing data. A single server is usually enough for small companies, while big organizations need several machines to run the system. DC also requires preinstalled Windows Server 2003/2008 with Microsoft SQL Server.

An on-premise distributed deployment model of DC is shown in Fig. 2. ASP.NET applications are composed into a Web Server Farm. They store frequently used data in a distributed cache that is usually located on a separate server. Backend engines are deployed separately as well. They require more powerful servers for heavy computations. A customer can choose the number of frontend and backend servers to achieve the required performance. A shared network folder plays the role of persistent file storage. Microsoft SQL Server is used as a database. End-users are usually located in the same environment where the system is running.

This on-premise deployment model gives several advantages. First, it keeps data and code physically close. It results in very low latencies and no bandwidth limitations. Second, sensitive data never goes outside the organization, which provides a high level of security. In some cases when users need to access the system outside the organization, a VPN connection is established to keep the transferred data protected.

Organizations are charged per installation depending on the number of users. There are different types of licenses available, including a personal license and a concurrent license.

Motivation for the Migration. There are several disadvantages of running DC on-premise in a customer environment. We briefly discuss here some of them as well as the benefits of migrating the application to the Cloud.

The biggest opportunity is the potential for more sales. DC is currently oriented to big and medium organizations that have enough resources, own infrastructure, and technical personnel to install and run the system. Furthermore, the license cost is quite high. Potential customers such as small companies cannot afford DC, facing too big financial commitments. Some of them would like to use the system inconstantly and pay only for the amount of compared data. SaaS version of DC can bring the product to such customers.

A cloud computing advantage would be easer installation and upgrade procedures. The system is currently distributed across many customers. InformaIT has to convince each customer to replace an on-premises package and then assist during the actual upgrading. Some customers still run older versions of the system, which brings an additional support overhead. The simple maintenance model of cloud computing will help to distribute resources more efficiently, leading to cost savings and business agility.

3.3 Suggested Cloud DC Architecture

Developers usually face a range of alternatives when implementing cloud-based systems. In this section we describe the chosen approach for our case and discuss different alternatives that can affect cost, architectural quality, and the amount of required changes.

Choosing a Cloud Provider. The first step when moving an on-premise application to the Cloud is to choose a proper cloud provider. We examined three major cloud providers (Amazon Web Services, Google AppEngine, and Microsoft Azure). Based on our finding we conclude that Google AppEngine is the worst candidate for DC because it does not support .NET applications, while Amazon AWS and Microsoft Azure both fit for the migration quite well. After further analysis we prefer Windows Azure to Amazon AWS for several reasons: i) it requires less configuration effort, ii) it has a faster deployment model, and iii) it allows consistent development experience for applications that are well-versed in Microsoft technologies.

Cloud DC Architecture. Once we have chosen a public cloud provider, we need to show how existing architectural components are mapped to abstractions provided by the platform. In our case this platform is Microsoft Azure.

The Frontend. Azure Web Role is an obvious choice for our ASP.NET frontend. Web Role has a preconfigured IIS and a built-in load balancer for web applications. Still, there are some limitations to keep in mind. For example, the Azure load balancer is not sticky, meaning that two requests from the same user can be processed by different Web Role instances. Also, Web Role supports only IIS 7.0 and requires .NET 3.5/4.0.

The Backend Engine. The backend maps to a Worker Role, since it suits perfectly for long running background tasks. It is worth noting that roles do not have administrative privileges in the environment. It restricts the execution of tasks that change OS configuration e.g. registration of a COM component or changing OS registry.

The Distributed Cache. Microsoft Azure has only one service for distributed cache so far, AppFabric Cache. Alternatively, cached data can be stored in either SQL Azure or regular Azure Storage. Though AppFabric Cache is considered to have better performance compared to the alternatives [16], it is quite expensive and limited in size (4GB maximum). We choose AppFabric Cache under the assumption that the size of data stored in cache will be significantly reduced. Otherwise we suggest using Table Storage.

The Database. On-premise DC version uses a Microsoft SQL Server database. We find SQL Azure to be a perfect cloud alternative. In most cases switching

Table 2. Identified compatibility issues

Compatibility issue	Required modification
Current solution uses .NET 2.0 and VS2005 that are not supported by Microsoft Azure. The platform uses the latest product versions.	The system should be migrated to .NET 3.5/4.0 and VS2010. This modification is quite simple due to full backwards compatibility of .NET 4.0 and 2.0.
The system cannot register COM components directly from code due to environment limitations.	There are some workarounds that allow using COM components for Azure applications: Registration-Free COM [18] and role startup scripts. We suggest using startup scripts because it is the easiest solution.
A local folder cannot be shared across Azure roles. Furthermore, suggested Blob Storage and Queue Storage have APIs that are not compatible with regular file APIs currently used by DC.	Change the code for accessing data in the file storage to use Blob Storage and Queue Storage APIs. Azure Drive is an alternative solution that eliminates these changes.
Standard ASP.NET session state modes do not suit Azure environment. In-Process mode is not an option because of a non-sticky load balancer.	The system needs distributed session storage in order to scale. We suggest using AppFabric Cache (or optionally Table Storage). Microsoft Azure offers an easy way of using these storages.

to SQL Azure is as simple as changing the connection string. In [8] it is argued that SQL Azure can become a bottleneck for systems that concurrently operate large amounts of data. However, it is not the case for DC.

The File Store. We have found out that the local file storage is not persistent and cannot be shared with other roles. All data stored locally gets lost if the role dies. The only persistent option for Azure applications is Azure Storage. We suggest using Queue Storage for messaging and Blob Storage for the files shared among roles. This approach leverages the cloud platform as much as possible. First, all data are automatically replicated and scaled. Second, Azure Storage can be accessed directly via REST calls, reducing the load on the frontend. Last but not least, Queue Storage provides a built-in reliable communication mechanism.

Fig. 3 presents a proposed deployment model of the system in the Cloud.

Identified Compatibility Issues. Even though Microsoft Azure fits well for the migration of DC, we have identified some compatibility issues that require changes in the current implementation. These issues are described in Table 2. In what follows, we recommend some design modifications in order to tune system performance, increase portability, and make the migration as smooth as possible.

Separate Data Layer from Business Logic Layer. InformaIT wants the system to be easily portable across both environments. However, this is not easy to achieve because of the need to switch from regular file system API to Azure Storage API. We suggest separating a data access layer from a business logic layer in order to increase portability. In other words, instead of using APIs directly, a business logic layer calls a data access layer interface. This loose coupling allows using regular file system or Azure Storage depending on the deployment environment.

Become as Stateless as Possible. Large amount of cached data will not only degrade the performance but also increase the cost. An additional 1GB of AppFabric cache costs around 100$, which is 1000 times more than Azure Storage cost. The bigger the session size, the more time required to serialize/de-serialize it. DC currently stores megabytes of data per a session, which is a big overhead. We suggest reducing the amount of cached data, making DC as stateless as possible. This suggestion can be applied for any web application that extensively uses session data.

Extensively Use Logging. Logging is very important for cloud applications, since debugging is impossible in the cloud environment. Logging helps developers to trace the behavior of the system and determine the reason of system failures. Furthermore it might be useful for identifying the level of resource utilization or just collecting statistical information.

4   Experiments

In this section we present experiments concerning cost and performance of running the DC application on the Cloud (under different conditions), and we compare those results with the on-premise implementation of DC. We are not concerned here with other issues as security and privacy.

In what follows we describe the environment these experiments are performed in. Experiments and measurements are done for North Europe deployment location of Microsoft Azure. This is the geographically closest location to the client testing environment located in Sweden (Gothenburg). All Azure compute instances have a small size, which provides 1.75 GB memory, 225 GB local disk space, moderate I/O performance, and CPU performance equivalent to one 1.6GHz core. We use small instances as a part of Azure free trial subscription, which gives necessary resources to perform our experiments for no fees. Testing on the client side is executed in a non-virtualized environment, external to the Cloud, with a direct connection to the Internet via a high-speed wired Ethernet. However, the cloud deployment location and the client environment are changed for some experiments. All experiments are performed at least 100 times to confirm that the results are stable.

4.1   Performance

As we identified earlier, a cloud environment entails increased latencies and unknown hardware underneath. Therefore, DC can have the following performance bottlenecks in the Cloud: the execution of heavy computational tasks (like digital document rendering) that require efficient hardware; and session handling that is latency sensitive. These operations represent the highest risk when moving DC to the cloud environment, because they might lead to significant system performance degradation.

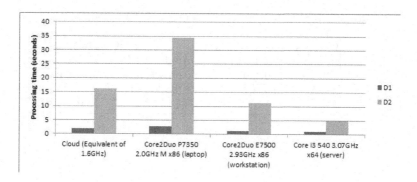

Fig. 4. Execution time comparison for cloud and on-premise environments

Execution Time. We have analyzed a production set of documents in order to suggest testing data for this experiment. We have classified two dominant types and picked up one document of each type (we reference to them as D1 and D2 accordingly). We then execute CPU heavy code for both documents and compare run time for cloud and on-premise DC versions. For a cloud version we use a small Azure compute instance (that has CPU performance equivalent to 1.6GHz), while on-premise installations have Core2Duo P7350 2.0GHz M x86 (laptop), Core2Duo E7500 2.93GHz x86 (workstation), Core i3 540 3.07GHz x64 (dedicated local server). Fig. 4 illustrates the results of our experiments. We have observed notably worse performance of one DC instance in the Cloud rather than on the dedicated server with powerful Intel Core i3 CPU (16.1 sec compared to 4.9 sec for D2). This means the system needs about three times more instances of the backend engine in the Cloud to achieve the same throughput.

Note that in contrast to the on-premise version where all files can be stored locally, cloud application needs to download and upload files to Blob Storage in order to process documents. However, it turned out that download and upload time together never exceeds 13% of total run time. Thus, our conclusion about computing capacity in the Cloud is still relevant.

Session Storing/Retrieving Time. In this section we compare on-premise and cloud DC session handling performance and also test two alternatives in Azure platform. For on-premise installation we evaluate standard ASP.NET in-process and state server modes. In-process mode stores session state data in memory, while state server mode uses a special process (separate from the ASP.NET worker process) for it. For cloud installation we evaluate AppFabric Cache, and a custom session handler that uses Azure Table. Session handling is very important for the frontend ASP.NET application, because it retrieves and stores session data on every page load as a part of the ASP.NET application lifecycle.

After putting an object into session, we measure the time it takes to load and save the session when handling an http request. We perform this experiment against different storages and object sizes: 1Kb, 1Mb, and 10Mb (assuming that session should not exceed 10Mb). Every object contains randomly generated

Table 3. Storing/retrieving time in seconds for session data

	On-premise DC installation		Cloud DC installation	
Session size	In-process	State server	AppFabric Cache	Table Storage
1 Kb	0.0/0.0	0.0/0.0	0.004/0.008	0.094/0.113
1 Mb	0.0/0.0	0.008/0.009	0.098/0.143	0.292/0.548
10 Mb	0.0/0.0	0.161/0.173	0.435/0.583	1.167/1.861

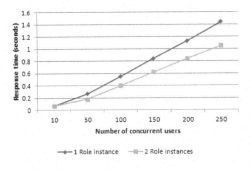

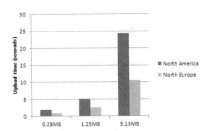

Fig. 5. Cloud DC page response time

Fig. 6. Response time file uploading

binary data. It is worth noting that serialization time depends on the number of objects stored in the session. In our case there is only one object. We also use the local Web server for state server mode, while a remote Web server would considerably increase session handling time.

Experiment observations are presented in Table 3 where we can see that on-premise DC requires significantly less time for session handling compared to the cloud installation. In-process mode is obviously the fastest, since all data is kept in memory all the time. However, when data is stored in another location like AppFabric Cache, it should also be serialized and de-serialized accordingly. We have observed that AppFabric Cache shows considerably better performance than Table Storage, especially for small amounts of data. It is approximately 3 times faster for 1Mb and 10Mb cases, and 17 times faster for 1Kb case (4/8ms compared to 94/113ms). Consequently, DC can have close to on-premise performance in the Cloud when operating smaller data amounts (kilobytes) stored in AppFabric Cache. Table Storage increases response time by 1.167+1.861, that is approximatively 3 sec, when storing 10Mb of data in session. On the other hand, it is much cheaper and has no capacity limits. Table Storage also shows a lower correlation between the time and session size, apparently caused by HTTP latencies to transfer the data.

Response Time. We have also tested response time of the frontend web application against different deployment locations and different scales. We try to reflect the actual time from the end-user perspective, because perceived response time dictates user-friendliness of the service. Response time can be decomposed into four parts: the latency to send a request from a client; the time to redirect the request by a load balancer (if there are several role instances); the time to process it by the application; and the latency to get a response back from the server. Even though these factors depend on network locality and traffic congestion, the main purpose is to show the difference in response time depending on different conditions. Variable conditions in our experiments are deployment location, number of role instances (scale), and load. In order to measure response time purely for a Web Role, we use a stateless .aspx page that does not include any external factors like session handling or document page rendering.

The first experiment evaluates page response time for a different number of role instances. The page makes some calculations and then generates dynamic output content. This dynamic data is needed to ensure that the page is not cached by any CDN service or in the client environment. We perform the experiment with a variable number of simulated clients accessing the service concurrently. In order to measure response time, we use Visual Studio 2010 Load Test[1] based on a Web Test that simply requests the page. All testing is done from outside the Cloud. We run the Load Test for a period of five minutes and perform it many times to confirm that the results are stable.

Fig. 5 shows the observed response time for both single instance and dual instance setups with an increasing number of concurrent users. Page time starts at about 80 ms for both cases and then grows linearly with different angular coefficients. Results show that an additional role instance decreases response time, especially for a heavy load. For 250 concurrent users a dual instance setup performs 400ms faster than a single instance setup.

The main goal of the second experiment is to show the difference in response time across different deployment locations. To do so, we execute Visual Studio 2010 Web Test that uploads a document to DC that is running in the cloud environment. This scenario reflects latency and bandwidth in a better way. We have picked up three random files of different sizes from the production document set: 0.28Mb, 1.25Mb, and 5.13Mb. The experiment is executed for two deployment locations: North America and North Europe, with testing performed in Sweden (Gothenburg). We repeat the experiment multiple times to confirm that the results are stable. The observed response time is presented on Fig. 6.

All three cases show approximately twice faster uploading time for North Europe zone compared to North America zone. The biggest file (5.13 MB) is uploaded to the first zone for 10 sec, while the second zone requires almost 24 sec. Consequently, a proper deployment location can significantly improve user experience by reducing interaction latencies.

4.2   Cost

In this section we estimate the cost of DC in the Cloud. For this purpose we model two real life scenarios that describe how cloud DC can be used. The cost for every scenario is estimated based on the Microsoft Azure pricing model.

---

[1] http://msdn.microsoft.com/en-us/library/ee923688.aspx

Table 4. DC estimated cost for Scenario 1 and Scenario 2

Service	Scenario 1		Scenario 2	
	Used capacity	Cost ($)	Used capacity	Cost ($)
Compute Instance	11 small instances (7920 hs)	950	3-11 small instances (3920 hs)	470
Relational database	1 GB	9.99	1 GB	9.99
Storage	500 GB	75	500 GB	75
Storage transactions	5000k transactions	5	5000k transactions	5
Data transfer	1000 GB	150	1000 GB	150
AppFabric Cache	512 MB	75	0-512 MB	55
Total:		1264.99 (1084.99)		764.99 (664.99)

Table 5. Cost distribution for Scenario 1 and Scenario 2

	Compute instance	Storage	Data transfer	Storage transactions	Cache	Database
Scenario 1	75%	6%	12%	0%	6%	1%
Scenario 2	61%	10%	20%	1%	7%	1%

Scenario 1: Production Installation. In Scenario 1 DC is used as a production installation with throughput equivalent to one dedicated server (without elastic scale). For this scenario we require DC to show the same throughout as the on-premise installation that is running on a server with Core i3 540 3.07GHz x64 processor, 500 GB available local storage and 4GB of memory. It uses three out of four cores for the backend and the rest one for the frontend. As we observed earlier, the backend engine shows three times worse performance in the Cloud. That means we need nine small compute instances for the Backend. The frontend application requires two small compute instances, since we do not expect big performance degradation for the ASP.NET application. We also include 512Mb AppFabric Cache. We perform all calculations for a 30 days period which is equivalent to one month. So we totally need 30*24*11 = 7920 compute hours that costs 2160*0.12 = 950 US dollars. Data storage costs 500*0.15=75$; outgoing traffic is 1000*0.15 = 150$; 5 million transactions cost only 5$; and 1 GB SQL Azure is 9.99$. Table 4 presents the total cost for this scenario, and Table 5 illustrates the cost distribution. The total cost in brackets represents an upfront payment case (using a subscription). For more information see the official Microsoft Azure page.

Scenario 2: Production Installation with Scaling. In Scenario 2 DC is used as a production installation with throughput equivalent to one dedicated server (using elastic scale). In this scenario we use the same capacities as in Scenario 2, but leveraging cloud elastic scalability. We assume DC has a typical enterprise system load pattern: high load during working hours (10 hours from

8AM to 6 PM) and almost no load during the rest time. That means we can scale our system down when the load is very low. We scale it down to three small instances to keep the system available. Also, the cache service is not needed when we have one Web Role. Assuming that there are 22 working days during a month we will need 30*24*3 + 22*10*8 = 3920 hours. The first term means that we need 3 instances all the time, and the second term means that we add 8 more instances during high load periods. The cache will cost 75*(22/30) = 55. However, using elasticity does not affect storage and outgoing traffic. The estimated cost is presented in Table 4. Table 5 shows the cost distribution among different services.

Based on our estimations we can conclude that compute services dominate in all scenarios. It makes up 75%, and 61% of the total cost for Scenario 1, and 2 accordingly. On the other hand, storage transactions have the least cost. SQL Azure also has a small cost share of 1%. However, this is because DC is not database centric. We found that the cost of DC can drop by 40 percent (764.99$ compared to 1264.99$) when leveraging elastic scalability. Even though choosing a proper scaling strategy is pretty straightforward for enterprise applications like ours, it might not be so trivial for other systems.

5   Related Work

Some work have been presented on the benefits, challenges, and consequences of adopting the Cloud. Armbrust et al [1] described their vision of cloud computing, emphasizing elasticity as an important economic benefit. Motahari-Nezhad et al [14] added that cloud computing significantly reduced upfront commitments and potentially reduced operational and maintenance costs are also important benefits of cloud computing from business prospective. Chappel [4] elaborated on different opportunities that cloud computing brings to ISV, including the potential for more sales and easier customer upgrades. Kim et al [9] made and extensive research on cloud computing issues, emphasizing security and availability as the most challenging ones. Security and privacy seems to be one of the mostly discussed obstacles for cloud computing adoption [5][21].

Various papers evaluated existing cloud implementations. Rimal et al [17] made a comparative technical study of cloud providers and suggested taxonomy for identifying similarities and differences among them. Later, Louridas [12] discussed the migration of applications to the Cloud, examining key features of cloud offerings based on the taxonomy from [17]. Li et al [10][11] suggested a set of metrics related to application performance and cost in a cloud environment, comparing cloud providers based on these metrics. The authors concluded that none of the cloud providers is clearly superior, even though they observed diverse performance and cost across different platforms.

However, we have not observed many publications on the consequences of the migration that would include for example cost, performance, or security comparison. Tran et al [19] provided a simple cost estimation model for cloud applications, based on the identified influential cost factors. Babar et al [2] shared experiences and observations regarding the migration of an existing system to a cloud environment, which also included some guidelines and suggestions. Still, none of the papers compared system behavior before and after the migration (or choosing different migration strategies), like we do in this paper.

6 Conclusion

In this paper we have shared our experience of cloud computing adoption based on a real case study from the industry.

We have implemented a cloud version of the on-premise enterprise application for Microsoft Azure platform. High compatibility with Azure and easy deployment were the main reasons for choosing this platform. The application cloud prototype was used to evaluate the performance and the cost of the system in a cloud environment. We have investigated the behavior of the system against different deployment locations, testing materials, scale and load. We could then make some extrapolations and suggest common practices based on our results. Our finding helped InformaIT to make a final decision regarding cloud adoption. Together with partners from InformaIT we have concluded that DC cloud implementation is feasible. We also found the estimated cost reasonable, especially when the system is dynamically scaled based on the load.

To our best knowledge there is no a unique metric that defines how well an application fits a cloud environment. The decision should be made separately for every system, based on the tradeoff between advantages and challenges. Existing systems are likely to face more challenges than new applications, due to the technological constraints of cloud platforms. In general, existing systems that are based on service oriented architecture with a focus on statelessness and low coupling fit the Cloud pretty well. Still, applications might require certain changes before being able to fully leverage a cloud environment. These changes are usually caused by environment limitations or the singularity of cloud storages. Based on our observations, the cloud version of a system is likely to show worse performance because of higher latencies and inferior computing hardware underneath. In order to tune system performance, we suggest eliminating unnecessary transfers between different system components, meaning both the amount of data and the number of calls. In particular, web applications should reduce the amount of data stored in session or become completely stateless; data intensive applications should also consider using local cache to store frequently used data. HPC applications will usually require more CPU cores (compute instances) in the Cloud to show the same throughput. Thus, such applications are likely to be costly. Last but not least, we suggest leveraging dynamic scalability in order to reduce the cost of a cloud application. This is especially important for systems with a changeable load. For example, enterprise application should scale up only during working hours; university web sites should scale up during application periods. However, monitoring is necessary when the load does not have a particular pattern. Furthermore, it might be ambiguous what metrics are the most relevant to monitor.

An extended version of the paper may be found online at `www.cse.chalmers.se/~gersch/ESOCC13-extended_version.pdf`.

References

1. Armbrust, M., Fox, A., Griffith, R., Joseph, A.D., Katz, R., Konwinski, A., Lee, G., Patterson, D., Rabkin, A., Stoica, I., Zaharia, M.: A view of cloud computing. Commun. ACM 53, 50–58 (2010)
2. Babar, M.A., Chauhan, M.A.: A tale of migration to cloud computing for sharing experiences and observations. In: SECLOUD 2011, pp. 50–56. ACM (2011)
3. Botteri, P., Cowan, D., Deeter, B., Fisher, A., Garg, D., Goodman, B., Levine, J., Messiana, G., Sarin, A., Tavel, S.: Bessemer's top 10 laws of cloud computing and saas (2010)
4. Chappell, D.: Windows azure and isvs: A guide for decision makers (July 2009)
5. Chow, R., Golle, P., Jakobsson, M., Shi, E., Staddon, J., Masuoka, R., Molina, J.: Controlling data in the cloud: outsourcing computation without outsourcing control. In: CCSW 2009, pp. 85–90. ACM (2009)
6. Driver, M.: Cloud application infrastructure technologies need seven years to mature. Research report, Gartner Inc., Stamford, USA (2008)
7. Hichkey, A.R.: Smb cloud spending to approach $100 billion by 2014 (2010)
8. Hill, Z., Li, J., Mao, M., Ruiz-Alvarez, A., Humphrey, M.: Early observations on the performance of windows azure. In: HPDC 2010, pp. 367–376. ACM (2010)
9. Kim, W., Kim, S.D., Lee, E., Lee, S.: Adoption issues for cloud computing. In: iiWAS 2009, pp. 3–6. ACM (2009)
10. Li, A., Yang, X., Kandula, S., Zhang, M.: Cloudcmp: comparing public cloud providers. In: IMC 2010, pp. 1–14. ACM (2010)
11. Li, A., Yang, X., Kandula, S., Zhang, M.: Comparing public-cloud providers. Internet Computing 15, 50–53 (2011)
12. Louridas, P.: Up in the air: Moving your applications to the cloud. IEEE Software 27, 6–10 (2010)
13. Mell, P., Grance, T.: The nist definition of cloud computing. Technical report, National Institute of Standards and Technology (2011)
14. Nezhad, H.M., Stephenson, B., Singhal, S.: Outsourcing business to cloud computing services: Opportunities and challenges. Technical report HPL-2009-23, HP Laboratories (2009)
15. Parkhill, D.F.: The Challenge of the Computer Utility. Addison-Wesley, US (1966)
16. Rabetski, P.: Migration of an on-premise application to the cloud. Master's thesis, Software Engineering and Management, Dept. of Computer Science and Engineering, Univ. of Gothenburg, Sweden (2011)
17. Rimal, B., Choi, E., Lumb, I.: A taxonomy and survey of cloud computing systems. In: 5th Int. Joint Conf. on INC, IMS and IDC, pp. 44–51. IEEE (2009)
18. Templin, D.: Simplify app deployment with clickonce and registration-free com (2005)
19. Tran, V., Keung, K., Liu, A., Fekete, A.: Application migration to cloud: a taxonomy of critical factors. In: SECLOUD 2011, pp. 22–28. ACM (2011)
20. Vaquero, L.M., Rodero-Merino, L., Caceres, J., Lindner, M.: A break in the clouds: towards a cloud definition. SIGCOMM Comp. Com. Rev. 39, 50–55 (2009)
21. Vouk, M.: Cloud computing - issues, research and implementations. CIT 16(4), 235–246 (2008)
22. Youseff, L., Butrico, M., da Silva, D.: Toward a unified ontology of cloud computing. In: GCE 2008, pp. 1–10. IEEE (November 2008)

Author Index

Ahtes, James   64
Álvarez, Pedro   196
Andrikopoulos, Vasilios   79
Aznag, Mustapha   19

Beauche, Sandrine   134
Bocconi, Stefano   64
Bouloukakis, Georgios   134

Canal, Carlos   180
Catan, Michel   1

D'Andria, Francesco   64
Díaz, Gregorio   119
Di Cosmo, Roberto   1

Eiche, Antoine   1
Evequoz, Florian   94
Ezpeleta, Joaquín   196

Fabra, Javier   196
Fischer, Robin   164

Garefalakis, Panagiotis   188
Georgantas, Nikolaos   134
Gómez Sáez, Santiago   79
Gouvas, Panagiotis   64
Gray, Birgit   4
Guillén, Joaquín   180

Hernández, Sergio   196
Hoffmann, Mario   149

Issarny, Valérie   134

Jarir, Zahi   19

Kamateri, Eleni   64
Katsaros, Gregory   4

Kieselmann, Markus   172
Konsolaki, Konstantina   188
Kritikos, Kyriakos   188

Lampe, Ulrich   172
Lascu, Tudor A.   1
Ledakis, Giannis   64
Lenk, Alexander   49
Leymann, Frank   79
Lienhardt, Michael   1
Llana, Luis   119
Lobunets, Oleksandr   64
Loutas, Nikolaos   64

Magoutis, Kostas   188
Mauro, Jacopo   1
Mentzas, Gregoris   34
Miede, André   172
Miranda, Javier   180
Murillo, Juan Manuel   180

Nanchen, Benjamin   94

Pahl, Claus   212
Pallas, Frank   49
Patiniotakis, Ioannis   34
Plexousakis, Dimitris   188

Quafafou, Mohamed   19

Rabetski, Pavel   227
Ravagli, Franco   64
Rizou, Stamatia   34
Rochd, El Mehdi   19

Saini, Arnita   94
Schill, Alexander   104
Schneider, Gerardo   227
Spillner, Josef   104
Springer, Thomas   104

Steinmetz, Ralf   172
Strauch, Steve   79

Tai, Stefan   4
Tarabanis, Konstantinos A.   64
Treinen, Ralf   1

Utlik, Anna   104

Verginadis, Yiannis   34

Walshe, Ray   212
Wittern, Erik   4, 164

Xiong, Huanhuan   212

Zacchiroli, Stefano   1
Zavattaro, Gianluigi   1
Zeginis, Chrysostomos   188
Zeginis, Dimitris   64
Zöller, Sebastian   172
Zwolakowski, Jakub   1